CONTEMPORARY
Black
Biography

ISSN-1058-1316

CONTEMPORARY

Black

Biography

Profiles from the International Black Community

Volume 80

GALE
CENGAGE Learning

Detroit • New York • San Francisco • New Haven, Conn • Waterville, Maine • London

Contemporary Black Biography, Volume 80

Kepos Media, Inc.: Derek Jacques, Janice Jorgensen, and Paula Kepos, editors

Project Editor: Margaret Mazurkiewicz

Image Research and Acquisitions: Leitha Etheridge-Sims

Editorial Support Services: Nataliya Mikheyeva

Rights and Permissions: Margaret Abendroth, Tracie Richardson

Manufacturing: Dorothy Maki, Rita Wimberley

Composition and Prepress: Mary Beth Trimper, Gary Leach

Imaging: John Watkins

Gale
27500 Drake Rd.
Farmington Hills, MI, 48331-3535

ISBN-13: 978-1-4144-4601-1
ISBN-10: 1-4144-4601-2

ISSN 1058-1316

This title is also available as an e-book.
ISBN 13: 978-1-4144-5697-3
ISBN-10: 1-4144-5697-2
Contact your Gale sales representative for ordering information.

Printed in the United States of America
1 2 3 4 5 6 7 14 13 12 11 10

Advisory Board

Contents

Introduction

Contemporary Black Biography provides informative biographical profiles of the important and influential persons of African heritage who form the international black community: men and women who have changed today's world and are shaping tomorrow's. *Contemporary Black Biography* covers persons of various nationalities in a wide variety of fields, including architecture, art, business, dance, education, fashion, film, industry, journalism, law, literature, medicine, music, politics and government, publishing, religion, science and technology, social issues, sports, television, theater, and others. In addition to in-depth coverage of names found in today's headlines, *Contemporary Black Biography* provides coverage of selected individuals from earlier in this century whose influence continues to impact on contemporary life. *Contemporary Black Biography* also provides coverage of important and influential persons who are not yet household names and are therefore likely to be ignored by other biographical reference series. Each volume also includes listee updates on names previously appearing in *CBB*.

Designed for Quick Research and Interesting Reading

- **Attractive page design** incorporates textual subheads, making it easy to find the information you're looking for.
- **Easy-to-locate data sections** provide quick access to vital personal statistics, career information, major awards, and mailing addresses, when available.
- **Informative biographical essays** trace the subject's personal and professional life with the kind of in-depth analysis you need.
- **To further enhance your appreciation** of the subject, most entries include photographic portraits.
- **Sources for additional information** direct the user to selected books, magazines, and newspapers where more information on the individuals can be obtained.

Helpful Indexes Make It Easy to Find the Information You Need

Contemporary Black Biography includes cumulative Nationality, Occupation, Subject, and Name indexes that make it easy to locate entries in a variety of useful ways.

Available in Electronic Formats

Diskette/Magnetic Tape. Contemporary Black Biography is available for licensing on magnetic tape or diskette in a fielded format. Either the complete database or a custom selection of entries may be ordered. The database is available for internal data processing and nonpublishing purposes only. For more information, call (800) 877-GALE.

On-line. Contemporary Black Biography is available on-line through Mead Data Central's NEXIS Service in the NEXIS, PEOPLE and SPORTS Libraries in the GALBIO file and Gale's Biography Resource Center.

Disclaimer

Contemporary Black Biography uses and lists websites as sources and these websites may become obsolete.

We Welcome Your Suggestions

The editors welcome your comments and suggestions for enhancing and improving *Contemporary Black Biography*. If you would like to suggest persons for inclusion in the series, please submit these names to the editors. Mail comments or suggestions to:

The Editor

Contemporary Black Biography

Gale, Cengage Learning

27500 Drake Rd.

Farmington Hills, MI 48331-3535

Phone: (800) 347-4253

Sharif Ahmed

1964—

President of Somalia

Ahmed, Sharif, photograph. AP Images.

Former geography teacher Sharif Ahmed became president of Somalia, a nation devastated by war, in January of 2009. Four years earlier Ahmed had emerged as a political leader when he became head of the Islamic Courts Union (ICU), a grassroots justice movement. "There is nothing left in Somalia. It is ruined," the new president told *Time* magazine's Abdiaziz Hassan about his nation, which has been mired in civil war since the early 1990s. "We need all kinds of assistance from the world in building up our national security forces, reconstructing destroyed cities and returning displaced people."

Born in 1964, Ahmed hails from Shabeellaha Dhexe, the Somali province that abuts the Indian Ocean. His family belonged to the Sufi branch of Islam, and his grandfather was a well-known Muslim cleric. In his youth Ahmed became a hafiz, or scholar who could recite the Koran, Islam's holy book, in its entirety. He was educated at religious schools and then went on to Kordofan University in Sudan, where he studied Arabic languages and geography. In 1998 he earned a law degree from Al-Jaamac Al-Maftuuxa University in Tripoli, Libya.

In 1991 Somalia's longtime authoritarian ruler, Mohammed Siad Barre, was ousted in a military coup. That event launched a long civil war that neither Somalia's army nor international peacekeeping forces could subdue. The conflict was exacerbated by long-standing tensions between the northern and southern sectors of the country, and by conflict among warlords who had historically controlled their large clans and local economies. There were several attempts at forming a government of national unity, but all of them failed.

Ahmed returned to Somalia in 2000 and settled in Mogadishu, the nation's capital. He started a pair of cultural organizations and then went to his home province, Shabeellaha Dhexe, to serve as a regional attorney. There he became involved in a special provincial Islamic court and was named its chairperson. At the time there were a handful of these special courts across Somalia, which had been established in response to an utter lack of government authority and legal process. The new courts had been funded in part by business leaders who were weary of the payments the warlords extorted from them. When Shabeellaha

At a Glance . . .

Born on July 25, 1964 in Shabeellaha Dhexe, Somalia; married; children: Ahmad, Abdullah. *Politics:* Islamic Courts Union of Somalia. *Religion:* Muslim. *Education:* Attended Sheikh Sufi Institute; studied Arabic languages with a minor in geography at Kordofan University of Sudan, 1992(?)–94; earned law degree from Al-Jaamac Al-Maftuuxa University, 1998.

Career: Founded two cultural organizations in Mogadishu, Somalia, after 2000; regional attorney for Shabeellaha Dhexe province; chair of the provincial court in Jowhar, 2001–02; geography teacher in Mogadishu, 2002–04; became chair of the Islamic Courts Union (ICU), 2005; president of Somalia, 2009—.

Addresses: *Web*—http://tfgsomalia.net/Home.

Dhexe was overrun by an unfriendly warlord, Ahmed and other members of the court were forced to flee.

In Mogadishu, Ahmed found work as a teacher but was spurred back into political action by the kidnapping of one of his students, a twelve-year-old boy. Such kidnappings had become common occurrences in Mogadishu, where armed gangs roamed the streets freely, taking hostages and demanding ransom. The city lacked almost any form of economy except the criminal, and most families lived in conditions of dire poverty. Like most, the family of Ahmed's student could not afford the ransom. Ahmed assembled a court to deal with the situation and eventually joined with the dozen or so similar Islamic-justice courts around the country to form the Islamic Courts Union, or ICU. Ahmed became the chief of the ICU, and an ICU militia arm took control of key sites in the capital and its surrounding roads. By June of 2006 that militia group had gained complete control of Mogadishu.

Ahmed first appeared in Western news reports when his group seized the Somali capital. Media stories initially portrayed the ICU as hardliner Islamists who planned to set up a Taliban-style theocracy in Somalia, and there were also reports that one of its founders, Adan Hashi Ayrow, had ties to Osama bin Laden's terrorist network, al-Qaeda. "We are a Muslim people, we want to live in a peaceful way, we want to live with the rest of the world in a peaceful way," Ahmed demurred in an interview with *New York Times* writer Marc Lacey. "We are not terrorists and we do not associate with terrorists."

Following the Mogadishu victory, the forces of the Somali Transitional Federal Government (TFG) began an offensive to push back the ICU. This opened yet another chapter in Somalia's fifteen-year civil war, and the ICU began losing ground. By December Ahmed and the ICU had fled to Kenya. Over the next several months Ahmed presided over an internal struggle within the ICU. The hardline faction of the ICU was ousted and formed its own organization, known as al-Shabaab (the Youth). From Yemen, across the Gulf of Aden, Ahmed regrouped and entered into negotiations with the TFG to become part of legitimate transitional government. Because Mogadishu was so troubled, the headquarters of the TFG had been established in Baidoa in south-central Somalia in 2004. The Somali parliament convened there as al-Shabaab began an offensive against Mogadishu, and the legislature had to flee the country entirely in January of 2009 when Baidoa was stormed by al-Shabaab units.

Ahmed was forced to flee with the TFG to the tiny nation of Djibouti, which had a large U.S. military presence at a former French Foreign Legion military base. The Somali parliament met there in late January of 2009 to elect a new president for the country, and Ahmed won after two rounds of balloting. He was sworn in at a luxury hotel on January 31. A few weeks later the TFG was able to return to Somalia and even made it back into Mogadishu. Ahmed moved into Villa Somalia, the heavily guarded presidential palace, but al-Shabaab forces remained a dire threat to the stability of his government.

Ahmed has concentrated on garnering support from international allies to restore a semblance of normal life to Somalia. In August of 2009 he traveled to Nairobi, Kenya, to discuss international aid with U.S. Secretary of State Hillary Rodham Clinton. Another major issue has been the need to combat piracy: because Somalia lacked a coast guard or viable navy for so many years, its coastal fishermen found their livelihood threatened when commercial fishing vessels from other countries began illegally trawling the waters off Somalia's coast. The Somali fishermen were forced to organize their own protection patrols, some of which evolved into outright pirate missions. "The pirates who hunt down ships are based on land," Ahmed told Hassan, the *Time* magazine reporter. "That's the reality. We can play our part by organizing locals to reject piracy on land. We have also started restructuring Somalia's navy."

Ahmed has also devoted time to recruiting educated Somalis who went abroad in the 1990s to return home and help rebuild the country's economy and infrastructure. "This government faced obstacles that were unparalleled," he told *New York Times* reporter Jeffrey Gettleman, who visited Villa Somalia and reported on the eerie quiet of the former capital. "We had to deal with international terrorist groups creating havoc elsewhere. Their plan was to topple the government soon after it arrived. The government proved it could last."

Sources

Periodicals

New York Times, June 19, 2006; September 17, 2009, p. A1.
Time, June 11, 2009.

Online

"Somalia's Moderate Islamist Leader," BBC News, http://news.bbc.co.uk/go/pr/fr/-/2/hi/africa/5072268.stm (accessed January 2, 2009).
"The President," Transitional Federal Government of Somalia, http://tfgsomalia.net/President (accessed January 2, 2009).

—Carol Brennan

Susana Baca

1954(?)—

Singer, educator, musicologist

Baca, Susana, photograph. AP Images.

Peruvian singer Susana Baca has been an international star since the mid-1990s. Her music is rooted in Afro-Peruvian culture, a rapidly vanishing heritage she has worked for decades to preserve. A largely self-trained musicologist and the founder of one of Peru's leading cultural institutes, she once said, in comments posted on the Web site of her primary record label (Luaka Bop), that she would like to be remembered not just for her voice, but "for helping to spread the music of my ancestors—all those people who were never recognized for their work or for their beautiful culture."

Born about 1954 in the Peruvian capital of Lima, Baca was raised just outside that city in Chorrillos, a poor suburb that has served for centuries as a center of Afro-Peruvian life. Although people of African descent have lived and worked in Peru—often as slaves or near-slaves—since the Spanish conquest in the sixteenth century, racial prejudice has remained strong. Many, the Baca family included, have struggled financially. Susana's parents were both employed by wealthy families, her father as a chauffeur and her mother as a cook and laundress. Despite the long hours these positions required, the Baca home seems to have been a warm and invigorating place. Music and dance had a central role in the family's life. Susana's father was a singer and guitarist whose repertoire included many folk songs of the sort she would later make famous. Her mother, meanwhile, made sure all her children knew how to dance.

Baca was attracted to the idea of a singing career from an early age, but she resisted the impulse for many years because her mother believed strongly that music was not a stable profession. After secondary school she made plans to become a teacher. While few details of her postsecondary education are available, there is no doubt that she took education courses, probably at the national university in Lima. Whether she received a degree is unclear. By the early 1980s, however, she was teaching dancing and music at schools around the capital. She was also working increasingly on her own singing, which to that point had been merely a hobby. A major influence in this period was Chabuca Granda, a Peruvian folk singer and songwriter revered throughout the nation for her poetic lyrics and commanding stage presence. In a 2000 interview with Jaime Manrique of *Bomb* magazine, Baca described meeting Granda at a poetry reading. The older singer, delighted with Baca's

At a Glance . . .

Born about 1954 in Lima, Peru; daughter of a chauffeur and a cook/laundress; married Ricardo Pereira. *Education:* University-level courses in education, 1970s.

Career: Various institutions, teacher, 1970s—; independent performing artist, 1980s—; Instituto Negro Continuo, co-founder and co-director, 1992(?)—.

Awards: Latin Grammy Award for Best Folk Album for *Lamento Negro,* 2002; fellowship, Rockefeller Foundation, 2005(?).

Addresses: *Office*—c/o Luaka Bop, 195 Chrystie St., #901F, New York, NY 10002.

voice, became her mentor. "She adopted me," Baca recalled. "My husband and I went to her house and made plans [for a music career]."

Granda died in 1983. Baca's husband Ricardo Pereira has continued to serve as her manager. "He organizes my life, my things, my work," she told Manrique. "I can dedicate myself to music." A native of Bolivia and a sociologist by training, Pereira helped Baca immerse herself in the study of Afro-Peruvian culture. In the early 1990s they founded a research organization, the Instituto Negro Continuo (Institute of the Black Continuum), to encourage further study of the subject.

By that time, Baca was performing regularly around Peru, and her reputation was growing steadily. When the major record companies she approached showed little interest, she recorded an album on her own. That record drew the attention of David Byrne, an American best known as the lead singer of The Talking Heads, one of the most influential rock bands of the 1980s. An enthusiastic fan of world music, Byrne was the founder in 1988 of a record label, Luaka Bop, dedicated to that genre. Several years later, he convinced Baca to contribute a song to a compilation he was preparing called *Afro-Peruvian Classics: The Soul of Black Peru.* Her track, "Maria Lando," became the album's standout hit on its release in 1995. "A ballad that poetically recounts the daily suffering of a black working woman," in the words of RootsWorld.com's Elisa Murray, the song proved a pivotal moment in Baca's career, introducing her to music fans beyond South America.

Following the success of "Maria Lando," Luaka Bop encouraged Baca to record a full-length solo album for the international market. Titled simply *Susana Baca,* it appeared in 1997. Subsequent albums, many on

Luaka Bop, have included *Eco de Sombras* (2000), *Lamento Negro* (2001), *Espíritu Vivo* (2002), and *Travesías* (2006). *Lamento Negro* won the 2002 Latin Grammy Award for Best Folk Album. An award of a different sort followed about three years later, when Baca won a Rockefeller Foundation fellowship to study the music of famed trumpeter and vocalist Louis Armstrong. Although her research in Armstrong's hometown of New Orleans, Louisiana, was interrupted by the devastating Hurricane Katrina in September of 2005, the break was only a temporary one. One of her long-term goals, she told Misha Berson of the *Seattle Times* in 2006, was to bring together a variety of styles, including the classic jazz Armstrong epitomized, to create "a mass that is sung for the poorest people, that will be a prayer for justice and [for] fulfilling the needs of the poor."

As of the fall of 2009, Baca was touring regularly in support of her album *Seis Poemas* (2009). Dedicated to the memory of Granda, it consists of six poems set to music. One track, "Los Lagartos," seemed particularly emblematic of Baca's career in its melding of Peruvian and non-Peruvian elements. The song's cadence and rhythms are Afro-Peruvian, while the lyrics are taken from a poem of the same name by the revered Spanish writer Federico García Lorca. Baca's willingness to weave together disparate elements can be taken as a reflection of her self-image as "a musical citizen of the world," in Berson's words. Many critics, however, have chosen instead to focus on what Spencer Harrington of AllMusic.com called her "splendid voice and equally impressive interpretive gifts."

Selected discography

Singles

"Maria Lando," included on *Afro-Peruvian Classics: The Soul of Black Peru,* Luaka Bop, 1995.

Albums

Susana Baca, Luaka Bop, 1997.
Del Fuego y del Agua, Tonga, 1999.
Eco de Sombras, Luaka Bop, 2000.
Vestida de Vida, Labrador, 2000.
Lamento Negro, Tumi, 2001.
Espíritu Vivo, Luaka Bop, 2002.
Travesías, Luaka Bop, 2006.
Seis Poemas (includes "Los Lagartos"), Luaka Bop, 2009.

Sources

Periodicals

Bomb, Winter 2000.
Seattle Times, October 25, 2006.

At a Glance . . .

Born in 1953 or 1954 in Ghana, probably in or around the town of Cape Coast; daughter of a skilled railroad worker and a shopkeeper.

Career: Embassy of Ghana, Washington, DC, secretary, 1979(?)—; king of Otuam, Ghana, 2009—.

Addresses: *Office*—c/o Embassy of Ghana, 3512 International Dr. NW, Washington, DC 20008.

Her coronation ceremony was likewise steeped in tradition. It was delayed for nearly fifteen months while she made preparations for the trip and accumulated the necessary vacation time. On her arrival in Ghana, she was greeted with the fanfare reserved for royalty. A retinue of servants escorted her to her "palace"—one of Otuam's largest homes. During the ceremony itself, she wore a heavy gold crown and was carried on a litter through the streets of the town. She also had to attend to some serious business, including her first meeting with the elders' council. She warned them not to try to take advantage of her. "If you step on my toes," she told them, in comments quoted by Paul Schwartzman of the *Washington Post,* "I will hit you where it hurts."

Bartels's installation as king came at a time when women were becoming increasingly prominent in local and national politics throughout West Africa. While men still dominated most political institutions, particularly traditional structures like kingships and elders' councils, women like Bartels and Liberia's Ellen Johnson Sirleaf, the first female head of state in post-independence Africa, posed a significant challenge to the status quo. Bartels, for her part, has pledged to increase the number of women among Otuam's elders.

According to a blog kept by Eleanor Herman, a friend who accompanied Bartels to Ghana, the new king planned a number of ambitious projects to improve Otuam's infrastructure, notably a new water system. The pipes for such a system already existed in many parts of the town but were not functional, so residents had to walk to a well in the countryside for water. As of the fall of 2009, Bartels was beginning the process of hiring engineers to assess the situation. She had also indicated her determination to improve the town's schools, in part by enhancing their computer resources.

Herman also noted that Bartels's story had generated considerable interest from movie producers. The prospect of a sizeable financial windfall from the sale of film rights, however, seems not to have altered the king's personal plans. According to Schwartzman of the *Post,* she intended to continue working for the embassy until 2014 or 2015. Upon her retirement, she told the newspaper, she would move to Otuam and take up her duties full time. In the meantime, Herman, a writer, was working on Bartels's biography. According to a summary posted on EleanorHerman.com, the book, tentatively titled *King Peggy: The Remarkable Journey of an American Female King in Ghana,* would feature "outrageous characters, moving scenarios, and a resourceful African lady who knows how to meet every challenge.".

Sources

Periodicals

Washington Post, September 16, 2009.

Online

Herman, Eleanor, "King Peggy: The Remarkable Journey of an American Female King in Ghana," EleanorHerman.com, http://www.eleanorherman.com/king_peggy/index.html (accessed November 4, 2009).
———, "Update from Otuam," EleanorHerman.Blogspot.com, September 26, 2009, http://eleanorherman.blogspot.com/2009/09/update-from-otuam.html (accessed November 2, 2009).
"Peggielene Bartels," Facebook.com, http://www.facebook.com/pages/Peggielene-Bartels/132308063405/pages/Peggielene-Bartels/132308063405?v (accessed November 2, 2009).
"Washington Secretary Is King in Africa," AOL.com, September 17, 2009, http://news.aol.com/article/secretary-peggielene-bartels-is-king-in/675463 (accessed November 2, 2009).

—R. Anthony Kugler

Carrie Best

1903–2001

Journalist, broadcaster

Carrie Best was a pioneering black journalist and broadcaster in Canada. In 1946 she launched Nova Scotia's first black-owned newspaper, the *Clarion.* Although the number of blacks in Canada would remain small until the early 1960s, when race restrictions on immigration were lifted, Best was one of Canada's early civil rights activists. Her newspaper served, said the *Toronto Star,* as "a voice for promoting interracial understanding and an outlet for her investigative journalism into discrimination [that] made federal and provincial officials take notice."

Best was born Carrie Prevoe on March 4, 1903, in New Glasgow, a coal mining town in Nova Scotia. There had been a sizable number of blacks in the area since the 1780s, when slaves who fought on the British side during the American Revolution in exchange for their freedom fled with their families across the border at the war's end. Over subsequent decades the descendants of those original three thousand were joined by fugitive American slaves who came to Canada via the Underground Railroad. All experienced tremendous discrimination in Nova Scotia and other provinces, including being forced to attend segregated schools, as Best and her siblings did.

Tensions in New Glasgow erupted into a violent race riot around 1918. As Best recalled in her 1977 autobiography, *That Lonesome Road,* "bands of roving white men armed with clubs had stationed themselves at different intersections allowing no Blacks to go beyond that point. We had learned of the riot from our father when he came home from work. My oldest brother was at work at the Norfolk House [hotel] and my mother who had been driven home by the chauffeur of the family for whom she had been working knew nothing of the situation." Her mother, Best remembered, decided she was going to the Norfolk House to retrieve her son. As she neared the hotel, "the crowd was waiting and as my mother drew near they hurled insults at her and threateningly ordered her to turn back." Fortunately one of the men recognized Best's mother and asked her why she was out on the streets. She gave them her reason, and "the young man ordered the crowd back and my mother continued on her way to the hotel. At that time there was a livery stable at the rear entrance to the hotel and it was there my mother found my frightened older brother and brought him safely home."

As a young woman Best considered the handful of career options open to her as a black woman in Canada. Her mother was a domestic, and she knew she wanted to avoid that drudgery. She thought about becoming a nurse, but no nursing schools in Canada admitted black students in that era. Teaching at a black school was another possibility, but she felt unsuited for that profession. In 1925 she wed a railroad porter, Albert T. Best, who had been born in Barbados. Their son was born a year later and came of age in the same restrictive atmosphere that Best had known in her youth. "When I was growing up in New Glasgow, you couldn't eat in a restaurant," Best told journalist Sharon Fraser for an interview that Fraser excerpted on the Rabble.ca Web site. "You couldn't get your hair cut. I went to jail. My son and I were at the movies; we sat

At a Glance . . .

Born Carrie Prevoe on March 4, 1903, in New Glasgow, Nova Scotia, Canada; died on July 24, 2001, in New Glasgow; daughter of James and Georgina (Ashe) Prevoe; married Albert T. Best (a railroad porter), 1925; children: son, J. Calbert Best; foster mother to four children.

Career: *The Clarion*, New Glasgow, NS, cofounder, 1946, and publisher, 1946–56; host of the radio show *The Quiet Corner*, 1952–64; columnist for the *Advocate*, Pictou Co., NS, 1968–75.

Awards: Member of the Order of Canada, Government of Canada, 1974; Officer of the Order of Canada, Government of Canada, 1979; Order of Nova Scotia, Government of Nova Scotia, 2002 (posthumous).

downstairs, we went to the movies three times a week and we'd sat in the same seats for years. Then one day, the usher came to me and said, 'You can't sit here. You have to go into the balcony.'"

This incident occurred in December of 1941, after another theater patron voiced a complaint. But Best and her fifteen-year-old son refused to move, and Best was arrested, convicted, and fined. Five years later a similar incident occurred involving another black woman, Viola Desmond, a Halifax hairdresser who was staying in New Glasgow. Desmond also refused to comply with the rule and was carried by a theater employee and a policeman to a waiting squad car. This time, a newly formed Nova Scotia Association for the Advancement of Coloured People took up the cause, which went all the way to the Nova Scotia Supreme Court.

Unfortunately, the provincial court upheld the charges against Desmond and the sentence meted out by the lower court, but the case attracted national attention. It also spurred Best to launch the *Clarion* with her son, J. Calbert Best, by then a university student in Halifax. It was the first black-owned newspaper in Nova Scotia, and Best made the Desmond case its inaugural editorial priority. Many Canadians felt their country superior to the United States, where stringent segregation laws ruled black life in the southern states. J. Calbert Best wrote a reply to this view in the pages of the *Clarion*. "We do have many of the privileges which are denied our southern brothers, but we often wonder if the kind of segregation we receive here is not more cruel in the very subtlety of its nature," he stated, according to *Globe & Mail* journalist Allison Lawlor. "Nowhere do we encounter signs that read 'No Colored' or the more

diplomatic little paste boards which say 'Select Clientele,' but at times it might be better. At least much consequent embarrassment might be saved for all concerned."

Best and other civil rights activists pushed for municipal by-laws similar to a statute already in force in Toronto that would prohibit businesses from discriminating on the basis of race, but they were initially unsuccessful. Her newspaper became the *Negro Citizen* in 1949 and five years later celebrated a major victory for black Canadians in Nova Scotia when school segregation was finally ended. Best's newspaper folded in 1956, but she remained an active presence in New Glasgow and the surrounding Pictou County area. She hosted a radio show called *The Quiet Corner* from 1952 to 1964 that featured poetry readings and classical music, and she also wrote a column for the Pictou *Advocate* from 1968 to 1975 in which she championed scores of social justice causes including the rights of Canada's First Nations, and opposed an attempt by New Glasgow officials to rezone and remove housing in its historically black neighborhood.

The Canadian government recognized Best with the Order of Canada in 1974 and made her an Officer of the Order of Canada in 1979. She died on July 24, 2001, at her home in New Glasgow. She was ninety-seven. Her son, J. Calbert Best, was a longtime civil servant and government official who in 1985 became Canada's first black high commissioner as the envoy to another British Commonwealth nation, Trinidad and Tobago.

Selected works

That Lonesome Road: The Autobiography of Carrie M. Best, Clarion Publishing, 1977.

Sources

Periodicals

Beaver: Exploring Canada's History, April–May 2009, p. 24.
Globe & Mail (Toronto), October 4, 2007, p. S9.
Pictou Advocate (Pictou County, NS) January 20, 1970.
Toronto Star, July 26, 2001.

Online

"Carrie Best: A Digital Archive," Pictou-Antagonish Regional Library, http://www.parl.ns.ca/carriebest/index.htm (accessed January 2, 2009).
Fraser, Sharon, "Carrie Best: 'As Good As Anyone, Better Than Most,'" Rabble.ca, February 20, 2006, http://www.rabble.ca/news/carrie-best-good-anyone-better-most (accessed January 2, 2009).

—Carol Brennan

Ali Ben Bongo

1959—

Politician

Politician Ali Ben Bongo stepped into the international spotlight in September of 2009 when he became president of Gabon, a small but resource-rich nation on the west coast of Africa. In doing so, he followed a course set by his father, El Hadj Omar Bongo Ondimba (generally known as Omar Bongo), who led the country for almost forty-two years, from the end of 1967 to his death in June of 2009. The elder Bongo's rule was marked by pervasive corruption, immense but poorly distributed oil wealth, and a political system that lent a veneer of democracy to what was, in all essential respects, an autocracy. In the fall of 2009 it was unclear whether Ali Ben Bongo would break the precedents set by his father.

Bongo, Ali Ben, photograph. Eric Feferberg/AFP/Getty Images.

Bongo was born February 9, 1959, in Brazzaville, a city on the Congo River that later became the capital of the Republic of the Congo (not to be confused with the much larger Democratic Republic of the Congo). At the time of Bongo's birth, the Brazzaville region—and Gabon—were both part of the Union of Central African Republics, a short-lived federation of French colonies formed in the course of their transition to full independence.

Bongo has revealed relatively little of his early life. By the time he had reached the equivalent of middle school, his father was president, so it is likely that his education was of the highest quality. According to Farai Sevenzo of the BBC, Bongo has referred in interviews to undergraduate work in the United States, but details have proved elusive, and the biographical statement available on his campaign Web site, Ali9.org, in the fall of 2009 mentioned only "law studies" in Paris.

Bongo entered politics in 1981, when he was only twenty-two. The primary focus of his work at that stage seems to have been the country's dominant political group, the Parti Démocratique Gabonais (Gabonese Democratic Party), generally known by its French acronym, PDG. Thereafter he held a wide variety of positions in the party, including seats on its Central Committee and Political Bureau. In the latter post, he served as the primary liaison between the presidential palace and party headquarters.

As the elder Bongo tightened his hold on power in the 1970s and 1980s, the lines between the ruling party and the state grew increasingly blurry. Few Gabonese were surprised, therefore, to find his son adding several

At a Glance . . .

Born Ali Ben Bongo Ondimba on February 9, 1959, in Brazzaville, Union of Central African Republics (later Republic of the Congo); son of El Hadj Omar Bongo Ondimba (a politician) and Patience Dabany; married Sylvia; children: four. *Politics:* Parti Démocratique Gabonais. *Education:* Undergraduate studies in the United States; law studies in France.

Career: Parti Démocratique Gabonais, variety of posts, 1981—; Gabonese Republic, foreign minister, 1989–91, National Assembly member, 1990–2009, defense minister, 1999–2009, president, 2009–.

Addresses: Office: c/o Embassy of Gabon, 2034 20th St. NW, Washington, DC, 20009.

government jobs to his PDG duties. A year after becoming foreign minister in 1989, he was elected to the National Assembly, the lower half of the country's bicameral legislature, in the first multiparty elections Gabon had seen since the 1960s. His tenure in the foreign ministry ended in 1991, but he retained his legislative seat for more than fifteen years, winning re-election three times. In 1999 he was appointed defense minister, an extremely influential post in a country that depended on the armed forces for the maintenance of law and order.

Bongo's father died in June of 2009. In accordance with the constitution, a veteran legislator named Rose Francine Rogombe became interim president while preparations were made for new elections. Bongo was the leading candidate from the outset. Well over a dozen candidates announced their intention to run; however, many were from minor parties, while others had significant business dealings with the Bongo family. As election day approached, it was clear that there were only three serious candidates: Bongo; Andre Mba Obame, once a minister in the elder Bongo's cabinet; and Pierre Mamboundou, a well-known opposition leader.

The campaign itself was relatively calm, but anger erupted in the streets of Libreville and Port-Gentil, the country's principal cities, shortly after the polls closed on August 30, 2009, as Bongo's opponents protested voting irregularities. Perhaps the most serious charge concerned the reliability of the electoral rolls, which contained more than eight hundred thousand

names—a suspiciously high number in a nation of 1.3 million people, many of them too young to vote. Similarly bloated rolls have been used around the world to add illicit votes, usually for the benefit of the party in power.

In the immediate aftermath of the election, all three major candidates declared victory. When the ballots were counted, Obame and Mamboundou had each won about 25 percent of the vote, while Bongo had 42 percent. Officially declared the victor on September 3, 2009, he began his seven-year term the following month. While calm had been restored throughout the country, there was no question that many Gabonese were unhappy with both the conduct of the election and the prospect of continued rule by the Bongo family. "They have trampled democracy," one man, Patrick Pambo, told Adam Nossiter of the *New York Times* after the outcome was announced. "These results are false."

As of November of 2009, it was far too early to assess the impact of Bongo's election. There was no question, however, that Gabon faced an array of severe problems. Many citizens had little access to health care, and the rate of infant mortality remained among the highest in the world. Gabon's extensive oil and timber resources were rapidly dwindling. Oil byproducts had already befouled many of the local waterways, while over-logging had destroyed much of the rainforest that once covered the region. While the Gabonese people dealt with these problems daily, the compensation they had long been promised remained largely out of their reach. Bongo made assurances throughout the campaign that he would redistribute oil and timber royalties to those most in need. As he completed his first months in office, the fulfillment of that promise had yet to be seen.

Sources

Periodicals

Economist, June 20, 2009.
New York Times, August 30, 2009; September 4, 2009.

Online

"Ali Bongo Ondimba," Ali9.org, http://www.ali9.org/homme.html (accessed October 30, 2009).
Sevenzo, Farai, "African View: Will the Bongo Dynasty Continue?" BBC.co.uk, August 30, 2009, http://news.bbc.co.uk/2/hi/africa/8226988.stm (accessed October 30, 2009).

—R. Anthony Kugler

Ernest Brown

1916–2009

Tap dancer, dance teacher

Tap dancer Ernest "Brownie" Brown spent eight decades as a popular entertainer, often appearing alongside bandleader Duke Ellington and other luminaries. Best known as one half of the vaudeville duo Cook and Brown, the Illinois native was also a founding member of the Copasetics, an all-star ensemble that helped to preserve the traditions of tap following the 1949 death of the genre's most famous practitioner, Bill "Bojangles" Robinson.

The youngest of a barber's nine children, Brown was born on April 25, 1916, in Chicago. Money was a constant worry for his hardworking parents. Without toys or other expensive amusements, he learned quickly to entertain himself, often by exploring the area around his home on the city's predominately African-American South Side. Impromptu dance performances were a staple of his neighborhood's vibrant street life, and it was in these that his grace and athletic ability first became apparent. When he was about twelve, a white entertainer named Sarah Venable recruited him to join her traveling vaudeville act. She did so at the suggestion of Charles "Cookie" Cook, one of her stars and Brown's good friend. The group's act, a mixture of tap dance, acrobatics, and comedy, was a leading attraction on the so-called "Keith circuit"—a nationwide chain of vaudeville houses—in the late 1920s.

Vaudeville's grueling schedule of shows, rehearsals, and travel put an end to Brown's formal schooling, although he received fairly regular lessons from tutors on the road. He and Cook became increasingly frustrated with the low pay they received as members of Ven-

able's troupe, and they left in about 1930 to form an act of their own. Cook and Brown, as the duo became known, quickly established a routine that served them well for the next forty-five years. Much taller and ostensibly more serious than his partner, Cook played the "straight man." Brown, in contrast, had what Jennifer Dunning of the *New York Times* called "an innocently joyous air and ease."

The 1930s were arguably the high point of Brown's long career. By the end of the decade, he and Cook had moved out of vaudeville into the better-paid world of nightclubs. Many of these were on the so-called "chitlin circuit." The term, derived from a traditional staple of African-American cooking (chitterlings or "chitlins"), referred to performance venues that welcomed African-American entertainers as headliners. At a time when racial segregation was still in force in much of the country, the circuit provided performers like Brown with crucial support. At venues like the Apollo Theater and the Cotton Club (both in New York), the duo frequently appeared on the same bill with some of the biggest stars in jazz, including Duke Ellington and the singers Lena Horne and Ella Fitzgerald. While Cook and Brown's prominence continued through the 1940s, it was clear by 1949 that tap was no longer the dominant force it had been only a few years earlier. As bebop jazz and, later, rock-and-roll attracted growing crowds, swing jazz, a genre closely associated with classic tap, began to decline, bringing the dance style down with it.

Another blow came with Robinson's death in November of 1949. To honor his memory, preserve the tap

At a Glance . . .

Born April 25, 1916, in Chicago, IL; died August 21, 2009, in Burbank, Illinois; son of a barber; married Hazel Coates (divorced); Patricia (died 1989); children: one daughter; several grandchildren and great-grandchildren.

Career: Member of Sarah Venable's vaudeville troupe, 1920s; Cook and Brown (dance duo), co-founder and principal, 1930?–70s; Copasetics (dance ensemble), founding member, 1949–60s; independent performer and teacher, 1970s–2009.

Awards: Tradition in Tap Award, Tradition in Tap, 2006; Tap Dance Hall of Fame (with Charlie Cook), American Tap Dance Foundation, 2008.

tradition, and improve his own business prospects, Brown joined other African-American dancers, choreographers, and musicians to form an ensemble called the Copasetics. The name was derived from "copasetic," a slang term for "great" that Robinson had popularized. Among the group's other founders, roughly twenty in number, were Cook, dancers Jimmy Slyde and Charles "Honi" Coles, and composer Billy Strayhorn.

Over the next two decades, the Copasetics had a considerable influence on popular dance, particularly in the New York area. Their shows, which featured improvised, highly individualistic routines by a rapid succession of dancers, inspired a new generation to study tap. After a 1966 performance at New York's Waldorf-Astoria Hotel, Charlotte Curtis of the *New York Times* wrote that the group "proved tap dancing did not die with Bill (Bojangles) Robinson." The style's popularity nevertheless continued to decline, and by the end of the 1960s the Copasetics had essentially disbanded, although individual members—and others unrelated to the original troupe—continued to use the name. Brown himself began to struggle financially. To support his family, he took a job as a messenger and security guard at one of New York's largest commercial banks. He continued to make occasional appearances with Cook into the 1970s.

As tap became increasingly popular again in the 1980s and 1990s, Brown returned to prominence as well. After moving back to Chicago, he focused much of his attention on teaching. One of his students, Reginald McLaughlin, better known as "Reggio the Hoofer," eventually became his partner; their association would last more than fifteen years. "We just kind of clicked," McLaughlin recalled to Sarah Halzack of the *Washington Post*. The duo's final performance took place in New York in 2008, when the senior partner was over ninety years of age.

Toward the end of his life, Brown won a number of awards, notably his induction with Cook into the American Tap Dance Foundation's Tap Dance Hall of Fame in 2008. These honors coincided with growing public interest in the history of the genre. As one of the few remaining vaudevillians and the last surviving Copasetic, Brown had a unique perspective on tap's development from a street-corner pastime to an internationally recognized art. His recollections, and video footage of some of his routines, were prominently featured in a popular documentary titled . The program, first broadcast nationally on the PBS network in 2001, received an Emmy nomination.

Brown died on August 21, 2009, in Burbank, Illinois, a Chicago suburb, at the age of ninety-three. Surviving him were a daughter, a sister, four grandchildren, and at least one great-grandchild.

Selected works

Theater

Kiss Me Kate, Broadway Theatre, 1952.

Television

Juba! Masters of Tap & Percussive Dance, PBS, 2001.

Sources

Periodicals

Dancer, August 1, 2006.
Los Angeles Times, August 26, 2009.
New York Times, February 14, 1966; August 25, 2009.
Washington Post, August 28, 2009.

—R. Anthony Kugler

James Cameron

1914–2006

Museum director, activist, businessman

Cameron, James, photograph. AP Images.

The only known survivor of a lynching, James Cameron used his memories of that horrific experience to promote racial harmony and reconciliation. An indefatigable civil rights activist, he was best known as the founder and director of America's Black Holocaust Museum, a Milwaukee institution dedicated to the history of racial violence in the United States.

Cameron was born on February 25, 1914, in La Crosse, Wisconsin, a city of modest size on the banks of the Mississippi River. Few details about his parents, James Herbert Cameron and Vera Carter Cameron, or his early life are available. It is known that the family moved from Wisconsin to Birmingham, Alabama, in about 1918 and from Alabama to Indiana in about 1926. After roughly two years in the city of Kokomo, Indiana, the Camerons settled in the nearby town of Marion.

In the summer of 1930, a white man, Claude Deeter, was found murdered in a parked automobile. A witness, Deeter's girlfriend Mary Ball, told police that the perpetrators were African American, that they had robbed Deeter before killing him, and that she had been raped. Three suspects were soon arrested: Thomas Shipp, nineteen; Abram Smith, nineteen; and Cameron, then sixteen. In his statement to police, Cameron acknowledged that the three had planned to rob the couple, but maintained that he had changed his mind and departed the scene before the events took place. Although Smith and Shipp confessed, they did so under extremely coercive conditions. Ball later recanted the rape charge. By that time, however, two lives had been lost.

On August 7, 1930, an enraged crowd of whites converged on the county jail and seized the three defendants. All were beaten badly. Cameron watched in horror, a rope already around his neck, as his acquaintances were hanged from a maple tree. Just as the crowd turned its attention to him, however, a voice that was never identified announced that he was uninvolved and ought to be released. The mob, surprisingly, relented and dispersed, leaving Cameron traumatized but alive. He later described his rescue as a miracle; the mysterious voice, he believed, had belonged to God.

The teenager's troubles did not end with the crowd's departure. Though the lynching's ringleaders were

At a Glance . . .

Born February 25, 1914, in La Crosse, WI; died June 11, 2006, in Milwaukee, WI; son of James Herbert Cameron and Vera Carter Cameron; married Virginia, 1938(?); children: five; numerous grandchildren and great-grandchildren. *Education:* Studied at Wayne State University and Milwaukee Area Technical College.

Career: Worker and independent businessman, 1930–80s; State of Indiana, director of civil liberties, 1942–50; America's Black Holocaust Museum, founder and director, 1988–2006.

Memberships: NAACP, founder of several local chapters.

Awards: Key to the City, City of Marion (IN), 1993; portion of North Ave. renamed in his honor, City of Milwaukee (WI), 2007.

never punished, Cameron was convicted of being an accessory to Deeter's homicide. On his release from prison in about 1935, he moved with his family's help to Detroit, Michigan, where he took classes at Wayne State University, married, and held a number of entry-level jobs. After about four years, he moved back to Indiana, settling in the town of Anderson, some thirty miles south of Marion. There he established what Yvonne Shinhoster Lamb of the *Washington Post* later described as "the only black business in town—a combination shoeshine parlor, record shop, and knickknack store."

Despite the demands of a growing family and long hours at his business, Cameron found the time to volunteer for civil rights organizations, particularly the NAACP. According to an article posted in 2006 on JSOnline.com, the *Milwaukee Journal Sentinel*'s Web site, he founded three separate NAACP chapters around Indiana, including one in Anderson. That work drew the attention of state officials, who were struggling to comply with new federal guidelines on the issue of segregation. Impressed with his organizational abilities, they hired him in 1942 as the state's Director of Civil Liberties. In that role, which he retained until 1950, he investigated complaints of racial injustice and advised local officials on civil rights issues.

In the early 1950s, Cameron moved with his family from Indiana to Milwaukee, where he remained for the rest of his life. Over the next three decades, he held jobs in a variety of industries, including brewing, pack-

aging, and retail. His passion, however, remained civil rights. Though his activism continued, particularly on the issue of housing discrimination, he increasingly approached the subject as a historian. He read widely, and his home became a repository of books, photographs, and artifacts, including a piece of the rope the Marion mob had placed around his neck. After a 1979 visit to the Yad Vashem Holocaust memorial in Israel, he decided to establish a museum to commemorate the victims of what he termed "the black holocaust." He focused on lynching, a crime that took the lives of an estimated four to five thousand African Americans between the 1880s and the 1960s.

America's Black Holocaust Museum opened in his basement in 1988, moving to larger quarters six years later. Attendance grew steadily, particularly after artifacts from a slave ship (the *Henrietta Marie*) were added in about 1999. Costs increased as well, however, and the museum often struggled to obtain grants and other financing. As of the mid-2000s, it was attracting roughly twenty-five thousand visitors a year.

The museum's growth and the publication of his memoir, entitled *A Time of Terror*, brought Cameron considerable attention from the media in the 1990s. By 1993, his story had drawn the interest of Indiana's governor, who apologized for Cameron's conviction in the 1930s and issued a full pardon. Officials in Marion, meanwhile, presented him with a key to the city. The most significant honor came in 2005, when he was invited to the U.S. Senate to receive an official apology for the federal government's failure to protect African Americans from lynching. "It's 100-something years late," he remarked, in comments quoted by Lamb of the *Post*. "But I'm glad they are doing it."

Cameron died on June 11, 2006, in Milwaukee; he was ninety-two. Surviving him were his wife, three of his five children, and a number of grandchildren and great-grandchildren. News of his death prompted tributes in Wisconsin and across the country. "He survived a lynching and never became bitter," judge and activist Vel R. Phillips remarked to the Milwaukee Journal Sentinel. "He epitomized what it takes to realize what faith is."

As of the fall of 2009, the future of Cameron's museum remained uncertain. Serious financial problems forced it to close two years after his death. The collections remained intact, however, and board members were hopeful that a new source of funding could be found.

Selected writings

A Time of Terror, self-published, 1982; reprinted by Black Classic Press, 1994.

Sources

Periodicals

Nation, June 12, 2006.
Washington Post, June 13, 2006.

Online

Durhams, Sharif, "America's Black Holocaust Museum Closing after 20 Years in Milwaukee," JSOnline.com, July 30, 2008, http://www.jsonline.com/entertain ment/29565784.html (accessed October 28, 2009).

"James Cameron: National Visionary," VisionaryProject.org, http://www.visionaryproject.org/cam eronjames/ (accessed October 28, 2009).

Jones, Meg, Leonard Sykes Jr., and Amy Rabideau Silvers, "Cameron Brought Light to Racial Injus tices," JSOnline.com, June 11, 2006, http://www3. jsonline.com/story/index.aspx?id=434456 (accessed October 28, 2009).

—R. Anthony Kugler

Frederick Chiluba

1943—

Former president of Zambia

Chiluba, Frederick, photograph. AP Images.

Frederick Chiluba was elected president of Zambia in 1991 in the country's first multi-party elections. A landlocked country in Africa, Zambia is heavily dependent on a single export commodity, copper, and as such has one of the highest levels of industrialization on the continent, and the most developed trade union movement, apart from that in South Africa. A self-made man and active trade unionist who grew up in a mining town in the Copperbelt region, Chiluba seemed an unlikely figure to unseat Kenneth Kaunda—known affectionately as "KK," the "father of the nation"—who had ruled the country since its independence from Britain in 1964. Indeed, Kaunda often referred to his successor as a "political dwarf", in part in reference to his diminutive stature of just over five feet. Chiluba, however, proved himself to be a shrewd politician and forceful leader, serving as Zambia's president until 2001. After leaving office he was targeted by an anticorruption investigation that culminated in his prosecution for embezzlement. Although found guilty in a British court in 2007, Chiluba refused to acknowledge the judgment of a foreign court and awaited a verdict in Zambia. That came in 2009 when he was cleared of the charges.

Most accounts report that the first elected president of Zambia was born Frederick Jacob Titus Chiluba on April 30, 1943, to Jacob Titus Chiluba Nkonde and Diana Kaimba, in the mining town of Kitwe on the Zambian Copperbelt. His parentage is not clear, however, and his political opponents challenged his eligibility to contest the 1996 presidential elections claiming that either he or his father was born in the Democratic Republic of Congo (formerly Zaire). There is no doubt, however, that he was raised on the Copperbelt, and this contributed to his early interest in and involvement with trade unionism. Information about Chiluba's education indicates that it was patchy at best. Chiluba worked many different, sometimes menial jobs. At the age of nineteen, he began work as a personnel clerk on a Tanzanian sisal plantation. On his return home in 1966 he worked as an account clerk and shop steward with the Swedish firm Atlas Copco, working there for many years during which time he met and married his wife, Vera, and was heavily involved in trade union activity. At the same time, he managed to complete his secondary education and courses on bookkeeping and credit collection via London correspondence courses. Once elected presi-

At a Glance . . .

Born Frederick Jacob Titus Chiluba on April 30, 1943, in Kitwe, Zambia; married Vera Chiluba (divorced); children: Helena, Miloyan, Hortensia, Castro, Patrice, Ekman, Hulda, Fred, and Vera. *Politics:* Movement for Multiparty Democracy. *Religion:* Christian. *Education:* Warwick University, MPhil, 1994.

Career: Atlas Copco, Zambia, various positions, 1966–90; Zambia Congress of Trade Unions, Zambia, chairman, 1974–91; Zambia, president, 1991–2001.

Memberships: Organization of African Unity (OAU), chairman.

Addresses: *Contact*—c/o Zambian Embassy, 2419 Massachusetts Ave. NW, Washington, DC 20008.

dent, Chiluba even completed a master's degree from Britain's Warwick University.

Acquired Power through the Labor Movement

Chiluba rose quickly through the ranks of the Zambia Congress of Trade Unions (ZCTU), the coordinating body of the country's nineteen major unions, to be elected chair in 1974. Established in 1964 by the ruling United National Independence Party (UNIP) as a means to communicate with the labor force, the ZCTU had historically supported UNIP. In the mid-1970s, Chiluba urged the government not to regard ZCTU as a pressure group and reiterated its support for the government. Throughout the 1980s, however, the relationship deteriorated as the ZCTU resisted attempts at government incorporation, and Chiluba's attitude changed from one of automatic support for the ruling party to one of monitoring its progress and performance. During this time of transition, however, the ZCTU maintained that it had no intention of becoming a political party. The year 1981 marked the first major conflict between the trade union movement and the government when Chiluba and sixteen other leading trade unionists were expelled from the party and imprisoned following their refusal to cooperate with the government's Local Administration Act. As the state of the economy deteriorated and the price of maize (corn) meal, a staple of the Zambian diet, doubled, the trade union movement called for strikes, and there were major uprisings in most urban centers in 1986.

As the largest and most powerful non-state organization in Zambia, ZCTU's expression of support for

multiparty democracy was a landmark in the country's journey towards democracy. Chiluba said in 1989 that "if the owners of socialism have withdrawn from the one party system who are the Africans to continue with it?" according to a *Times of Zambia* article quoted in *Comparative Politics.* Kaunda lifted the ban to organize opposition parties in July of 1990, and within days the Movement for Multiparty Democracy (MMD) was officially established as a party. In 1991 ZCTU broke its alliance with UNIP to support the new party. Apart from UNIP no other association had a comparable organizational network, and MMD benefited greatly from the union's organizational apparatus, which along with resources and manpower, were harnessed in support of MMD. MMD was not, however, a labor movement, but rather a broad-based, diverse coalition of interests. Chiluba, who was elected chair at the party's first national convention in 1991, served as a unifying symbol with whom the Zambian population identified, and his history as a labor leader concealed the dominance within MMD of business and former members of UNIP. A former labor leader may have led the party to victory, but business had funded MMD with at least $10 million.

In elections declared to be free and fair both by international and local monitors, the MMD was swept to victory winning almost three-quarters of the vote and 125 out of 150 seats in the National Assembly in October of 1991. Kaunda immediately and gracefully accepted his loss of office, enabling Chiluba to preside over what was to be the first of a series of government handovers through the ballot box to be witnessed in sub-Saharan Africa, and as such Zambia was hailed by the international community as a pioneer of democracy and duly rewarded with considerable amounts of aid. Chiluba became president November 2, 1991, and in his inaugural speech declared that "the hour has come to build a new Zambia," as quoted in *African Affairs.* Shortly after his election, Chiluba, a born-again Christian who had discovered religion during imprisonment, declared Zambia a Christian nation. He pledged to instill biblical values into the political life of the country, but apart from the peppering of biblical references in his speeches, and one other visible Christian member of the ruling party, this declaration did not translate into noticeable changes in how the country was run.

Overcame Coup Plot in 1993

Two years into Chiluba's presidency, in March of 1993, a coup plot—called "zero option," a plan to incite widespread disobedience—was discovered and the government responded by declaring a state of emergency. Chiluba explained his decision: "Zambia is threatened. Our young democracy is at stake. The danger is real, and the consequences if not attended to are grave," as quoted by Melissa Ham in *Africa Report.* While Chiluba argued that the declaration of a state of emergency was necessary to protect the young democracy, others, including some within the government, saw the declaration itself as an assault on democracy, for it was reminiscent of the tactics employed by the previous government. On discovery of the plot, eleven members of UNIP, among them one of Kaunda's sons, were arrested and detained, but none of the arrests led to any convictions.

Questions about economic liberalization that were the center of debate during the 1991 elections contrasted with the rhetoric regarding citizenship that accompanied the 1996 elections. In spite of opposition among the donor community, parliament passed a constitutional amendment barring anyone whose parentage was not Zambian from standing for the presidency. Given that Kaunda's parents were from the area that is now Malawi, despite being the most credible alternative to Chiluba, he was effectively disqualified from standing for election. Chiluba's own claims to Zambian citizenship did not go unchallenged, and his political opposition produced a birth certificate which they claimed proved that the president had been born in the Democratic Republic of Congo (former Zaire)—a document that the Zambian government declared to be fake. In spite of a call from Kaunda for a boycott of the elections, they went ahead, and the MMD won all but three seats. Less than half of those eligible to vote were registered and less than half of those registered did go to the polls. It was a hollow victory that lacked the legitimacy of the elections that swept Chiluba to power, and both international and local observers united in declaring the elections neither free nor fair.

Kaunda voiced concern over the election results and continued his efforts against Chiluba. In October of the following year, a few days after he predicted that an "explosion" would occur, a group of soldiers took over Zambia's radio station and declared that they had deposed Chiluba, according to an article on the *Amnesty International* Web site. It was a premature declaration, however, and the army moved in swiftly to subdue the situation. Chiluba announced a state of emergency for the second time during his rule and had Kaunda arrested. In March of 1998 all charges against him were dropped, and the state of emergency lifted.

Sought to Fix the Ravaged Economy

The prevailing consensus among international donors as to the best way to achieve development was that political and economic liberalization should be undertaken simultaneously, and it was on such a ticket that Chiluba was elected. His government inherited a hugely indebted economy that was in shatters. Chiluba thus swiftly implemented a series of market-oriented reforms, such as the removal of subsidies on maize meal and petroleum imports, the liberalization of foreign exchange, and wholesale privatization. Chiluba is quoted in *Forbes* as saying, "We are determined to move away from a life of subsidy and consumption to a

life of sacrifice and production." The commitment to transform Zambia's economy from one dominated by large state companies and parastatals (companies managed—fully or in part—by a national government) to a market-driven, private-sector-led economy was not to last, however. In 1993, for example, figures spearheading the economic reform effort were removed from office.

For many observers, the litmus test would be whether Zambia Consolidated Copper Mines (ZCCM) made it into private hands or remained a national industry. Given that the economy depended upon copper for 80 percent of its exports, the issue was inexorably politically charged. Debates raged throughout the ten years of Chiluba's presidency, and the decision was repeatedly delayed. The mines were finally privatized in 2000, but in the following year the government reneged on its commitment to privatize a number of public utilities, opting for commercialization instead. In defense of this decision, Chiluba told a rally organized by the MMD that his government had learned from their privatization of other parastatals in the earlier years of his tenure that foreign companies—who would most likely become the new owners of ZCCM—would be unlikely to feel any obligation to contribute towards Zambia's economic welfare or to provide services at affordable rates. This stand garnered the support of trade unionists, human rights organizations, and opposition groups.

Accusations of corruption, drug smuggling, and human rights abuses among high level ministers and officials were not uncommon during Chiluba's ten years in office. Analysts focused in large part upon Chiluba's lack of political experience to explain his inability to discipline and rein in his corrupt ministers, some of whom were business tycoons and political veterans who had been longstanding members of the UNIP government.

Although by the end of Chiluba's tenure as president in 2001, real GDP grew at a rate of 3.5 percent and inflation fell to its lowest in two decades, as indicated by World Bank figures, few Zambians had benefited from this newfound macroeconomic stability. Extensive privatization and the removal of subsidies contributed to the deterioration of living standards, and as Chiluba left office more than 80 percent of the population were living below the poverty line.

Faced Corruption Charges after Leaving Office

Toward the end of Chiluba's second term, speculation was rife that he sought a third, and would change both the national and his party constitution to do so. Although he vehemently denied this, such rumors were given credence when activists protesting a third term were denied entry to an extraordinary MMD convention. Arguably frustrated by popular pressure Chiluba announced that he had never sought a third term and appointed as presidential candidate Levy Mwanawasa, who had served as vice-president until 1994 when he resigned in protest against corruption. He was widely considered a weak character, so his selection was seen as an attempt by Chiluba to maintain a hold on power from behind the scenes. The *Post of Zambia* alleged he was "of Chiluba, by Chiluba, and for Chiluba," as quoted by David J. Simon in a report on the *Freedom House* Web site.

If it was indeed Chiluba's intention to maintain control, it was frustrated, for shortly after Mwanawasa's election in 2001 he declared a "war on corruption and economic plunder" and established a task force to investigate corruption in his predecessor's government. After Mwanawasa alleged that Chiluba had stolen approximately $80 million during his ten-year tenure, parliament voted unanimously that Chiluba's immunity be lifted in 2002. Although Chiluba challenged the decision, observers noted that he had trampled over the immunity of his own predecessor when he had Kaunda arrested in 1997, and in February of 2004 the Supreme Court affirmed parliament's lifting of his immunity. Chiluba faced fifty-nine charges of theft and abuse of office, all of which he denied. Other top officials from his government were also charged, but complaints surfaced from a Zambian group called Citizens' Forum that the war on corruption had become too centered upon the former president.

In November of 2006 Chiluba was declared medically unfit to continue his corruption trial and sought treatment in South Africa for a heart condition. The following spring, however, he was convicted in a British court of embezzling $46 million from the Zambian government. The ruling was largely symbolic, however, as Chiluba did not submit to the court's authority, and maintained that only local courts had jurisdiction in the case. Mwanawasa offered a plea deal in which charges would be dropped if Chiluba admitted wrongdoing and returned 75 percent of the nearly $500,00 he was alleged to have stolen while in office. Chiluba declined the offer, and continued to deny the allegations.

Although Mwanawasa died in 2008, the case he instigated against Chiluba lived on in the courts. In August of 2009 Chiluba was cleared of the charges against him when a judge ruled that prosecutors had failed to prove that government funds were used by Chiluba to make extravagant purchases. Chiluba testified that the money had come from campaign contributions and corporate supporters, not from government sources. (Using political contributions for private purposes is not illegal in Zambia.) In the months following the trial, some anticorruption activists protested the verdict and called for an appeal. However, an appeal was not sought, and Maxwell Nkole, the head of Zambia's anticorruption task force, was fired. Critics of the prosecution, including President Rupia Banda,

noted that more than $13 million had been spent in the attempt to convict Chiluba, financial resources that could have been better spent on education and health care needs in the impoverished country. For his part Nkole expressed disappointment in the trial outcome, but noted, "The very fact that they were able to prosecute a former head of state sets a very important precedent." For his part, Chiluba expressed relief. "I want to thank the Almighty God," he said. "For eight long years the devil has tried to put the stigma of a thief on me. The Lord has dealt with that."

Selected works

Books

Chiluba, Frederick, *Democracy: The Challenge of Change,* Multimedia Publications, 1995.

Sources

Books

Chiluba, Frederick, *Democracy: The Challenge of Change,* Multimedia Publications, 1995.
Rakner, Lise, *Political and Economic Liberalization in Zambia 1991–2001,* Nordic Africa Institute, 2003.
——, *Trade Unions in Processes of Democratization: A Study of Party Labor Relations in Zambia,* Chr. Michelsen Institute, Department of Social Science and Development, 1992.

Periodicals

African Affairs, 91, 1992.
African Business, April 2001; September 2002.
Africa Report, May-June, 1993; March 1994.
Canadian Journal of African Studies, 29, 1995.
Christianity Today, April 1995.
Comparative Politics, 24(4), 1992.
The Economist, August 22, 2009, p. 33EU.
Forbes, September 1993.
Journal of Modern African Studies, 36(1), 1998.
Journal of Southern African Studies, 26(3), 2000.
New African, June 2001; May 2002.
New York Times, August 17, 2009.
Privatisation International, December 1994.

Online

Berger, Sebastien, "Zambia's Ex-president Frederick Chiluba Cleared of Theft," Telegraph.co.uk, August 17, 2009, http://www.telegraph.co.uk/news/world news/africaandindianocean/zambia/6044417/Zam bias-ex-president-Frederick-Chiluba-cleared-of-theft. html (accessed December 29, 2009).
"Country Brief: Zambia," World Bank, September 2009, http://web.worldbank.org/WBSITE/EXTER NAL/COUNTRIES/AFRICAEXT/ZAMBIAEXTN/

0,,menuPK:375684~pagePK:141132~piPK:14110
7~theSitePK:375589,00.html (accessed December
29, 2009).

"Zambia: Misrule of Law: Human Rights in a State of
Emergency," Amnesty International, March 2, 1998,
http://www.amnesty.org/en/library/info/AFR63/
004/1998/en (accessed December 29, 2009).

"Zambia's Chiluba Guilty of Graft," BBC News, May 4,
2007, http://news.bbc.co.uk/2/hi/africa/662454
7.stm (accessed December 29, 2009).

"Zambia's Chiluba Unfit for Trial," BBC News, November 17, 2006, http://news.bbc.co.uk/2/hi/africa/
6157990.stm (accessed December 29, 2009).

—Naira Antoun and Laurie DiMauro

Alice Coles

1951(?)—

Community activist

Coles, Alice, photograph. AP Images.

Alice Coles has been credited with almost single-handedly reviving her impoverished community of Bayview, Virginia. Until 2003 the Eastern Shore village was home to fifth-generation African-American residents who lived in two-room tar-paper shacks that lacked indoor plumbing. Coles rallied her neighbors, rural poverty specialists, and state and federal officials to join her crusade to reconstruct Bayview. Residents began moving into newly built homes in the fall of 2003. "The bottom line of everything that Bayview did was that we looked around," Coles explained to CBS News reporter Rebecca Leung. "We had everything to gain. We didn't have nothing to lose. So we put everything in it."

Born in the early 1950s, Coles was raised in a family of eleven children in Portsmouth, Virginia, a well-populated Atlantic seaboard port. Her father worked for the railroad, but every summer Coles and several siblings would go with their mother to stay with relatives in the small farming community of Bayview on Virginia's Eastern Shore. The Eastern Shore is a spit of land between Chesapeake Bay and the Atlantic Ocean. Its flat farming terrain and nearby shoals with plentiful oyster and clam beds had provided a modest but independent way of life for generations of residents. Bayview was a settlement that had been home to freed slaves after the end of the Civil War, and some families had roots in the area that dated back to the eighteenth century.

Coles and her siblings picked potatoes in Bayview every summer, and she liked the small-town feel of it so much that she moved there at the age of sixteen and graduated from the area's Northampton High School. Hoping to find a secretarial job, she was dismayed to learn that the few local employers rarely hired blacks for office jobs. When she applied at the Perdue chicken processing factory, she was offered a job on the line trimming chicken livers for $2.03 an hour, which she accepted. Over the next few years she became a union official at the plant and in 1974 finally moved to a desk job. She left Bayview for Norfolk in 1977 when she married and started a family.

Coles returned to Bayview in 1981 to care for her mother, who had retired there. By then, the small farms had largely disappeared. She found a seafood factory job as a crab-picker, but this was seasonal work, and she earned just $5,000 a year. For a time she ran a juke

At a Glance . . .

Born in 1951(?) in Virginia; daughter of Carlisle (a railroad worker) and Mary (Fisher) Coles; children: Nikita, Reginald.

Career: Worked at a chicken-processing factory, 1969(?)–77, and at a butcher shop, 1977(?)–81; also worked at a crab-processing factory and a solar-panel factory in the 1980s and 1990s; founded Bayview Citizens for Social Justice (BCSJ), 1995.

Addresses: *Home*—Bayview, VA. *Office*—Bayview Citizens for Social Justice, 22807 Bayview Cir., Cape Charles, VA 23310.

joint where she sold beer and took a cut of every card game. "I took it from very poor people and then watched them suffer for the whole month," she told *Virginian Pilot* writer Sylvia Moreno. "It was their rent money, school money, bread money and I was profiting."

Bayview was the type of small, rural Southern community that sprang up after the Civil War but seemed to have been passed by in the progress of the twentieth century. There were a total of fifty-two households, most of them renters who paid between $30 and $50 a month. Only six of the homes had running water; the toilets were outhouses that overflowed during the rainy season or chamber pots inside the house that were emptied into the outhouses. Water for drinking and bathing came from shallow wells that occasionally turned toxic from contamination by human waste. The provision of electricity, too, was substandard, with exposed wiring that sparked frequent fires, some of them deadly. In the winter months, heat was provided by wood stoves or kerosene heaters.

Coles lived in one of the six houses that had running water. She was spurred into activism in 1994 when Virginia officials announced plans to build a maximum-security prison on lands adjacent to Bayview. The cost would be $85 million, and some residents were swayed to support the project by the state's promise of five hundred new jobs. On the opposing side of the issue were affluent property owners on the Eastern Shore who allied with environmentalists in deeming the project a terrible idea. Coles joined their efforts and traveled to the state capital for the first time in her life to persuade the Virginia state assembly to halt the prison plan. "I said: 'We bathed your children—we took in your wash,'" she recalled in an interview with Anne Raver in the *New York Times.* "'And now you are leaving us to rot.'"

The grassroots effort worked, and the state abandoned the prison plan. The land had already been purchased, however, and the state was looking for a buyer. "If we left it open," Coles explained to Raver in the *New York Times* article, "somebody was going to come in and build a smelly old fish plant or condos." The community activists Coles had met helped her form a nonprofit organization, Bayview Citizens for Social Justice (BCSJ), which then applied for a loan to purchase the land. Coles also recruited a University of Virginia professor of architecture and expert on sustainable design, who counseled her on how to apply for Environmental Protection Agency grants first to study the well-water and outhouse issue and then to build new and improved deepwater wells and sanitary privies.

Coles dreamed of entirely new housing for Bayview and began working to win federal and state grants to construct low-income housing subsidized through U.S. Department of Agriculture rural-poverty relief grants. When her project seemed to stall, she invited a disaster-relief expert from the National Association for the Advancement of Colored People (NAACP) to inspect the town; he was appalled by the conditions in Bayview. The NAACP's involvement led to interest from news outlets, who sent in journalists, photographers, and camera crews to document the living conditions in Bayview that NAACP officials likened to those in South African black townships under apartheid. With that, Virginia officials took notice of Coles's efforts, and in the end the BCSJ won $4 million from the state, an amount matched by the federal government. Another $2 million was raised through other sources. In 1999 Coles left her job at a solar-panel factory in nearby Exmore to become the full-time executive director of the BCSJ.

The first residents moved into the $7.8 million New Bayview Rural Village in October of 2003. That historic event was captured by camera crews from the CBS News program *60 Minutes* as well as by makers of a 2004 documentary film, *The Black Soil: A Story of Resistance and Rebirth.* Coles's efforts went beyond housing: a community center, job-training school, community garden, child- and elder-care centers, and laundromat were already erected or in the planning stages, and Coles began thinking about new economic opportunities to ensure Bayview's long-term survival, too. Asked by Leung, the CBS News journalist, if one person can make a difference, she said yes. "They don't make all of the difference. Just one little piece ... like big doors. They hang them on small hinges. And if I couldn't be the door that opened, you know, to a better life, I'll be the hinge to hold the door."

Sources

Periodicals

Crisis, May–June 2005, p. 2.
Essence, April 2004, p. 40.

New York Times, August 21, 2003, p. F1.
People, October 6, 2003, p. 105.
Virginian Pilot, January 3, 1999, p. E1.

Online

Leung, Rebecca, "Alice Coles of Bayview," 60 Minutes, CBS News, July 18, 2004, http://www.cbs news.com/stories/2003/11/26/60minutes/main 585793.shtml (accessed January 2, 2009).

McMoore, Terry, "Community Builder, Activist Alice Coles to Speak at APSU Library," Clarksville Online, http://www.clarksvilleonline.com/2008/03/24/community-builder-alice-coles-to-speak-at-apsu-library-athenaeum/ (accessed January 2, 2009).

—Carol Brennan

Cardiss Collins

1931—

Legislator

Collins, Cardiss, photograph. Bettmann/Corbis.

Cardiss Collins is among the longest-serving African-American women in the U.S. House of Representatives. The first African-American wo-man to be elected to Congress from the state of Illinois, Collins was elected in June of 1973 in a special election to fill the seat left vacant when her husband, Congressman George W. Collins, was killed in an airplane crash. Just two days after her election, Collins started working on a bill to combat credit discrimination against women, just one of several issues concerning women, African Americans, and other minorities that Collins routinely brought to the attention of federal lawmakers. During more than two decades in Congress, Collins held positions in numerous subcommittees, including the House Government Operations subcommittee on Manpower and Housing and the Commerce, Consumer Protection and Competitiveness subcommittee. She retired from Congress in 1996 and later chaired an independent task force charged with improving racial equality in the methods used to assess television viewership.

Replaced Deceased Husband in Congress

Collins was born in St. Louis, Missouri, in 1931. At age ten she moved with her family to Detroit, Michigan, where she was educated and graduated from the High School of Commerce. She moved to Illinois, where she lived with her maternal grandmother, and married the Chicago politician George Collins in 1958. Through her husband, Collins became active in the local Democratic political organization and served as a committeewoman and campaign worker. Collins earned an accounting degree from Northwestern University and began working in a series of office positions in the Illinois state government. When her husband was elected to Congress in 1970, Collins's involvement in politics increased, and after his tragic death she was determined to carry on with the work he had begun on behalf of their Chicago district.

As chairwoman of the Government Activities and Transportation (GAT) subcommittee from 1983 to 1991, Collins pushed for groundbreaking laws to control the transport of toxic materials and to provide safer and more secure air travel. Growing concern about plans to locate landfills and incinerators in minority or poor neighborhoods led her to sponsor a bill that would give communities like Chicago's Southeast Side the

At a Glance . . .

Born Cardiss Hortense Robertson on September 24, 1931, in St. Louis, MO; daughter of Finley Robertson and Rosia Mae Robertson; married George Collins (a congressman; died 1972); children: Kevin. *Politics:* Democrat. *Religion:* Baptist. *Education:* Northwestern University, completed accounting degree, 1967.

Career: Illinois Department of Labor, stenographer; Illinois Department of Revenue, secretary, then accountant, then revenue auditor; elected to U.S. House of Representatives' Seventh Illinois District, 1973–96; chair of Task Force on Television Measurement, Nielsen Media Research, 2004–05.

Memberships: Alpha Kappa Alpha; Black Women's Agenda; Chicago Urban League; Coalition of 100 Black Women; National Association for the Advancement of Colored People (NAACP); National Council of Negro Women; National Women's Political Caucus. Served on numerous committees, including Congressional Caucus on Women's Issues, secretary; Congressional Black Caucus, vice-chairman; Congressional Black Caucus Task Force on Intercollegiate Athletics, chair; and Congressional Black Caucus Foundation Inc., chair.

Awards: Honored for government service, American Black Achievement Awards, 1991; Sportsperson of the Year, Black Coaches Association, 1994; received honorary degrees from Spelman College, Winston-Salem State University, and Barber-Scotia College.

Addresses: *Office*—Democratic National Committee, Member at-Large, 430 S. Capitol St. SE, Washington, DC 20003. *Home*—1110 Roundhouse Lane, Alexandria, VA 22314-5934.

power to forestall landfills and incinerators proposed for their areas. The bill was "meant to keep such neighborhoods from becoming concentrated dumping grounds for garbage and hazardous industrial waste," the *Chicago Tribune* reported.

In 1985 Collins called on Congress to cut funding to federal agencies including the National Endowment for the Humanities, the Federal Trade Commission, and the U.S. Justice Department that did not supply information regarding goals and timetables of their affirmative action programs, as required by law. In the mid-1980s Collins conducted inquiries into the employment practices of the nation's airline industry, investigations that showed that most airlines—including TWA and United—hired few African-American and minority employees. At United Airlines in 1985, *Jet* reported, 1.2 percent of pilot applicants were black, but fewer than 1 percent were hired. Fewer than 1 percent of the airline's black employees were classified as "professionals." These investigations resulted in the airlines taking steps to improve affirmative-action programs.

In 1987 Collins launched an inquiry into allegations that Eastern Airlines failed to repair critical safety equipment on its planes, an investigation that led to a Federal Aviation Administration inspection of the airline and an unprecedented financial review of Eastern's parent company, Texas Air Corp. The lax maintenance practices identified by the investigation led to criminal charges being filed against the airline and nine of its managers. Among Collins's other legislative achievements on behalf of minorities and women was an amendment to the Airport and Airway Safety, Capacity, and Expansion Act of 1987, which required a 10 percent participation level in all airport concessions by minority and women-owned businesses.

Supported Legislation Promoting Women and Minorities

Collins introduced legislation that would deny federal tax write-offs to major Madison Avenue advertising firms that ignored black-owned communications media, both print and broadcast. She introduced the Non-Discrimination in Advertising Act, "designed to correct a serious injustice against black and other minority-owned media," discrimination identified through a 1990 study by the Government Accounting Office (GAO, later the Government Accountability Office).

In their examination of the federal government's use of minority-owned advertising agencies and broadcast stations, the GAO discovered that the Department of Defense, which accounts for 95 percent of federal advertising, had failed to comply with non-discrimination regulations. There was little contracting with minority-owned media and advertising companies, *Jet* reported. Officials of the National Association of Black-Owned Broadcasters complained that they were subject to "systematic discrimination," a situation that Collins found intolerable, especially in instances in which ad agencies and their clients refused to advertise in media owned by blacks even when minorities were the targeted audience.

Prodding from Collins led the National Collegiate Athletic Association (NCAA) to improve opportunities for women athletes as mandated by Title IX of the Education Amendments of 1972. In a commentary in *USA Today,* Collins took issue with suggestions that the equal treatment of women collegiate athletes would somehow diminish men's athletic programs. She stated that the NCAA would have to "do a better job" of enforcing Title IX or Congress would have to step in. On February 17, 1993, Collins introduced H.R. 921, the Equity in Athletics Disclosure Act, designed to amend the Higher Education Act of 1965 to require institutions of higher education to disclose gender participation rates and program expenditures.

Supported Health Care Reform Legislation

A longtime advocate for universal health insurance, Collins co-sponsored both the Universal Health Care Act of 1993 and President Clinton's Health Security Act. She chaired one of four subcommittees to which Clinton's health plan was referred during 1993. As part of the latter Act, Collins argued fiercely for the establishment of a federal Office on Minority Health to increase research and track the health care needs of America's minority population. "Little use has been made of studies on minority prone diseases despite the significant disproportionate array of health conditions," she noted in hearings before the House Energy and Commerce Committee.

From 1991 to 1993, the House of Representatives adopted Collins's resolution designating October as National Breast Cancer Awareness Month. Collins wrote the 1990 law expanding Medicare coverage to include mammography screening for millions of elderly and disabled women. She also sponsored the Medicaid Infant Mortality Act of 1991, as well as legislation to provide Medicaid coverage for Pap smears enabling the early detection of cervical and uterine cancer. In 1993 Collins authored the Child Safety Protection Act, legislation requiring warning labels on dangerous toys as well as federal safety standards for bicycle helmets.

Although Collins continued to maintain a somewhat low public profile, in 1994 she found herself engaged in sharp, bitter debate with fellow Illinois Representative Henry Hyde over renewal of the Hyde Amendment, a restriction on the use of federal funds for abortion that was first approved in 1976. Collins and other African-American women representatives led the unsuccessful move to repeal the ban on federal funding of abortions for poor women under Medicaid.

In late 1995 Collins announced that she would not seek re-election the following year. With the Republicans in the majority in Congress at the time, her influence was somewhat diminished, and no Democrats were elected to chair positions on legislative committees. At the time of her announcement, she told *Jet* simply, "I'm going to be sixty-five next year and that's the time many people retire. Now is the time for me to move on."

Collins retired to Alexandria, Virginia, but continued her role as a minority advocate as a private citizen. In 2004 she chaired an independent Task Force on Television Measurement created by the Nielsen media company with input from Representative Charles Rangel of New York. The task force sought to increase the number of minorities included among viewers surveyed by Nielsen in order to better reflect minority viewing habits. In addition to Collins, the multiracial task force included advertising professionals, media executives, and minority advocates. The task force issued a final report in March of 2005 that made specific recommendations to Nielsen, including increasing the number of minority households sampled, strengthening training and recruitment efforts among women and minorities, and improving incentives paid to ratings participants. Concluding her work on the panel, Collins noted, "I am quite proud of the hard work that the Task Force members have devoted to this project, and I believe the report will be extremely helpful in [Nielsen's] efforts to ensure accurate measurement of persons of color."

Sources

Periodicals

Chicago Tribune, April 30, 1993, sec. 2C, p. 3; July 1, 1993, p. S1.
Congressional Yellow Book, summer 1994, pp. II–59.
Ebony, January 1992, p. 66.
Emerge, October 1993, p. 26.
Jet, December 22, 1986, p. 4; March 23, 1987, p. 8; January 28, 1991, p. 5; March 29, 1993, p. 29; March 7, 1994, pp. 6–7; April 25, 1994, p. 33; June 5, 1995, p. 10; November 27, 1995, p. 14.
New York Times, December 14, 1993, p. B15.
PR Newswire, June 8, 2004; March 23, 2005.
Rolling Stone, May 19, 1994, p. 43.
USA Today, February 10, 1993, p. A11.

Online

"Nielsen: We're Upping Our Ethnic Mix," Media Life, March 24, 2005, http://www.medialifemagazine.com/news2005/mar05/mar21/4_thurs/news1thursday.html (accessed December 28, 2009).

—Laurie Freeman and Laurie DiMauro

Camille Cosby

1945—

Philanthropist, entrepreneur, executive

Cosby, Camille, photograph. Scott Wintrow/Getty Images.

Camille Cosby is married to one of the most recognized faces in the entertainment industry, yet has maintained a low profile throughout much of husband Bill Cosby's career. She has preferred to work behind the scenes, raising five children, returning to school to finish her education, and helping to manage her husband's career and estimated $300 million fortune. A large portion of that fortune has been given away to historic African-American colleges and universities in an ongoing, one-family philanthropic mission. At the same time, Cosby has undertaken significant projects of her own, including a stage play based on a best-selling book, a documentary film about a mentoring program, and a project to record oral histories of African-American elders.

Camille Olivia Hanks was born in Washington, DC, in 1945, the eldest of Guy and Catherine Hanks's four children. After attending Catholic schools, she enrolled in the University of Maryland as a psychology major. During her sophomore year friends convinced her to go on a blind date. Her escort to the movies was a 26-year-old comedian named Bill Cosby. She eventually dropped out of school and married the rising star in

1964. Camille began traveling with Bill every few weeks as he performed throughout the country. Less than a year after their marriage, Bill Cosby's appearance on the *Tonight Show* landed him a role on the prime-time television show *I Spy.* As Alexander Scott, Bill Cosby became the first African-American to star in a leading dramatic role on a television series.

Assumed Role of Financial Manager

The Cosbys soon began a family that would number five in all—Ericka, Erinn, Ennis, Evin, and Ensa. Yet fame also came with a price tag. "We moved to California, and all of a sudden we were successful people," Cosby recalled in an interview with Stephanie Stokes Oliver of *Essence.* "All of a sudden we had money coming in, and it changed our lives.... Bill is seven years older than I am, but neither of us had the experience of managing money, of dealing with beggars, and of saying no a lot." Following the dismissal of a dishonest financial manager, Cosby realized that she was the best person to manage her husband's money. "When Bill released his manager, I realized that I had to become a participant," Cosby recalled in an interview

At a Glance . . .

Born Camille Olivia Hanks, in 1945, in Washington, DC; daughter of Guy and Catherine Hanks; married Bill Cosby (an entertainment personality), January 25, 1964; children: Ericka, Erinn, Ennis (deceased, 1997), Evin, and Ensa. *Education:* University of Massachusetts, MEd, 1980, PhD, 1992.

Career: Business manager for her husband, comedian, author, and television actor Bill Cosby; oversees all financial, philanthropic and staffing matters. Also president of COC Productions, a film production company, and C&J Productions, a stage production company; co-founder of the National Visionary Leadership Project.

Memberships: Board member, Essence Communications, National Council of Negro Women, National Rainbow Coalition; honorary member of Delta Sigma Theta.

Awards: Honorary doctorate, Spelman College, 1989.

Addresses: *Home*—Shelburne Falls, MA.

with Sharon Fitzgerald for *American Visions.* "In this kind of business, you have to protect each other. I think it is difficult for a performer to totally immerse himself or herself in creativity and watch everything else, too."

In the 1970s the Cosbys moved to Amherst, Massachusetts, and once several of her children were in school Camille Cosby decided to return as well. By 1980 she had earned a master's degree in education from the University of Massachusetts. "Education empowers you," Cosby told Fitzgerald. "It places you in a position to verbally challenge people who are giving you a whole lot of nonsense." Her dissertation focused on historically black educational institutions, such as Howard University in Washington, DC, which her mother had attended, and Fisk University in Nashville, Tennessee, from which her father had earned his master's degree.

Collaborated in Husband's Career

Over the years, Cosby has played an integral role in working with her husband on the details of his various projects. These projects have included comedy recordings and videos, stand-up engagements across the

country, Bill's role as a spokesperson for Jell-O products, and the phenomenally successful NBC-TV sitcom *The Cosby Show* and its spin-off, *A Different World.* The role of Claire Huxtable—the wife of Bill Cosby's character on *The Cosby Show*—was based, in part, on Camille Cosby. The mother of the fictional Huxtable family was cast as an attorney, opposite her obstetrician husband, and the show made important strides in showing a side of African-American life not often seen on television. The Huxtables were a financially successful, educated, African-American family that was as proud of their heritage as any other American family. The show stressed several important ideals: respect your elders, take pride in your race, and have a serious attitude toward your education. The set of the Huxtable home was also adorned with the works of African-American artists. The Cosby vision behind the show was a carefully presented one. "There are zillions of wonderful stories to tell, but they—meaning television's controlling, hegemonic strata—won't deal with those stories," Camille Cosby told *American Visions.* "They only want to perpetuate what they have always perpetuated: that we are buffoons and mammies and lazy."

While at work on her master's degree, Cosby visited eight historically black colleges and universities. In the course of her research, she found that many of these venerable institutions were suffering from dwindling enrollment and severe financial difficulties. A majority of alumni were uninterested in making financial contributions or sending their own children to African-American institutions, as civil rights gains had made it easier for African Americans to attend traditionally white colleges and universities. The Cosbys began working to remedy this situation by promoting historically black colleges and universities on *The Cosby Show.* Dr. Huxtable wore sweatshirts form these institutions on episodes of the program, and the eldest Huxtable daughter eventually enrolled in an African-American college, resulting in the campus-based spin-off *A Different World.*

Supported African-American Colleges and Universities

In addition to championing African-American colleges and universities on television, Camille and Bill Cosby began making large financial contributions to individual institutions. "We were forgetting about the history of black institutions and the fact that they had educated so many of our prominent leaders," Camille Cosby explained to Fitzgerald in *American Visions.* "So my husband and I were inspired to contribute and to make those contributions public so that the importance of the schools would be known." They began making large bequests in 1986, including a $20 million gift to Atlanta's Spelman College, which one of their daughters had attended. At the time the gift was the largest ever made to any of the 112 historically black colleges and universities in the United States. In thanks, Spelman designated a "Camille Cosby Day" in 1989 and invited her to give the commencement address. A large part of the donation was used to construct the Camille Olivia Hanks Cosby Academic Center on campus.

The concept of mentoring is an important one to Cosby. When she hired an Atlanta couple, Wesley and Thelma Williams, for a catering job, she learned that they were using their business to mentor several at-risk male teens. Their story became the 1994 documentary *No Dreams Deferred,* produced by Cosby, who took a hands-on role in the project. "I wanted to put something on film that would project positive images of young African-American males," she told Fitzgerald in *American Visions.* "The idea was also to show what one can do in an environment that is affirming, an environment that has discipline with love."

Completed PhD

Over the next several years, Cosby pursued a PhD. By this time, some of her own children were college-age. "The children have been very supportive," Cosby told Robert E. Johnson of *Jet,* "And I suspect, as a matter of fact, I think that because I was in school hitting those books diligently that it made my children more diligent students." She has publicly spoken about dyslexia, a reading disability that affected three of her five children, and the need to recognize differing developmental processes. As she told Johnson, "I think that the educational system as a whole has not been established to educate all children. That's one of the problems and that is why they will not acknowledge people with different learning styles."

In 1992 Cosby completed her PhD at the University of Massachusetts. Her dissertation was published in 1994 in book form under the title *Television's Imageable Influences: The Self-Perceptions of Young African-Americans.* It is a topic that is one of Cosby's most passionate pursuits. Her book examines the influence the media has over young African Americans between the ages of eighteen and twenty-five. Cosby asserts that the American entertainment industry, especially television, has not ventured very far from the stereotypical, racist minstrel images of the early twentieth century. "If you project blacks as human beings, then it makes it difficult to come up with a reason why they should be oppressed," Cosby told *New York Times* reporter Lena Williams.

Working diligently to alter those stereotypes, Cosby acquired the stage rights to *Having Our Say,* the remarkable 1992 biography of two North Carolina centenarians, Bessie and Sadie Delany. The daughters of a former slave, the charismatic sisters had attended college, gone on to complete advanced degrees, and watched history develop over the course of their long lives. C&J Productions—a joint venture of Cosby and her friend Judith Rutherford James—brought the Delany sisters' story to Broadway in 1995. Four years later Cosby served as executive producer of a television adaptation starring Ruby Dee as Bessie and Diahann Carroll as Sadie.

Lost Son

In January of 1997 the Cosbys experienced tragedy when their twenty-seven-year-old son, Ennis, was murdered in a robbery attempt as he was changing a tire beside a Los Angeles freeway. Diagnosed with dyslexia in college, Ennis had been working toward a PhD in special education at Columbia University and hoped to open a school for children with learning disabilities. He was remembered by his friends, students, and colleagues as someone who had succeeded despite his learning disability and sought to inspire others to do the same. On May 27th, Columbia granted Ennis Cosby a posthumous master's degree in recognition of his accomplishments.

Two days after Ennis's death the Cosbys were embroiled in a tabloid-fueled scandal when a young woman claiming to be Bill Cosby's illegitimate daughter was arrested on charges of attempting to extort $24 million from the entertainer in return for her silence. While Bill Cosby admitted to having had an affair with the woman's mother and had paid some of the woman's educational expenses over the years, he adamantly maintained that he was not her father, and when she demanded money as payment to refrain from selling her story to a tabloid newspaper, Cosby contacted the authorities.

The publicity-shy Cosbys were appalled to come under the media scrutiny that followed the tragic death of their son and the scandal that emerged so soon after. In an editorial in *USA Today,* Camille Cosby lashed out at the tabloid media for their "overt lies" and their treatment of her in particular. When her son was killed, she wrote, she was ignored as though "Ennis William Cosby did not have a mother," but when the scandal erupted she was on the covers of tabloids depicting her as "being out of control; emotionally and psychologically unstable and "on the verge of a nervous breakdown'…. Needless to say, I am outraged."

In 1998, after her son's killer was convicted, Cosby once again made a public statement in *USA Today,* this time with the assertion that American society had taught the killer, a young Ukrainian immigrant, to hate blacks. She stated, "African Americans, as well as all Americans, are brainwashed every day to respect and revere slave-owners and people who clearly waffled about race." Cosby went on to conclude: "All African Americans, regardless of their educational and economic accomplishments, have been and are at risk in America simply because of their skin colors. Sadly, my family and I experienced that to be one of America's racial truths."

Cosby's philanthropic work was unabated by the turmoil in her personal life and the backlash against her statements about race, which many found controversial. Indeed, a mere three weeks after Ennis's death, she and her husband responded to a solicitation for financial support from the founder of the *Black Star News,* a start-up publication intended to serve an African-American readership in New York City.

Founded National Visionary Leadership Project

In 2001 Cosby joined with former television correspondent and documentary filmmaker Renee Poussaint to establish the National Visionary Leadership Project (NVLP), an initiative to collect oral histories of older African Americans. The project's stated mission was to "ensure that the wisdom of our country's extraordinary African American elders is preserved by and passed on to the young people who will lead us tomorrow." Videos of the interviews were made freely available on the NVLP Web site and were permanently archived by the Library of Congress. In 2004 Cosby and Poussaint compiled *A Wealth of Wisdom: Legendary African American Elders Speak,* drawn from the archives of the NVLP. Speaking with Robin D. Stone of *Essence* about the importance of the project, Cosby said, "We must become critical thinkers. And the only way to be a critical thinker is to know the truth about our history. All of us have been guilty of just absorbing what the media tells us about ourselves. But we must question what we're told. And listening to oral histories will give us a different view of ourselves."

Selected works

(Author of foreward) *Our Family Table: Recipes and Food Memories from African-American Life Mod-*
els, by Thelma Williams, Diane Publishing Co., 1993.

Television's Imageable Influences: The Self-Perceptions of Young African-Americans, University Press of America, 1994.

(Co-author of introduction with William H. Cosby Jr.) David C. Driskell, *The Other Side of Color: African American Art in the Collection of Camille O. and William H. Crosby, Jr.,* biographies by Rene Hanks, Pomegranate, 2001.

(Editor, with Renee Poussaint) *A Wealth of Wisdom: Legendary African American Elders Speak,* Atria Books, 2004.

Sources

Periodicals

American Visions, December 1994, pp. 20–25.

Black Issues in Higher Education, March 21, 1996, p. 18.

Ebony, May 1989, p. 25.

Essence, December 1989, pp. 62–64, 114, 118; February 2004, p. 153.

Jet, June 15, 1992, pp. 12–17; May 1, 1995; March 18, 1996, p. 22; February 24, 1997; July 27, 1998.

New York Times, December 15, 1994, p. C1; January 17, 1997; January 21, 1997; April 17, 1999.

Time, January 27, 1997, pp. 22–27.

Online

National Visionary Leadership Project, http://visionaryproject.org/ (accessed January 7, 2010).

—Carol Brennan and Paula Kepos

Oscar Stanton De Priest

1871–1951

Politician

De Priest, Oscar Stanton, photograph. Chicago History Museum/
Hulton Archive/Getty Images.

In 1928 Oscar Stanton De Priest became the first African American elected to the U.S. Congress from a northern state. The Illinois Republican spent six years on Capitol Hill and endured some shocking indignities from a handful of hostile colleagues. He made headlines in 1934 by fighting to end an unofficial policy in the House dining room that permitted him to eat there, but forbade his bringing guests if they were black. "If we allow segregation and the denial of constitutional rights under the Dome of the Capitol," he asked his fellow lawmakers, according to *Jim Crow America: A Documentary History,* "where in God's name will we get them?"

De Priest was a native of Florence, Alabama, where he was born on March 9, 1871, thirteen months after Congress ratified the Fifteenth Amendment, which prohibited discrimination at the voting booth on the basis of a person's "race, color, or previous condition of servitude." Both of his parents had been slaves. Their hope for a better future following the Emancipation Proclamation and the passage of the Fifteenth Amendment was short-lived, as southern states began enacting strict new codes in response to the federally imposed Reconstruction-era laws. De Priest's father, Alexander, was a cart driver, and decided to move the family to Kansas as part of the "Exoduster" migration during which former slaves left the South for fear that slavery might be reinstituted. The De Priests left for Kansas in 1878, where De Priest attended public schools and learned some building trades. As a young man he took business and bookkeeping courses at Salina Normal School before moving to Chicago around 1889.

Elected to Chicago City Council

De Priest found steady work in the booming city as an apprentice plasterer, house painter, and decorator. His South Side contracting business evolved into a real estate brokerage, and he became active in Republican Party politics in the city. In 1904 he won a seat on the board of commissioners for Cook County, the county that includes Chicago, and was reelected to a second two-year term in 1906. He lost his 1908 bid, but won an important ally in Martin Madden, an influential Chicago Republican. In the spring of 1915 De Priest made Chicago history by becoming the city's first

African-American alderman, as Chicago's council members are called. He was elected from the Second Ward, which had a predominantly black population. Two years later he was forced to resign after allegations that he took money from an illegal gambling enterprise. He hired famed attorney Clarence Darrow to represent him; Darrow proved that the charges were politically motivated and won an acquittal for De Priest.

Chicago was undergoing a massive demographic shift during this same period, as blacks fled the repressive climate of the South for better-paying jobs in the growing urban industrial centers of the North and Midwest. De Priest founded the People's Movement Club, the first African-American political organization in the city. Over the next decade it emerged to become a key player in Chicago politics as the city's black population continued to grow.

Madden, De Priest's mentor, died in April of 1928 in Washington, DC, where he had been serving for the past twenty-three years as a Republican from Illinois's First Congressional District. De Priest's strong ties to the city's political machine helped him secure a spot on the ballot as Madden's replacement. He won the November election by three thousand votes, despite another attempt to block his ambitions through a grand jury indictment.

Before his swearing-in on April 15, 1929, there was another move to prevent him from taking office based on the vice charges of which he had previously been cleared. The Speaker of the House was an Ohio Republican, Nicholas Longworth, whose wife was Alice Roosevelt Longworth, daughter of Theodore Roosevelt. Alice was close friends with another newly elected lawmaker from Illinois, Ruth McCormick, who convinced Nicholas Longworth to make a change in procedure. "The Speaker dispensed with the traditional procedure for swearing in Members by state delegation," explained the Web site Black Americans in Congress, "and administered the oath of office simultaneously to prevent Members sworn in before De Priest from disputing the legality of his joining the 71st Congress." De Priest thus entered Congress as its only black member at the time. There had been a few African-American lawmakers before him who had been elected during the Reconstruction era, but the last to sit in the House had been George H. White of North Carolina, who left office in 1901.

Battled Lingering Prejudices

Further acts of discrimination followed. De Priest's wife, Jessie, found herself in the middle of a minor fracas over an invitation to the White House traditionally extended by the First Lady to congressional wives. When Lou Henry Hoover, wife of President Herbert Hoover, included Jessie De Priest's name on the official invitation, some southern segregationists erupted in protest. A few state legislatures even passed resolutions in opposition to the invitation. Mrs. Hoover was forced to hold the tea in four separate shifts to avoid placing De Priest's wife in an uncomfortable situation with hostile congressional wives.

De Priest had a difficult time finding office space in the nation's capital. A senior House member blocked his application for space in the House office building, but a Republican from New York, Fiorello LaGuardia, spoke up in De Priest's defense. "It is manifestly unfair to embarrass a new member and I believe it is our duty to assist new members rather than humiliate them," the future mayor of New York City told his colleagues, according to a *New York Times* report.

De Priest served three two-year terms in Congress. He held committee assignments on the House Indian Affairs, Invalid Pensions, Enrolled Bills, and Post Office committees. During his six years on Capitol Hill, he supported several issues pertinent to African Americans of the era, the most important of these an amendment to the 1933 act that created the Civilian Conservation Corps (CCC), a work-relief program. The amendment prohibited discrimination on the basis of race, creed, or criminal convictions, and was a small but significant milestone among civil rights statutes in the United States at a time when even the military was segregated by race. De Priest also introduced two anti-lynching bills, which sought to classify these acts as federal crimes. Neither bill passed.

Target of Death Threats

De Priest introduced another piece of landmark legislation, as well, which passed after he had left office. This was a 1933 bill that permitted court cases to be transferred to another jurisdiction if the defendant's lawyers could demonstrate that it would be impossible for their client to receive a fair trial because of blatant biases held by the community at large. The impetus behind the legislation was the notorious Scottsboro Nine case, in which nine African-American men from Alabama were falsely accused of sexual assault and sentenced by an all-white jury to the death penalty.

De Priest was fearless in pursuing his public life. He received death threats, but traveled to the South for speaking engagements anyway. In September of 1930 he was the target of an extortion scheme in which three Chicago men demanded $10,000 from him not to carry out a supposed contract killing on him. But it was one of De Priest's House colleagues who entered into the fiercest battle against the lawmaker, regarding the privileges accorded to members of Congress within the Capitol Building itself. Lindsay C. Warren, a North Carolina Democrat, objected to the presence of black congressional staffers in the House dining room. Technically, De Priest was allowed to eat there, but other African Americans were expected to eat in a separate basement room. Although this custom had been largely ignored in recent years, in January of 1934 De Priest's secretary, Morris W. Lewis, was turned away on the orders of Warren, who was chair of the House Committee on Accounts, which oversaw the dining room.

De Priest introduced a resolution on the House floor requesting an inquiry into the matter, but it was blocked. Turning to another option of parliamentary procedure, he drew up a petition and began to gather the number of signatures necessary to authorize the inquiry. Speaking on the House floor on March 21, 1934, De Priest conceded that his colleagues from the South brought their own beliefs with them to Washington. "I appreciate the conditions that pertain in the territory where [Warren] comes from, and nobody knows that better than I do," he said, according to the book *Jim Crow America: A Documentary History.* "But North Carolina is not the United States of America; it is but a part of it, a one forty-eighth part." Arguing in support of a formal inquiry he remarked further, "If we allow this challenge to go without correcting it, it will set an example where people will say Congress itself approves of segregation." In the end, the southerners prevailed, claiming that the dining room was not a public venue and therefore was not subject to the terms of the Fourteenth Amendment.

Lost 1934 Race

While a liberal on matters of social justice, De Priest was a conservative on fiscal issues. Although he served a constituency severely hit by the Great Depression, as a Republican he stayed with his party in opposing federal relief programs launched in 1933 by the new Democratic administration of Franklin D. Roosevelt. He lost his 1934 reelection bid to a black Democrat, Arthur W. Mitchell, who became the first black Democrat ever elected to Congress. This event also marked the first Congressional race between a pair of African-American candidates. Mitchell's election signified a shift that would influence American politics for the rest of the century, as northern Democrats began to court black voters, who had traditionally favored the Republican party because it was originally founded on an antislavery platform.

De Priest returned to Chicago and to local politics. He was again elected to the Chicago City Council, this time from the Third Ward, and served from 1943 to 1947. He died on May 12, 1951, from a kidney ailment at Provident Hospital, Chicago's black-owned, black-operated medical facility. He and his wife had two sons: Laurence, who died in his teens in 1916, and Oscar Jr., who died in 1983. The apartment building that De Priest owned in the 4500 block of King Drive South in Chicago was later designated a National Historic Landmark by the National Parks Service.

Sources

Books

Jim Crow America: A Documentary History, edited by Catherine M. Lewis, University of Arkansas Press, 2009, pp. 97–98.

Periodicals

New York Times, April 9, 1929, p. 64; June 26, 1929, p. 9.

Online

"Oscar Stanton De Priest," Black Americans in Congress, http://baic.house.gov/member-profiles/profile.html?intID=28 (accessed January 2, 2009).

—Carol Brennan

Shirley Franklin

1945—

Politician, executive, educator

Shirley Clarke Franklin made history in January 2002, when she was inaugurated as the first woman mayor of the city of Atlanta, Georgia, and the first African-American woman elected as mayor of any major city in the southern United States. After a career that had included three stints in city government, time as a business executive and entrepreneur, and a key role in bringing the Summer Olympics to Atlanta in 1996, Franklin came to run a city crippled by corruption scandals and fiscal mismanagement. During her eight years as Atlanta's top executive, Franklin tightened budgets, improved city services, oversaw a major investment in the city's water management system, and was repeatedly recognized as one of the best mayors in the country.

Shirley Clarke was born in Philadelphia on May 10, 1945, to Eugene Haywood Clarke and Ruth Lyons White. There she attended an all-girl's high school, which she told USA Today left her "believing that I could really do anything or be anything that I wanted to." However, public service was definitely not what she had in mind. "My dream as a child was to be a dancer. I wasn't the class president or the student government president or anything like that. The first time I ever ran for a major office was to be mayor," she continued. Following high school she attended Howard University, where she was active in the civil rights movement. There she earned a Bachelor of Arts degree in sociology in 1968. A year later she earned a Masters in sociology at University of Pennsylvania. In 1972 she married David McCoy Franklin and settled in Atlanta. They had three children, Kai Ayanna, Cabral Holsey,

and Kali Jamilla, who they raised in the same house on the southwest side of the city where she continued to live until her election. She and Franklin were divorced in 1986.

Franklin's first taste of city politics came in 1973 when her then-husband worked as a key player in the election of Maynard Jackson, Atlanta's—and the South's—first black mayor. In 1978 she joined Jackson's team as the commissioner of cultural affairs. When Andrew Young took over the mayoral office a few years later, Franklin was appointed city manager—becoming one of the first women in the nation to hold such a post in city government. She was responsible for the daily operations of Atlanta with a $1 billion budget and nearly 8,000 employees. During her tenure from 1982 to 1990 she oversaw the development of Atlanta's airport, a new city hall and court buildings, and over 14,000 new housing units. According Wendy Johnson of the Progressive Media Project, during this time she "gained the title of 'Mayor Shirley,' since Young's globe-trotting deal-making made him scarce at city hall." When Jackson returned for a third term as mayor, Franklin was appointed executive officer for operations, a post she held from 1990 to 1991.

Brought Olympics to Atlanta

In 1991 Franklin became the top-ranking woman on the team responsible for bringing the Olympics to Atlanta—the Atlanta Committee for the Olympic Games. She served as the senior vice president for external relations and was a key player in developing

Centennial Olympic Park. She was also the main negotiator with everyone from labor unions to environmentalist groups. In 1997 she parlayed her administrative and management skill into Shirley Clarke Franklin & Associates, a consulting firm for community and public affairs and strategic planning. In 1998 Franklin became a majority partner in Urban Environmental Solutions. She returned to politics later that year when she was appointed to serve on newly elected governor Roy Barnes's transition team. In 1999 she joined the Georgia Regional Transportation Authority as vice-chair. She held this post until 2000 when she officially announced her candidacy for mayor of Atlanta and resigned to begin campaigning.

During her years working in governmental and administrative posts, Franklin was very active in civil and cultural organizations, serving on more than thirty boards, including the Atlanta Symphony Orchestra, the Georgia Council for the Arts, the National Endowment for the Arts, the United Way, Spelman College, and the National Urban Coalition. She was also a member of the Democratic National Committee and served as treasurer of the Democratic Party of Georgia. Her activism and commitment to her community did not go unnoticed, and Franklin was the recipient of many civic honors, including the 1995 Legacy Award from the Big Brothers—Big Sisters of Metro Atlanta, the 1996 Woman of the Year Award from the YWCA, the 1987 Leadership award from the Atlanta chapter of the NAACP, and the 1983 Distinguished Alumni award from the National Association for Equal Opportunity in Higher Education.

Embarked on Two-Year Campaign

Although she was extremely experienced in city management and politics, running for office did not come naturally for Franklin. A naturally shy person, she was more comfortable as a team player in the background than as the person in the limelight. She was also concerned about the effect running for office would have on her family. However, she was able to overcome this reluctance. As she told *Newsweek* in 2007, "At some point, I looked in the mirror and said, 'You cannot give another graduation or baccalaureate speech, or another pep talk to a young woman that she has no boundaries and no limits if you in fact are limiting yourself by your fear.'"

Once she decided to run for mayor, her commitment to the cause was complete. The Progressive Media Project described her campaigning style as "well-organized, to-the-point and no-nonsense." Her first step was to take a full two years to campaign. "All of my [female] predecessors were well—educated, articulate, experienced African Americans who had been elected to other offices before," she explained to *USA Today*. "I looked at why they didn't win the mayoral race and discovered that they all ran for very short periods of time, like four months. They couldn't break down psychological barriers or raise enough funds in that kind of time. People have to see you, shake your hand and get to know you. So I spent two years running my campaign, getting out there and meeting the people." She also committed to full financial disclosure. She listed all of her donors on her campaign Web site and publicly released her last four federal tax returns. Her fundraising was stunning in its success, exceeding the funds raised by her nearest political rival, seasoned politician and former City Council President Robb Pitts, by nearly two to one. When the election was over it was revealed that she had raised and spent more than $3 million, the most ever spent by an Atlanta mayoral candidate.

As she campaigned, Franklin's indomitable personality came to light. A recognizable figure around town because of her blonde dye job and the large flowers she wore on her lapel, Franklin also became known for her openness and availability to constituents on the campaign trail. Her style was refreshing in a city beleaguered by problems including crime and poor city services and tired of the city officials who let these problems multiply. Although there were dissenters, mainly among well-off business leaders, when Election Day finally arrived, Franklin pulled in just over fifty percent of the vote—not a landslide by any means, but enough to avoid the run-off election many pundits had predicted.

Franklin further established her style with her inauguration celebration held in January of 2002. A far cry from the tuxedoed, invitation-only affairs Atlanta mayoral inaugurations were known for, Franklin's fete kicked off with a party complete with local acts including rappers Outkast and comedian Chris Tucker. The event was open to members of the public, who only needed to go to City Hall to pick up tickets. "People from every corner of the city supported her, and she really wanted this party to be about them as a way to say thank you instead of an inaugural celebration focused on her," Franklin's spokesperson Imara Canady told the Atlanta Journal-Constitution.

Faced Major Budget Crisis

It was a good party, but the festive mood died down quickly after Franklin took her oath of office and set about tackling the problems facing the city. The day after her swearing-in ceremony she announced that the city budget was running a deficit of $82 million—nearly $30 million more than the previous mayor had acknowledged. "The public in Atlanta had not counted ... on the city being in such bad shape," she later told Newsweek. "I had to give them the bad news that we were close to bankruptcy, and that we would all have to really take a step back and reorder our priorities if we were to get through it."

Franklin led a citywide belt-tightening effort by example, laying off half of her staff and slicing her own salary by $40,000. She also cut nearly 1,000 municipal jobs. She brought in top auditing firms to analyze the city's systems, including human resources and technology. "For some reason, people were skeptical," Franklin told the Atlanta Journal-Constitution. "They doubted that I could do the review audits. Not only are we doing it, but we raised $2 million from the private sector to do it."

While she wrestled with the budget and the audits, Franklin also initiated two major public relations coups—the "pothole posse" and ethics legislation. Atlanta's streets had been neglected by the previous administration, and potholes were a major problem for the city's motorists. Soon after her election she began a program to fill them, setting up a telephone hotline and promising action within seventy-two business hours. The public and the media loved it. "It was symbolic, but substantive. Nuts and bolts is what a city is all about," Bob Holmes, director of the Southern Center for Studies in Public Policy told the Atlanta Journal-Constitution. "It established a standard that things are going to be done the way they should be. If she is concerned about potholes, she is concerned about everything else." Another popular initiative she spearheaded was the creation of ethics legislation as part of the standards to guide public officials. "Everyone who ran for City Council, school board and mayor spoke the words of 'I will hold myself to a high standard; you can trust me, I am honest.' But translating that into city policy with ethics legislation took work," Franklin told the Atlanta Journal-Constitution. "I get almost as many calls about ethics legislation as I do about potholes. It was important to set a new tone for ethics."

It would take even more hard work to modernize Atlanta's water and sewer systems. In the 1990s, it became evident that Atlanta's antiquated water infrastructure was incapable of keeping up with the city's rapid growth. Raw sewage regularly overflowed into Atlanta's streams, creating a public health hazard, and the city was embroiled in continuous litigation with environmental groups and the federal Environmental Protection Agency. Between 1992 and 1998 the city paid more than $19 million in fines for violations of the Clean Water Act. Prior to Franklin coming into office, Atlanta was saddled with a multibillion-dollar court-mandated plan to remake the city's water and sewer systems, with deadlines that seemed impossible.

"No one thought that we could do it except for a federal judge and some strong environmental groups," Franklin admitted to the Atlanta Press Club in 2009. "[At first] I actually thought that we would fail, and that ultimately the federal government would take over the water system." Despite long odds, and the fact that it would require unpopular tax increases, Franklin threw herself into the job with her trademark dedication, dubbing herself "the Sewer Mayor," and lobbying the state legislature for a sales tax increase to help pay for the project. By 2008, Thomas Thrash, the federal judge who oversaw compliance with the Clean Water plan, was impressed with the city's progress, "Frankly, I expected excuses, delays, obstruction, incompetence, and, under Mayor Franklin's administration, none of that's happened. The work's been done. It's been done on time, I think pretty much done within budget. And it really is a remarkable accomplishment."

Won Re-election in a Landslide

Franklin's accomplishments did not go unnoticed. In 2004, *Governing* named her its public official of the year, praising her "straightforward attitude" and "just-do-it style." The following year, *Time* touted her as one of the five best mayors in the country, *U.S. News and World Report* profiled her as one of "America's Best Leaders," and *Esquire* featured her as one of the year's "Best & Brightest." Franklin was also awarded the 2005 John F. Kennedy Profile in Courage Award. Announcing the award, Caroline Kennedy praised Franklin for her "willingness to make the difficult and unpopular decisions necessary for good governance."

Franklin came into her second Election Day with not only this fistful of honors, but also with three straight balanced budgets and a comprehensive homeless strategy that combined carrot (a $5 million "gateway center" to help see to the personal and health needs of the homeless) and stick (a new law that made panhandling illegal in certain neighborhoods, police arresting "aggressive" panhandlers) bolstering her popularity. She beat three obscure challengers, garnering more than 90 percent of the vote.

In 2006 Franklin spearheaded the effort to keep a large collection of Dr. Martin Luther King Jr.'s papers and personal effects from being sold at auction, raising more than $30 million to ensure the collection would remain available to the public. She also focused on community beautification and development projects, increasing the size of the police force, curbing illegal handguns, and raising awareness of child trafficking. She became one of the first Georgia Democrats to throw her support behind Barack Obama in his 2008 presidential bid against party favorite Hillary Clinton. In turn, she was made one of the co-chairs of the Democratic National Convention in Denver that year.

Even at the height of her popularity, Franklin faced adversity and missteps. In 2004 Franklin's son-in-law, Tremayne Graham, was indicted as part of a major drug-dealing ring, and he eventually received a life sentence. Although Franklin herself was not implicated in any way, the authorities pursued Graham's wife, Kai Franklin, on money laundering charges, to which she pleaded guilty in 2007. In 2005 Franklin launched the Brand Atlanta campaign, which unsuccessfully tried to generate tourism for the city and was generally consid-

ered a waste of time and money. One of Franklin's signature projects, the Beltline, a proposed system of transit and parks based around a twenty-two-mile loop of unused rail tracks, ran into all manner of obstacles, ranging from lawsuits and greedy developers to last-minute threats by AMTRAK and the Georgia Department of Transit to condemn parts of the property for their own use.

However, the biggest setback the Franklin administration faced was the city's economic downturn. In January 2008 Franklin announced that Atlanta was facing a $70 million budget shortfall. She urged the City Council to take immediate steps, including a small tax increase, to keep the city from cutting essential services. The Council not only disregarded regarded her recommendations, but they voted to cut taxes instead. Months later, when the full extent of national recession became evident, the council members regretted their decision, as they had to pass a much larger tax increase the following year. Meanwhile Franklin, restricted by term limits from running for re-election, ended her second term as she had begun her first: tightening the city's belt with layoffs and furloughs—including shuttering City Hall one day a week—to save money.

The cuts, which included closing firehouses, reducing garbage collection, and furloughing firefighters and police officers, were painful to Atlanta's residents. In combination with her administration's lame duck status, the reductions in services took a real toll on Franklin's popularity. In her final press conference as mayor, Franklin related a conversation she had years earlier with then–City Council President Marvin Arrington Sr.: "We made a pact that when it was over, we would know it was over and move on. That was 20 years ago. I know when it's over. I'm moving on." For Franklin, moving on started in January 2010 with a one-year endowed professorship at Spelman College, where she would teach about gender, politics, urban policy, and leadership. In the last days of her administration, Franklin resisted grading her performance or discussing her legacy. As she told Shaila Dewan of the *New York Times,* "If you have to worry about your legacy, you don't have one. I would hope my legacy would be that a woman was up to the job."

Sources

Periodicals

Atlanta Journal-Constitution, January 4, 2002; April 17, 2002; April 18, 2002.
Christian Science Monitor, January 16, 2002.
Governing, November, 2004.
Jet, November 26, 2001, p. 4; January 28, 2002, p. 4.
Newsweek, October 15, 2007.
New York Times, October 10, 2006; September 8, 2009, p. A11.
Time, April 17, 2005.

USA Today, January 8, 2002.
U.S. News and World Report, October 30, 2005.

Online

"Atlanta: A Clean Water Success Story," City of Atlanta Online, http://www.atlantaga.gov/media/nr_cleanwater_080509.aspx (accessed January 8, 2010).

"Atlanta Mayor Shirley Franklin Signs Off (We Think)," PBA Online, December 17, 2009, http://www.publicbroadcasting.net/wabe/news.newsmain/article/0/2866/1590337/Atlanta.Morning.Edition/Atlanta.Mayor.Shirley.Franklin.signs.off.(we.think) (accessed January 8, 2010).

"Award Announcement," John F. Kennedy Presidential Library & Museum, March 10, 2005, http://www.jfklibrary.org/Education+and+Public+Programs/Profile+in+Courage+Award/Award+Recip ients/Shirley+Franklin/Award+Announcement.htm (accessed January 8, 2010).

"Mayor Shirley Franklin and the Ford Foundation's Alison Bernstein to Join Spelman College as Cosby Endowed Professors," Spelman College, News& Events, November 23, 2009, http://www.spelman.edu/_ezpost/data/23134.shtml (accessed January 8, 2010).

"Mayor Shirley Franklin Managing Atlanta's Future," NPR, April 15, 2008, http://www.npr.org/templates/story/story.php?storyId=89655308 (accessed January 8, 2010).

"Shirley Franklin Meets the Press," Forum Network, January 13, 2009, http://forum-network.org/lecture/atlanta-mayor-shirley-franklin-meets-press (accessed January 8, 2010).

—Candace LaBalle and Derek Jacques

Dorothy J. Gaiter

1950(?)—

Journalist, author, wine critic

Dorothy J. Gaiter is a prominent journalist and a leading authority on fine wine. She has worked as a reporter, editor, and columnist for some of the nation's most influential newspapers, including the *Miami Herald, New York Times,* and *Wall Street Journal.* She is best known, however, as a wine critic. With her husband, fellow journalist John Brecher, she has reviewed thousands of wines for "Tastings," the *Journal's* widely read wine column, since its debut in 1998.

Gaiter, known to many of her friends as "Dottie," was born in 1950 or 1951 in Red Bank, a small town in New Jersey. Her father, a professor in the field of industrial production, took the family soon after her birth to Tallahassee, Florida, where he joined the faculty of Florida A&M University, a predominately African-American institution in what was then a largely segregated region. One of the most formative periods in her childhood began in about 1957, when she moved to Indonesia, where her father was working. There she attended an international school, an experience that gave her an early appreciation for multiculturalism, diversity, and tolerance.

After her sojourn abroad, Gaiter received a shock when she returned to the United States in about 1960 and recognized the pervasiveness of racial discrimination in U.S. society. The civil rights movement was intensifying, and she quickly came to admire its activists, particularly journalists. The decision to become a journalist herself was made at the age of about ten. After high school, she entered the University of Missouri (MU), home to the world's first school of journalism,

established in 1908. She received a wide range of practical training, including a proofreading internship at a local newspaper. She later recalled these on-the-job experiences—a hallmark of the so-called "Missouri Method"—as an invaluable part of her professional development. The proofreading job, in particular, "reinforced [the idea] that you are accountable for what you do," she told MU's Yanan Zou. "The thing that made the School [of Journalism] special was that you got real-life work experience." During her student years Gaiter was also a founding editor of *Blackout,* a campus newspaper focusing on African-American life. As of 2009, the student-run publication was still in existence.

After receiving her bachelor's degree in journalism in 1973, Gaiter moved to Florida to begin work as a reporter for the *Miami Herald.* She remained there for roughly the next six years, focusing primarily on local issues. By about 1979, her work had drawn the attention of a rival publication, the *Miami News,* which hired her to fill the important position of night news editor. Her time at that paper was curtailed, however, when *Herald* staffer Brecher, whom she had recently married, took a job in New York City. Upon moving there to join him in about 1980, Gaiter found a job as a reporter at the *New York Times.* That position lasted until 1984, when the couple moved back to Miami to rejoin the *Herald.* There she received a substantial promotion, becoming the first African-American woman with a regular column on the paper's editorial pages. With new freedom to choose her own stories,

At a Glance . . .

Born in 1950 or 1951 in Red Bank, NJ; daughter of a college professor; married John Brecher; children: two daughters. *Education:* University of Missouri, BJ, 1973.

Career: *Miami Herald,* reporter, 1973–79(?); *Miami News,* night news editor, 1979(?)–80(?); *New York Times,* reporter, 1980(?)–84; *Miami Herald,* editorial writer and op-ed columnist, 1984–90; *Wall Street Journal,* reporter, 1990–96, national news editor for urban affairs, 1996–2000, wine columnist, 1998—.

Memberships: *Blackout* (student newspaper at the University of Missouri), co-founder, 1969.

Awards: Nominated several times for a Pulitzer Prize, 1990s–2000s.

Addresses: *Office*—c/o "Tastings," Wall Street Journal, 1211 Avenue of the Americas, New York, NY 10036.

she concentrated on ethnic and cultural diversity and socioeconomic issues.

As Gaiter's prominence in Miami grew, she began to receive offers from newspapers around the country. One of these was the *Wall Street Journal,* which hired her—and Brecher—in 1990. For the next six years, she traveled the country as a reporter, focusing on diversity in the business world. Pleased with her performance, the *Journal* appointed her national news editor for urban affairs in 1996. Two years later, the paper, aware that she and Brecher shared an interest in wine, offered the couple a chance to start a weekly column devoted to that subject. "Tastings" debuted shortly thereafter. It was initially treated as an adjunct to the authors' regular duties but became their primary responsibility in 2000.

"Tastings" quickly won strong reviews from consumers and wine professionals alike. Its relaxed and colloquial tone stood in sharp contrast to the staid style long associated with the subject. Gaiter and Brecher took particular care to avoid wine "lingo." Their rating system, for example, comprised a simple scale ranging from "Yech" to "Delicious!"

Encouraged by the column's success, the couple began work on a series of wine books, including *The Wall Street Journal Guide to Wine* (1999), which was in its second edition by 2002. They also completed a joint memoir, entitled *Love by the Glass: Tasting Notes from a Marriage* (2002). Alder Yarrow of Vinography. com, a leading wine blog, called the latter "a meditation on the subtle ways that wine and love both touch us deeply." The authors, who began dating at a time when interracial relationships (Brecher is white) were rare, designed the book, in part, to illustrate how society's growing appreciation for diversity has enhanced personal life.

In February of 2000, Gaiter and Brecher began what quickly became an annual event around the world: Open That Bottle Night, often known by the acronym OTBN. "On a special Saturday night in February," a Web site devoted to the event noted in 2009, "friends, couples and groups around the world get together to enjoy particular bottles of wine, champagne and spirits. The bottle that you enjoy, traditionally, is one that you have been saving for some special event that, so far, has never quite happened." Participants are encouraged to share the stories that result by posting them online.

Gaiter has received several honors in the course of her career, including Pulitzer Prize nominations for her work at the *Journal.* In May of 2009, she was asked to give the keynote address at her alma mater, MU's School of Journalism. "I am encouraged, looking at you, that so many smart young people are excited about doing this kind of work," she told the assembled graduates, "for it is necessary to keep democracies strong."

Selected writings

(With John Brecher) *The Wall Street Journal Guide to Wine,* Broadway, 1999 (revised 2002).
(With John Brecher) *Love by the Glass: Tasting Notes from a Marriage,* Villard, 2002.
(With John Brecher) *Wine for Every Day and Every Occasion: Red, White, and Bubbly to Celebrate the Joy of Living,* William Morrow, 2004.

Sources

Periodicals

Wall Street Journal, December 20, 2008.

Online

"About Open That Bottle Night," OpenThatBottle-Night.com, http://openthatbottlenight.com/index. shtml (accessed November 10, 2009).
"Missouri School of Journalism to Recognize 505 Graduates at Spring Commencement Ceremonies," Missouri.edu, May 8, 2009, http://www.journalism. missouri.edu/news/2009/05-08-commencement. html (accessed November 8, 2009).
Yarrow, Alder, "Book Review: *Love by the Glass* by Dorothy Gaiter and John Brecher," Vinography. com, February 3, 2008, http://www.vinography.

com/archives/2008/02/book_review_love_by_the_
glass.html (accessed November 8, 2009).

Zou, Yanan, "Missouri Journalism Alumni: Dorothy
Gaiter," Missouri.edu, May 8, 2009, http://www
.journalism.missouri.edu/alumni/dorothy-gaiter-73
.html (accessed November 8, 2009).

—R. Anthony Kugler

Eddie George

1973—

Athlete, business owner

Eddie George accumulated a slew of college football honors prior to his nine seasons in the National Football League. Before retiring from the game in 2004, the running back earned a reputation as one of the hardest-working athletes in the league, starting in 128 consecutive games. He spent most of his career with the Tennessee Titans, compiling impressive annual rushing and touchdown numbers well into his thirties.

George was born in 1973 and named after his father, a disabled military veteran whom he saw only intermittently while growing up in Philadelphia. George and his older sister were raised by their mother, a factory worker who later became a flight attendant, with help from one of his grandmothers. His ardor for the game dated to elementary school: at the age of eight he informed his family that he planned to win the Heisman Trophy, given to the top collegiate football player, and then go on to a professional career.

Packed off to Boarding School

George's plans were nearly derailed by his teenage hijinks. "I had a mind of my own," he told writer Beverly Keel for the Nashville Scene Web site. "I didn't

George, Eddie, photograph. Jemal Countess/Getty Images.

care about other people's feelings. I didn't care about authority." After his sophomore year at suburban Abington Township Senior High School, George asked his mother to pay for summer school so that he could improve his math skills; in reality the class was a mandatory make-up math course that required no tuition fee. His mother discovered the ruse and decided to ship him off to military school. She chose Fork Union Military Academy in Fork Union, Virginia, an eight-hour drive from Philadelphia.

George protested his mother's decision adamantly, even pleading with other family members to intervene. Once he had settled in at Fork Union, however, he recognized the opportunity. "It instilled discipline in me," he told *Football Digest* writer Larry Mayer. "I think I lacked that at that particular time in my life. It was very crucial for me to leave and go to Fork Union because I was on a path headed to nowhere. So I had to really get focused and decide on what I wanted to do with my life. I was young, but time was starting to run out on me." He credited a classic self-help book, *Think and Grow Rich,* as a great influence on him during this period of his life.

At a Glance . . .

Born Edward Nathan George Jr. on September 24, 1973, in Philadelphia, PA; son of Edward Sr. and Donna George (a flight attendant); married Tamara (Taj) Johnson-George (a singer, television personality, and author), June 2004; children: Jaire David; (with Johnson-George) Eriq Michael. *Education:* Degree in landscape architecture from Ohio State University, 1996; Northwestern University, MBA, 2009.

Career: Drafted fourteenth in the first round of the 1996 National Football League draft by the Houston Oilers (later the Tennessee Titans); played eight seasons with the Oilers/Titans; played part of the 2004 season with the Dallas Cowboys; The Edge Group (a landscape design firm), principal; partner in Eddie George's Grille 27 (Columbus, OH), and in Eddie George's Sports Grille (Nashville, TN); with wife, Tamara (Taj) Johnson-George, founder of a domestic violence awareness organization, Visions with Infinite Possibilities (VIP).

Awards: Player of the Year, Walter Camp Football Foundation, 1995; Doak Walker Award, Southern Methodist University, 1995; Heisman Memorial Trophy, Heisman Trophy Trust, 1995; Rookie of the Year, National Football League, 1996.

Addresses: *Office*—c/o Visions with Infinite Possibilities, P.O. Box 150283, Nashville, TN 37215.

Fork Union belonged to a prep-school athletic league, and even though George proved himself on the gridiron there was little interest from college scouts. "There were a lot of people around me saying, 'You can't do this, you can't do that. He's an OK athlete, but he won't go Division One,'" George recalled in the interview with Keel for Nashville Scene.com. "That was a big thing. I wanted to go to a big-time school and play in a great program, but no one necessarily believed it but me." In his senior year George scored twenty touchdowns and rushed more than fifteen hundred yards, but no full scholarship offers came his way. He even cold-called colleges himself, he told *New York Times* journalist Thomas George. "I told them all that I was 6 feet 3 and 220 pounds, but I really weighed about 200 then. I told them I was working on my S.A.T. I said I was a hard worker and my best football was ahead of me. They all kind of blew me off."

Won Heisman Trophy

George stayed on at Fork Union for an extra senior year, and finally garnered the attention of Big Ten recruiters for his performance in the 1991 season. He chose Ohio State University in Columbus, and in the season opener in September of 1992 the Buckeyes trounced Syracuse in a nationally televised game. George scored three touchdowns in the 35–12 rout. In the third game of the season, however, he fumbled twice, and he saw little action for the rest of the year. He was the third-string running back his sophomore year, but started for the Buckeyes again in the 1994 season. During that junior year, George rushed a total of 1,442 yards and scored twelve touchdowns. He surpassed those numbers in his senior year, totaling twenty-four touchdowns and 1,927 yards rushed, a school record. George set another Buckeye record that year, for 314 yards rushed in a single game. The Buckeyes finished that season 10–2, and George beat out several other accomplished contenders to win the Heisman Memorial Trophy, awarded to the most outstanding college player of the year. He also won two other top honors: the Walter Camp Player of the Year award and the Doak Walker Award for the season's leading collegiate running back.

In the 1996 National Football League draft, George was the fourteenth player selected in the first round. The Houston Oilers signed him to a five-year contract worth $7 million, but the team's owners had already announced their decision to move the franchise to Nashville, Tennessee, so George played the home games of his rookie season before sparse Astrodome crowds. His performance won him the NFL Rookie of the Year honors. The newly renamed Tennessee Titans team played at the Liberty Bowl in Memphis for the 1997 season, and at Nashville's Vanderbilt Stadium in 1998. In 1999 the all-new Adelphia Coliseum was at last ready to host Titans' home games.

George was voted onto Pro Bowl teams four times between 1997 and 2000 and helped lead the Titans to their first Super Bowl appearance in January of 2000. While the Titans lost there to the St. Louis Rams, George made two touchdowns and rushed 95 yards. In 2004, following a dispute over salary, the Titans released George from his contract. In July of that year he announced that he was joining the Dallas Cowboys. He started in eight games as their running back before his first-string position was usurped by Julius Jones.

Endured Dismal Final Season

In June of 2004 George married his girlfriend of several years, Tamara "Taj" Johnson, of the R&B group SWV. The two had met the night in December of 1995 when he accepted the Heisman honor, but did not begin dating until a few years later. When the newlyweds moved to Dallas, Tamara was expecting their first child. "We would turn on the TV and it was like, 'He is washed up. He is no good,'" Tamara recalled in the interview with Keel for the Nashville Scene Web site. "He had to go through a lot, and it just gave him a sense of endurance because it can tear you to pieces if you let it."

George left pro football at the end of the 2004 season, but had already been planning for his postgame career. With his degree in landscape architecture from Ohio State, he started his own environmental-design firm, the Edge Group, in Columbus. He teamed with some backers to open a sports bar–restaurant in the city, and then second one in Nashville, the city he had made his primary residence. Fox Sports hired him as a pregame analyst, and he also appeared on the Big Ten Network cable channel. His business ventures prompted him to seek an advanced degree from Northwestern University's Kellogg School of Management, which awarded him an MBA in December of 2009.

George remained close to his mother and focused on family life. In 2007 the Georges opened up their home to a reality-television crew from TV One. Producers of the series *I Married a Baller* hooked the show on George's accomplished wife, R&B singer Taj Johnson-George, who had returned to school to earn a bachelor's degree. Johnson-George had two older daughters in addition to her son with George and was stepmother to George's son from a previous relationship. George said he enjoyed the television experience. "You just see how precious and blessed you are to have your kids and your wife and the things you do have," he told *Columbus Dispatch* writer Molly Willow.

Selected works

I Married A Baller (television series, as subject), TV One, 2007.

Sources

Periodicals

Columbus Dispatch (Columbus, OH), April 18, 2007.
Football Digest, August 2000, p. 42.
New York Times, December 10, 1995, p. 81; November 5, 1997, p. C6.
Sports Illustrated, January 24, 2000, p. 50.

Online

Keel, Beverly, "The Longest Yard," NashvilleScene. com, March 17, 2005, http://www.nashvillescene. com/content/printVersion/15127 (accessed January 2, 2009).

—Carol Brennan

Haile Gerima

1946—

Film producer, film director, screenwriter

Gerima, Haile, photograph. AP Images.

Haile Gerima is an Ethiopian-born filmmaker best known for his 1993 film *Sankofa,* which follows a modern African woman as she is transported back in time to become a slave. The word *sankofa* means to go back to the past in order to move forward. It is an apt summation of the filmmaker's life. When he began making films, Gerima mined the richness of his Ethiopian culture as well as the horrors of African slavery. In doing so, he created a new form of African cinema with blacks as heroes and the Diaspora (the dispersion via slavery of African peoples throughout the world) as the landscape. He weaves together history and traditional storytelling to create a provocative filmmaking style. Along the way he has become one of the most highly regarded independent filmmakers in the world. Throughout his career Gerima has struggled for funding and been ignored by Hollywood, yet he has not stopped filming. When he found he could not get his films distributed, he founded a distribution company. When video rental chains refused to stock his films, he opened a video shop. When no theaters would carry his films, he rented out theaters across the country and presented the films himself. "We feel we are making our last stand in the cultural struggle—that is the struggle to make our own image," he told Esther Iverem on SeeingBlack.com. By reclaiming his past with film, Gerima is doing just that and creating a future for African and African-American cinema in the process.

Learned Western Culture in School, Cinema

The fourth of ten children, Haile Gerima was born in Gondor, Ethiopia, on March 4, 1946. His parents were both teachers, his mother at a primary school and his father for the Ministry of Education. His father, Tafeka Gerima, was also a playwright and founded a theater troupe with which the young Gerima often performed. His father's plays celebrated Ethiopian history and culture, a departure from the lessons Gerima learned in school.

He and his sister attended a school taught by well-meaning U.S. Peace Corps volunteers who emphasized Western culture and cut local culture and history from the curriculum. At his local theater nothing but American movies played. "I felt we [Africans] were savages," he told the Knight Ridder/Tribune News Service. "I learned from *Tarzan* that everybody has to

At a Glance . . .

Born on March 4, 1946, in Gondor, Ethiopia; son of Tafeka Gerima (a playwright) and his wife (a teacher) ; married Shirikiana Aina; children: six. *Education:* Studied at Goodman School of Drama (now the Theatre School at DePaul University), 1968–70; University of California at Los Angeles, BA, 1972, MFA, film, 1976.

Career: Filmmaker, 1971—. Professor of film, Howard University, 1975—. Founded film companies Negod Gwad Productions (production), Mypheduh Films (distribution, 1982—), and Sankofa Video and Bookstore (sales, 1996—).

Memberships: African Committee of Filmmakers; Pan-African Federation of Filmmakers.

Awards: Grand Prix Award, Lisbon International Film Festival, Silver Leopard Award, Locarno International Film Festival, and Oscar Micheaux Award for Best Feature Film, Black Filmmakers Hall of Fame, all 1976, for *Harvest: 3000 Years*; FIPRESCI Award, Berlin International Film Festival, London Film Festival Outstanding Production, and International Film Critics Award, all 1983, for *Ashes and Embers*; Best Cinematography Award, Pan African Film and Television Festival of Ouagadougou (FESPACO), Oscar Micheaux Award, Black Filmmakers Hall of Fame, and Mayor's Arts Award for Excellence, Washington, DC, all 1993, for *Sankofa*; Paul Robeson Award, Howard University Department of Radio, Television, and Film, 2001; Dioraphte Award, Rotterdam International Film Festival, Best Screenplay and Golden Prize for Cinematography, Carthage International Film Festival, Best Screenplay and Special Jury Prize, Venice Film Festival, all 2008, and First Prize, FESPACO, 2009, for *Teza*.

Addresses: *Office*—Mypheduh Films Inc., 2714 Georgia Ave. NW, Washington DC 20002.

---

can culture he had grown up admiring was not ready to accept him. At Goodman he was relegated to minor roles as a servant or criminal. Gerima recalled his frustration during a speech at Mount Holyoke University: "I was writing plays at home for my high school or my pre-high school. I was in my father's plays, and here I am now [in the] background. And it creates certain alienation in me." Distanced from his own culture and rejected by Chicago's theater scene, Gerima found refuge in the Black Power Movement that was gaining momentum throughout the country.

Used Film to Reclaim African Culture

In 1969 Gerima moved to California and shifted his focus from theater to film. He also began to turn a critical eye to the American movies he had devoured as a child. "At UCLA, I was intermingling with students from Brazil and Mexico. We shared a collective rage," he told the Knight Ridder/Tribune News Service. "We realized we had been betrayed by the movies." Hollywood had misrepresented his culture and that of countless others, including that of African Americans. Gerima decided to make movies that told the truth.

While in graduate school, Gerima made the short film *Bush Mama* about the political awakening of a young black mother on welfare. "When I made the movie … Black people were so hungry," he recalled in his speech at Mount Holyoke. "In Oakland they saw my movie and they thought it was a miracle movie and hugged me and cried and wrote poems about me." It was a very important experience for Gerima and validated for him the need for his work. His first feature film followed. Released in 1975, *Mirt Sost Shi Amit* (also known as *Harvest: 3000 Years*) depicts an Ethiopian peasant village that overthrows its landlord after centuries of oppression. The drama drew international acclaim and earned Gerima the Oscar Micheaux Award for Best Feature Film from the Black Filmmakers Hall of Fame. (Micheaux was an important African-American filmmaker from the 1920s and an inspiration to Gerima.)

In the filmmaking industry a graduate degree from UCLA's famed film school is considered a launching board for a career in Hollywood. However, Gerima had other ideas. In 1975 he moved to Washington, DC, and took a teaching position at Howard University, where he continued as a professor in the radio, television, and film department in 2009. "[Hollywood] doesn't have an appeal to me because it only inducts or recruits people to serve its interest," Gerima told the Web site Addis Tewlid. "That is why I even came to Howard to teach and be a part-time filmmaker. Because I didn't want to be subservient to the white Euro-centric cultural power in Hollywood." He concluded, "They wouldn't want me, nor do I want them."

Gerima's next few films documented the struggles of the African-American community. His 1977 documen-

---

go to America to become human." After a brief stint at the Creative Art Center at Haile Selassie I University, Gerima did just that, emigrating to the United States to study drama.

Gerima enrolled in the Goodman School of Drama in Chicago in 1967 and soon discovered that the Ameri-

tary *Wilmington 10–USA 10,000* told the story of ten African Americans, including former NAACP leader Benjamin Chavis, who were jailed on questionable charges for the fire-bombing of a white-owned grocery during riots in Wilmington, North Carolina. The convictions were overturned after Amnesty International intervened. In 1982 Gerima released the powerful *Ashes and Embers.* Described by the *Nation* as "honest and brave," the film documents an African-American soldier's return from Vietnam and the realization that he does not have a place in his country—neither within the white power structure, nor with black activists.

Though both these films were well received, neither of them drew the attention of Hollywood, and Gerima experienced difficulty getting them distributed. In response he founded Mypheduh Films which became one of the leading distributors of films by people of African descent. Mypheduh, from the Ethiopian Geze language, was a name given Gerima by his father and means "sacred shield of culture"—a fitting description of the goal of the company.

Depicted Slave Experience in Sankofa

Gerima first conceived the idea for *Sankofa* in the early 1980s. He wanted to tell the story of slavery from a slave's point of view and honor the forgotten history of the many slaves who escaped to freedom on their own. "Hollywood makes stories like *Cry Freedom* and *Mississippi Burning* where blacks are either spectators or victims to be freed by whites," he told the Knight Ridder/Tribune News Service. "This cripples the African-American viewer's self-esteem." Upon completing the screenplay Gerima encountered massive hurdles in securing funding.

It was not until 1991 that Gerima had enough money to begin filming. Two years later *Sankofa* premiered at the Berlin Film Festival. It won international critical acclaim and several awards, including prizes from the Pan African Film and Television Festival of Ouagadougou, the Black Filmmakers Hall of Fame, and the mayor of Washington, DC. However, U.S. distributors were not interested. "One distributor said it was too black," Gerima recalled to the Knight Ridder/Tribune News Service. "Then another said they couldn't market this movie. Yet another said the black audience would not go see 'serious' films." In response, Gerima rented out theaters across the country and marketed the film directly to African-American activists and leaders. Buzz about the film soon filled the black press, and in each city where *Sankofa* played, it played to full houses. "In city after city, audiences weep at Gerima's saga of Shola, an African woman who is shackled, then sent across the sea to toil on a sugar plantation in the Americas before rebelling against her slave-owners," wrote the Knight Ridder/Tribune News Service. Both

blacks and whites flocked to see the film, and it became clear that not only was there an audience for the film, but that audiences felt a need to see it.

In 1996, with some of the proceeds from *Sankofa,* Gerima opened the Sankofa Video and Bookstore in Washington, partly in response to the refusal of video rental chains to stock his and other African filmmakers' work. The store also housed Mypheduh Films and Gerima's film production company, Negod Gwad Productions. Gerima's wife Shirikiana Aina, with whom he has five children, is his business partner in these ventures. The store stocks mainstream black films as well as independent and foreign films about the African Diaspora.

Reflected Intellectual Displacement in Teza

Gerima's next major film documented the 1896 defeat of invading Italian armies by the Ethiopian people wielding little more than spears and an incredible conviction to defend their land. "It is a major event, but very underplayed not only to other people, but even to myself," Gerima told Michele Reaves in the *Washington Times.* Part documentary, part historical drama, *Adwa: An African Victory* released in 2000, required Gerima to travel back to his homeland and interview elders who knew first-hand accounts of the battle and could pinpoint the areas where fighting took place. Again, Gerima distributed the film himself, booking theaters across the United States and marketing it straight to the African-American community through the black media.

In 2008 Gerima released *Teza,* a film chronicling the experiences of Anberber, a young intellectual who leaves Ethiopia to study medicine abroad. He relocates to Germany, where he experiences harsh racism, embraces socialism, and forms an idealistic plan to return home to help those suffering in his impoverished homeland. Anberber returns to Ethiopia during a period of Marxist oppression in the 1980s and soon becomes disillusioned with his former political ideals. He settles with his mother but finds that he no longer fits in to village life and retreats into memories of his idyllic childhood.

Mike Collett-White reported for Reuters UK that Gerima told a press audience at the Venice Film Festival in 2008 that he was inspired by a dream to make the film. "The dream is basically about intellectual displacement.... When I translated my dream it was about being displaced, unable to live up to your peasant life, your peasant family and at the same time reconcile [that] with your modern world." Gerima explained to Ruth McCann in the *Washington Post,* that the story of Anberber, while not autobiographical, reflects many of the issues he encountered personally when he returned to Ethiopia as a visitor after being educated in the

United States. "What I do is I really look at that generation, the idealism that we felt…. It was very easy: We're going to go abroad, we're going to reclaim and come back." *Teza* won numerous international film awards, including trophies at festivals in Rotterdam, Carthage, Venice, and Ouagadougou, Burkina Faso.

Through his continuing efforts to write, produce, and distribute stories that reflect true African and black experiences, Gerima hopes to overcome generations of misrepresentation by white-oriented Hollywood films. "How can black people be anything if they are not culturally anchored?" Gerima asked during his speech at Mount Holyoke. "If one doesn't have cultural peace with oneself, does not respect one's origin, one's soul, one's spirit, one's physical appearance, how can they succeed in anything?" His solution is to turn to the past. "Many of us have disconnected our antennae," Gerima told the *Knight Ridder/Tribune News Service.* "But those people in shackles who crossed the ocean are trying to speak to us." Through his films, Gerima is giving them a voice.

Selected works

Films (as director)

Child of Resistance, Mypheduh Films, 1972.
(And producer and screenwriter) *Mirt Sost Shi Amit;* also known as *Harvest: 3000 Years,* Mypheduh Films, 1975.
(And producer and screenwriter) *Bush Mama,* Tricontinental Film Center, 1976.
(And producer and screenwriter) *Ashes and Embers* (television), Mypheduh Films, 1982.
(And producer and screenwriter) *Wilmington 10–USA 10,000* (documentary), Mypheduh Films, 1982.
After Winter: Sterling Brown (documentary), Mypheduh Films, 1985.
(And producer and screenwriter) *Sankofa,* Channel Four Films, 1993.

(And producer and screenwriter) *Adwa: An African Victory,* Mypheduh Films, 1999.
(And producer and screenwriter) *Teza,* Negod Gwad Productions, 2008.

Sources

Periodicals

Hollywood Reporter, September 2, 2008.
Knight Ridder/Tribune News Service, August 31, 1994.
Nation, January 20, 1992, p. 64.
Washington Post, September 21, 2009.
Washington Times, November 20, 1999, p. 4.

Online

Collett-White, Mike, "Ethiopian Film Explores Nation's Recent Violent Past," Reuters UK, September 2, 2008, http://uk.reuters.com/article/idUKL23453720080902 (accessed December 30, 2009).
Gerima, Haile, "Transcript of Lecture by Haile Gerima, Given at Mount Holyoke College on March 30, 1995," Mount Holyoke, April 5, 1995, http://www.mtholyoke.edu/offices/comm/csj/950405SE/transcript.html (accessed December 30, 2009).
Interview with Haile Gerima, Addis Tewlid, http://www.addistewlid.com/indexnew2.html (not active December 30, 2009).
Iverem, Esther, "Blackbuster: Haile Gerima's DC Store Rents a Different Kind of Black Film," SeeingBlack.com, http://www.seeingblack.com/x040901/sankofa.shtml, April 9, 2001 (accessed December 30, 2009).
Salouka, P. Boureima, "Ethiopian Film Maker, Haile Gerima, Does It Again," Afrik.com, March 9, 2009, http://en.afrik.com/article15401.html (accessed December 30, 2009).

—Candace LaBalle and Laurie DiMauro

George Gervin

1952—

Professional basketball player, nonprofit executive

Gervin, George, photograph. AP Images.

Basketball player George Gervin earned his nickname, the Iceman, for his cool demeanor on the court and effortless style of play. He regularly landed long outside shots as if they were simple free-throws, and he perfected his signature finger roll—a difficult maneuver pioneered by Wilt Chamberlain—while other players were busy dunking. He was so laid back that some players and coaches wondered whether he was bored.

But Gervin's outward reserve belied a fierce sense of competition. He was one of the most prolific scorers in basketball, averaging 25.1 points per game and 25,595 total points during his 14-year career in the American Basketball Association (ABA) and National Basketball Association (NBA), putting him among the best of all time. He won the NBA scoring title four times and racked up double-digit points in an incredible 407 consecutive games. In all nine of his NBA seasons—which included eight years with the San Antonio Spurs and one year with the Chicago Bulls—Gervin led his team to the playoffs and earned a trip to the All-Star Game. In 1996 Gervin was inducted into the Naismith Memorial Basketball Hall of Fame for his remarkable achievements.

Loved Basketball as a Boy

Gervin was born on April 27, 1952, in Detroit, Michigan, one of six children. His father left the family when George was a toddler and his mother struggled to make ends meet. As a boy, Gervin played basketball in his neighborhood with childhood friend Ralph Simpson, who later would star with the ABA's Denver Nuggets, and at the local YMCA. The game kept Gervin out of trouble and gave him an outlet for his youthful energies. "I was just running the streets like any other kid, but the difference was that I was in love with basketball," he explained, according to the National Basketball Association Encyclopedia Web site. "You live in a city like that and you're living in a state of war. You don't realize it then. You just take it day by day."

At Martin Luther King High School, Gervin tried out for the basketball team as a sophomore. At only five feet eight inches, and so thin that friends called him "Twiggy," he did not look like a promising player and was nearly cut from the team. Gervin struck a deal with

At a Glance . . .

Born on April 27, 1952, in Detroit, MI; married Joyce King, 1976; children: George Jr., Jared, Tia Monique. *Education:* Long Beach State University; Eastern Michigan University, 1970–72.

Career: Virginia Squires, forward, 1972–74; San Antonio Spurs, forward/guard, 1974–85, director of community relations, 1986–92, 1994–95, assistant coach, 1992–94; Chicago Bulls, guard/forward, 1985–86; Banco Roma, guard, 1986–87; Quad City Thunder, guard, 1989–90; George Gervin Youth Center, founder and director, 1995—.

Awards: All-Rookie Team, American Basketball Association (ABA), 1974; All-Star Game, ABA, 1974–76; All-Star Game, National Basketball Association (NBA), 1977–85; All-Star Game Most Valuable Player, NBA, 1980; Naismith Memorial Basketball Hall of Fame, 1996; Fiftieth Anniversary All-Time Team, NBA, 1996.

Addresses: *Office*—George Gervin Youth Center, 6903 S. Sunbelt Dr., San Antonio, TX 78218-3336.

the school janitor, who allowed the teenager to shoot hoops in the gym after hours—sometimes as many as 600 baskets a night—as long as he swept up before he went home. Gervin improved his skills on the court but struggled in the classroom, forcing him to miss half of his junior season. As a senior, however, Gervin, who had shot up to six feet four inches in two years, hit his stride, averaging thirty-one points and twenty rebounds per game and taking his team to the state quarterfinals.

Gervin earned a scholarship to play basketball at Long Beach State University under Coach Jerry Tarkanian. But Gervin immediately became homesick and left school during his first semester, transferring to Eastern Michigan University, located not too far from Detroit. He played two seasons of college ball, scoring 29.5 points per game in 1971–72 and leading the Hurons to the National Collegiate Athletic Association tournament. During a playoff game, however, the usually mild-mannered Gervin punched a player from the opposing team after getting elbowed. The following year he was suspended and then later kicked off the team, losing his scholarship; soon he quit school altogether. "That's the only time I remember crying, because I wanted [the scholarship] so much," he told *People* magazine in 1980.

Began Professional Career

Returning to Detroit, Gervin signed with the semiprofessional Pontiac Chapparrals of the Continental Basketball Association. During one game, scout Johnny Kerr turned out to see the young phenom, who scored a whopping fifty-two points that night. Gervin soon was drafted by the ABA's Virginia Squires, where he would be a teammate of Julius "Dr. J" Erving. Fellow Squire Roland "Fatty" Taylor was the first to dub Gervin "The Iceman" for his calm, cool manner on the court.

In 1974, as the Squires faced financial difficulties, Gervin was sold to the San Antonio Spurs of the ABA and he quickly distinguished himself as a top scorer. In his first season with the Spurs, he averaged 23.4 points per game, ranking fourth in the league. Two years later, the Spurs joined the NBA when the two leagues merged, and Gervin continued to dominate, even after switching positions, from forward to guard. He led the league in scoring four times in his first five years in the NBA (only Wilt Chamberlain and Michael Jordan earned more career scoring titles) and took the Spurs to the playoffs in eight consecutive seasons, although a championship title eluded him.

Gervin was known for making long outside shots—three-pointers after the NBA adopted the three-point rule in 1979—and his signature was the "finger roll," a one-handed move in which the ball is rolled off the player's fingertips, sending it high above the heads of defenders who might otherwise block the shot. The finger roll was notoriously difficult to master, and much less flashy than the dunk—a perfect match for Gervin's understated personality. Living up to his nickname, the Iceman had a reputation for his stoic, expressionless demeanor. "On the court he is a study in composition. He looks as if he is merely killing time in a playground, waiting to play winners. He shows only what he must show," Malcolm Moran wrote in the *New York Times* in 1979.

Following the 1984–85 season, the Spurs traded Gervin to the Chicago Bulls, where he played a single season before being released in 1986. He played in Italy with Banco Roma in 1986–87 and with the Quad City Thunder of the Continental Basketball League in 1989–90 before retiring from the game. Over the course of his ABA/NBA career, Gervin averaged 25.1 points per game (10th all-time), accumulated a total of 26,595 points (13th all-time), and made a dozen All-Star appearances.

Turned Life Around after Setback

In retirement, Gervin struggled to make the transition to life off the court. He had begun using cocaine near the end of his career and in 1989 he suffered an apparent drug overdose. "I couldn't deal with not being in the league anymore," he told *Sports Illustrated* in 1996. "I didn't feel I was worth very much. That's when the disease took hold of me and wouldn't let go."

Gervin sought counseling at a drug treatment center and turned his life around. He served as community relations director for the San Antonio Spurs until 1992, when he became an assistant coach for the team under John Lucas. In 1994 he returned to community relations; the following year he founded the George Gervin Youth Center, a nonprofit organization that reaches out to troubled youth and their families. "The key to everything is to give back. To help those that are unfortunate," Gervin told the Web site Good Point. "I give back because I'm a product of being an underprivileged kid…. It was tough times for me coming up as a young person, but I made it through."

In 1987 his number 44 was retired by the San Antonio Spurs. In 1996 Gervin was inducted into the Basketball Hall of Fame and named to the NBA's Fiftieth Anniversary All-Time Team.

Sources

Books

Hickok, Ralph, *A Who's Who of Sports Champions: Their Stories and Records,* Houghton Mifflin, 1995.

Periodicals

New York Times, January 29, 1979, p. C1.
People, February 4, 1980, p. 76.
Sports Illustrated, March 6, 1978; May 6, 1996.

Online

"George Gervin," Naismith Memorial Basketball Hall of Fame, http://www.hoophall.com/hall-of-famers/tag/george-gervin (accessed December 3, 2009).

"George Gervin," National Basketball Association Encyclopedia: Playoff Edition, http://www.nba.com/history/players/gervin_bio.html (accessed October 18, 2009).

Kent, Austin, "The Man and the Monument: How George Gervin Became Champion of the People," Good Point, October 13, 2008, http://www.thegoodpoint.com/basketball/oct08/the-man-and-the-monument-how-george-gervin-became-champion-of-the-people.html (accessed December 3, 2009).

—Deborah A. Ring

Angela Griffin

1976—

Actress

Griffin, Angela, photograph. JAB Promotions/WireImage/Getty Images.

Angela Griffin is an English actress best known for her role on the long-running television serial *Coronation Street.* After leaving the show in 1998, Griffin went on to roles in the medical drama *Holby City* and in *Waterloo Road,* a series set at a fictional urban high school in England. "I've had a completely charmed existence, I've just managed to go from one thing to another," she admitted to Nina Myskow, a journalist for the London tabloid the *Mirror.*

Griffin is of mixed heritage. Her father Desmond was a native of the Caribbean island of Nevis and moved to Britain in the late 1950s in the first major wave of West Indian immigration. He settled in Leeds, an industrial center in England's north, where he met Griffin's English mother, Sheila, while both were working for the bus company. Griffin, born on July 19, 1976, was the last of their three children and their only daughter. The family lived on a council estate, as public housing complexes are called in Britain, and struggled financially. As Griffin recalled in an interview with another *Mirror* journalist, Helen Weathers, her father's extravagant spending habits exasperated her mother, who divorced him when Griffin was still quite young. He departed England permanently, heading to the United States. "I was only four but I remember crying my eyes out on the back seat," she told Weathers. "I knew he was going away for good."

Won Soap Opera Part

Griffin's father had run up enormous debts before he left England. Her mother eventually remarried, but they stayed in council housing. "I spent most of my childhood being hard up," Griffin told Ali Hussain in the *Sunday Times.* "My mum had, on average, three jobs at any one time and my step-dad worked at Leeds council clearing up after the market." For Griffin and her brothers, their mixed heritage was also a difficult issue. "Where we grew up we were the only black family so we stood out," she told the *Mirror*'s Weathers. "As soon as I went to school I realised I wasn't like the other kids.... I had no hang-ups about it because as far I was concerned everyone got picked on at school. I did it myself."

Griffin discovered her calling at the Leeds Children's Theatre, where her aunt brought her for Saturday

At a Glance . . .

Born on July 19, 1976, in Leeds, England; daughter of Desmond and Sheila Griffin; married Jason Milligan (an actor), July 27, 2006; children: Tallulah Jae, Melissa.

Career: Made television debut on Yorkshire Television, 1990; cast in the British soap opera *Coronation Street*, 1993; continuing work as British television actress and host, 1999—.

Addresses: *Office*—c/o Sky 1, Grant Way, Isleworth, Middlesex TW7 5QD, England.

performance workshops. She appeared on that stage and with the South Leeds Youth Theatre, and her first television appearance was in a children's story dramatization on Yorkshire Television in 1990. She was fourteen at the time and had already started working in the fast-food industry in addition to shouldering her school obligations. In the interview with Myskow for the *Mirror*, Griffin recalled that entering high school was a turning point. "Leeds then was not the most multi-cultural place," she remarked. "But when I went to high school when I was 13, there were loads of brown people everywhere, and I was like, 'Oh my God, this is fantastic! I didn't realise there were so many of us.'"

Griffin earned excellent grades at Leeds Comprehensive School and was planning to study psychology at the university level when she won a part on a long-running British drama series, *Emmerdale,* which is produced by Yorkshire Television. Then sixteen, she decided to audition for another small part on *Coronation Street,* the longest-running soap opera on British television. "Corrie," as fans call it, has been on the air since 1960 and is set in a working-class neighborhood in Manchester, England. At that tryout was another Leeds performer, Melanie Brown, who was a year older than Griffin and also biracial; the two knew one another from school, and Brown would later become famous as "Mel B" of the Spice Girls.

"It Was Just a Job"

Griffin beat out the future Spice Girl for the *Coronation Street* part and made her debut as hairdresser Fiona Middleton in March of 1993. "I came into it so gradually, it was a year before anyone noticed me," Griffin recalled in the interview with Myskow for the *Mirror.* "I used to do an episode here and there. My normal life was working at Burger King. Because I was

16, I didn't realise what I had. I hadn't watched Corrie, I didn't see it as a big thing. It was just a job. I was earning money and I was on telly."

With a five-year run behind her Griffin decided that it was time to leave the show. She had no other job options, which made it a risky decision. "I soon discovered just how many bad scripts there are out there," she told Jim Taylor, a reporter for the Glasgow *Daily Record.* "For one they wanted me to be Cleopatra in a sitcom. I knew it wasn't for me." Griffin soon landed on *Holby City,* a hospital drama that debuted on BBC1, a British Broadcasting Corporation station, in January of 1999. The show was a spin-off of *Casualty,* a BBC emergency-room drama that had been on the air since 1986. Griffin was cast as Nurse Jasmine Hopkins and stayed until midway through the program's third season, leaving at the end of 2000.

In the fall of 2001 Griffin hosted a special program on Britain's Channel 4 about the nation's increasingly multicultural character. For *Brown Britain,* she interviewed other notable entertainment industry figures about their backgrounds and the challenges they faced growing up. She also interviewed her mother on camera, which "brought home to me all kinds of things about being a mixed race person," she told Edinburgh *Evening News* writer Olovia Convey. "My mum was so honest talking about what it was like in the Seventies being in a predominantly white area bringing home kids that were brown."

In 2002 Griffin appeared on several episodes of *Babyfather,* a romantic comedy series, and then joined the cast of *Cutting It,* a BBC show about hairdressers, where she stayed for three years in the role of Darcey Henshall. Her next regular series was *Waterloo Road,* set at an urban comprehensive school beset by an array of problems, in which she played teacher Kim Campbell. She departed in 2007 as she was about to have her second child, a daughter she named Melissa. Griffin and her partner, actor Jason Milligan, were married in July of 2006. Their first daughter, Tallulah Jae, was born in 2004. Griffin rejoined the cast of *Waterloo Road* in early 2009 and later that year began hosting an afternoon talk show, *Angela and Friends,* on the satellite television channel Sky 1. Her co-hosts were her two longtime friends and fellow *Holby City* alumnae, Lisa Faulkner and Nicola Stephenson.

Asked how she avoided being typecast as the spunky heroine after spending five years on one of the most popular shows in the history of British television, Griffin told the *Wales on Sunday* newspaper that moving on from *Coronation Street* was "just a happy accident. I'd love to say I planned my career, but I haven't…. It's just been what jobs have come up, what interviews have come up and which ones I've managed to get, and I think the rest of my career will be exactly the same."

Selected works

Coronation Street, Granada, 1993–98.
Holby City, BBC1, 1999–2000.
Brown Britain (documentary, as host), BBC 4, 2001.
Babyfather, BBC2, 2001–02.
Cutting It, BBC, 2002–05.
Waterloo Road, BBC, 2006–07, 2009—.
Boy Meets Girl, ITV, 2009—.
Angela & Friends (talk show, as host), ITV, 2009—.

Sources

Periodicals

Daily Record (Glasgow), January 2, 1999, p. 48.
Evening News (Edinburgh), June 16, 2001, p. 16.
Independent (London), October 20, 2002; May 15, 2008.
Mirror (London), November 29, 1997, p. 12; January 26, 2001, p. 32.
Sunday Times (London), May 11, 2008, p. 10.
Telegraph (London), April 4, 2001.
Wales on Sunday (Cardiff), March 29, 2009, p. 2.

—Carol Brennan

Bryant Gumbel

1948—

Television journalist

Gumbel, Bryant, photograph. AP Images.

Best known as the long-time host of NBC's *Today* morning news program, Bryant Gumbel has distinguished himself as one of the most skillful and quick-thinking news hosts on television during his fifteen-year tenure on *Today* and in numerous other diverse and high-profile assignments. Gumbel has hosted coverage of the Olympics, co-anchored coverage of a presidential election, hosted a prime-time newsmagazine show and a public affairs show, and served as an NFL play-by-play announcer. His work has won four Emmy Awards and numerous other honors. A combination of characteristics make Gumbel a tremendous asset on live television: his unfailingly thorough preparation and phenomenal memory are matched with an ability to speak fluently and act calmly when on-air pressures are at their peak. Off-camera, however, Gumbel's perfectionism has sometimes made him a difficult colleague, and his friction with co-workers has resulted in some unflattering headlines.

Born in New Orleans in 1948, Gumbel grew up with two younger sisters and older brother Greg—who is now a well-known network sportscaster—in the Hyde Park neighborhood of Chicago. His father Richard was a Cook County probate judge who had worked two jobs to put himself through law school at Georgetown University. Richard Gumbel instilled in Bryant his focus on the importance of reading and of writing and speaking well. He also taught him how to play baseball, feeding his son's growing passion for sports. As a student majoring in Russian history at Maine's Bates College, Bryant played baseball and football. However, his hope of becoming a professional athlete was ended by a wrist injury. Instead, Gumbel moved to New York City to work as a salesman for Westvaco Corporation, an industrial paper company; he quit this job after six months. While his parents hoped that he would attend law school, Gumbel was determined to try his hand at sports reporting. He soon landed a job with *Black Sports* magazine and, within the year, was promoted to editor.

Wowed TV Broadcasters

In 1972 Gumbel was about to take a job with the *Baltimore Sun* when his father died of a heart attack. Regretfully, Richard Gumbel never lived to see his son's

At a Glance . . .

Born Bryant Charles Gumbel, September 29, 1948, in New Orleans, LA; son of Richard Dunbar (a probate judge) and Rhea Alice (a city clerk; LeCesne) Gumbel; married June Baranco, December 1, 1973 (divorced 2001); married Hilary Quinlan, August 24, 2002; children (with Baranco): Jillian and Bradley. *Education:* Bates College, Lewiston, ME, BA, 1970.

Career: *Black Sports Magazine,* writer, 1971, editor, 1972; KNBC-TV, Burbank, CA, sportscaster, 1972–76, sports director, 1976–81; NBC, sports host, 1975–82, *Today* host, 1982–97; HBO, *Real Sports with Bryant Gumbel* host, 1995—; CBS, *Public Eye with Bryant Gumbel* host, 1997–98, *The Early Show* host, 1999–2002; PBS, *Flashpoints* co-host, 2003—; NFL Network, play-by-play announcer, 2006–08.

Memberships: American Federation of Television and Radio Artists; serves on boards of the United Way of New York City, Xavier University, and Bates College.

Awards: Golden Mike Award, Los Angeles Press Club, 1978, 1979; Edward R. Murrow Award, Overseas Press Club, 1984; Best Morning TV News Interviewer, *Washington Journal Review,* 1986; Journalist of the Year, National Association of Black Journalists, 1993; four Emmy Awards; Edward Weintal Prize for diplomatic reporting; George Foster Peabody Award; Frederick D. Patterson Award, United Negro College Fund; Martin Luther King Award, Congress of Racial Equality; three NAACP Image Awards; International Journalism Award, TransAfrica; Africa's Future Award, U.S Committee for UNICEF; leadership award, African American Institute; honorary doctorates from Bates College, Xavier University, College of the Holy Cross, Providence College, and Clark Atlanta University.

Addresses: *Office*— HBO, 1100 Avenue of the Americas, New York, NY 10036

clear that he had a special talent for his new job. The station had suggested that Bryant change his last name because of the possibility of nicknames like "Stumble-Gumbel"; instead, he became known as "Never-Fumble Gumbel." At the 1974 World Series, NBC network executives who saw him doing "stand-ups" in one take were impressed by Gumbel's fluidity and precision. NBC sports producer Michael Weisman recalled in *Sports Illustrated* the first impressions of the then chubby, long-haired sportscaster, "We were dumbfounded. We had experienced network guys who would've taken two hours to do what he did in two minutes." The network staffers at NBC immediately began asking for Bryant's name and that of his agent.

The next year, Gumbel received his first assignment for NBC as co-host of a weekend sports show called *Grandstand.* He outlasted two co-hosts because, as Rick Reilly smirked in *Sports Illustrated,* "Next to Gumbel, everybody else clunked like a dryer full of tennis shoes." In 1976 he began commuting from Los Angeles to New York to anchor professional football, baseball, and college basketball broadcasts for the network. Gumbel went to work for NBC full time in 1980, when he began doing three sports stories per week on *Today.* Eventually, he served as a substitute host when anchors Jane Pauley or Tom Brokaw were absent. When Brokaw left *Today* in 1981 to anchor NBC's evening news, Gumbel replaced him as a host.

When Gumbel first appeared as a *Today* host on January 4, 1982, he was one of three co-hosts, with Jane Pauley and Chris Wallace. Within the year, however, Wallace left the show and Gumbel teamed with Pauley as a main anchor. In 1984 Gumbel won the Edward R. Murrow Award for outstanding foreign affairs broadcast reporting for a series of *Today* interviews with high-ranking Soviet officials in Moscow. NBC proceeded to give Gumbel increased duties. In 1985 he became the host of *Main Street,* an afternoon monthly news program, and in 1988 he was the key anchor for the Olympic Games in Seoul, South Korea. This second assignment was "the fattest enchilada ever handed out by NBC," noted Rick Reilly in *Sports Illustrated,* "and the ultimate testament to Gumbel's talent is that no one has yet mentioned that it went to a black man." Writing for the *New York Times,* John J. O'Connor wrote, "Mr. Gumbel sets the tone for the prime-time coverage and he does so with remarkable style. He is smooth and articulate. Better yet, he has a sense of humor and perspective."

Negative Publicity Mounted

In 1988 Rick Reilly wrote a highly critical profile of Gumbel in *Sports Illustrated,* calling him a "strange man. Stubborn man." This was the beginning of media coverage that closely examined the journalist's private life and off-camera personality and often presented Gumbel in an unfavorable light. Reilly described Gum-

success as a journalist. Just a week after his father's funeral, Gumbel was asked to audition for the position of weekend sportscaster at Los Angeles's KNBC-TV. Although Gumbel believed that he got the job because the station wanted a black reporter, it soon became

bel as a man who was too hard on his friends, his mother, and people in general. Gumbel's professional enemies were numbered and an unflattering interview with his estranged mother was included in the article. In addition, the article focused on Gumbel's seeming obsession with his deceased father and even suggested that Gumbel proposed to his wife because his father spoke of her so highly.

In 1989 Gumbel's image was further tarnished when the contents of a confidential interoffice memo sent by Gumbel to the *Today* show's executive producer was leaked to the press. In the memo, Gumbel characterized the behavior of the *Today* show's weatherman Willard Scott as unprofessional and offered criticism of almost every aspect of his program. However, his assertion that Scott was "holding the show hostage to his assortment of whims, wishes, birthdays and bad taste" received the most notice. The press leak was followed by a highly publicized squabble between Scott and Gumbel, and *TV Guide* dubbed the entire incident "Gumblegate." Walter Goodman editorialized in the *New York Times* that given *Today's* formula of "straight news to straight nonsense," the incident gave Gumbel "the appearance of a vaudeville piano player clucking his tongue over how the jugglers are distracting the customers from his Liszt concertos."

The fallout from "Gumblegate" affected the show's cast and ratings. Willard Scott "made up" with Gumbel by giving him a kiss on the air, but proceeded to shift his weather reports to remote locations. Gumbel was essentially unapologetic. In an interview with the *New York Times* he remarked, "Maybe the worst somebody would *ever* say of me was: He was fairly undiplomatic in the way he tried to get things done. But at least he tried to get things done." In 1990 Deborah Norville was added to the *Today* show cast, a move which may have contributed to Jane Pauley's departure. Although Pauley had been a popular figure on the show, it was rumored that Gumbel didn't think she worked hard enough. The addition of Norville was not well received by *Today* viewers. The show's ratings plummeted, and it lost the distinction of being America's most popular morning program to ABC's *Good Morning, America.*

Firmly Anchored on Today

Eight years into Gumbel's stint on *Today,* the *New York Times Magazine* profiled the host, focusing on his reaction to such criticism and his role in revitalizing the morning news program. Writer Bill Carter noted that Gumbel had not responded publicly to the uproar surrounding the infamous *Today* memo, despite the urging of NBC management, and—contrary to the opinions of some friends—did not blame the incident on racial motivation. It was clear, however, that Gumbel was still determined to improve *Today* according to his agenda and that his talent had won him a key role in directing this effort. Carter offered this analysis of Gumbel as host: "With his seamless elocution, assidu-

ous preparation and astonishing memory for detail, Gumbel can speak cogently and off-the-cuff on virtually any subject—though he acknowledges a weakness in economics—and has a reputation for being unflappable, equally deft with a script or without, a man who can handle any broadcast crisis without flinching on the air."

In 1992 former *Today* staffer Judy Kessler published the book *Inside Today: The Battle for the Morning,* which included harsh criticism of Gumbel as a sexist who was aggressive and juvenile. However, the book did not receive much media attention beyond two excerpts in *TV Guide.* Moreover, Gumbel remained firmly entrenched as one of the main *Today* hosts. In November of 1992 the show regained the top ratings position for morning network news from *Good Morning America,* after the addition of Gumbel's latest co-host, Katie Couric.

Left Today for New Challenges

Bryant Gumbel always said how much he enjoyed hosting *Today,* but by 1992 it was clear that he was looking for a new challenge. With the program ahead in ratings, and with an award from the National Association of Black Journalists for a *Today* series shot in Africa—a five-year effort on Gumbel's part—the television journalist sounded restless. In January of 1996 he finally announced that he would leave *Today* in 1997 after fifteen years on the show. Having begun hosting HBO's *Real Sports with Bryant Gumbel* the year before, Gumbel decided to move on to other, as yet undetermined, projects. By the time he hosted his last *Today* show, on January 3, 1997, Gumbel had interviewed an estimated twelve thousand guests. His final episode was a two-hour tribute to Gumbel himself, with accolades from a parade of celebrities. Guests included Muhammad Ali, Maya Angelou, and the artist formerly known as Prince, while Tom Cruise and Hillary Clinton appeared on video. Moved to tears, Gumbel said, "I am humbled, I am grateful, and I am proud to have the friends and colleagues I do on this show."

Three months later, Gumbel had signed a five-year contract with CBS at an estimated $5 to $7 million per year to host a prime-time news magazine program. Called *Public Eye with Bryant Gumbel,* the show had its debut in September of 1997 but lasted barely a year before being cancelled due to weak ratings. According to Gumbel, the show failed for two reasons: the taped format failed to take advantage of his strength as a live interviewer, and he was given insufficient resources by CBS. "They went out and got a free-agent quarterback," he said. "But they had no offensive line, no running backs, no defense, no coaching staff, no scouting staff, no stadium. But they said: 'O.K., you're the quarterback. You win the ball game.' And, frankly, I wasn't good enough to do it."

Returned to Morning Television

In 1999 Gumbel returned to morning television as the host of CBS's morning news show, the perennial third-place finisher in the three major networks' morning TV wars. In first place, *Today* was seen by an estimated 5.5 million viewers, followed by *Good Morning America* on ABC with 3.3 million, while *CBS This Morning* brought up the rear with 2.5 million. According to estimates by Nielsen Media Research, *Today*'s dominance translated into profits of about $100 million for NBC in 1998. Renamed *The Early Show* and revamped at a cost of $30 million, the CBS program debuted in November of 1999 to great expectations. By early 2002, *The Early Show* had added approximately 200,000 viewers; at the same time, however, *Today* had gained more than a million and *Good Morning America* more than two million, in one of the few segments of network television that was gaining viewers rather than losing them to cable. By 2002 *Today*'s profits were estimated at $250 million, compared to $25 to $40 million for *The Early Show*. With his contract up, Gumbel chose to leave CBS and morning news behind.

Gumbel's tenure on *The Early Show* coincided with a bitter divorce that was highly publicized by the tabloids. Gumbel had left his wife, June, to whom he had been married since 1973, for another woman, Hilary Quinlan. A devout Catholic, June Gumbel was reluctant to accept a divorce despite her husband's very public affair with Quinlan. "People just accept infidelity from celebrities like it's okay or fashionable—I think it's disgusting," she said. "I don't think you can have happiness with someone else on the pain you've caused your family." The proceedings turned uglier when she sued him for "emergency financial relief," maintaining that Gumbel was providing her with a mere $250 per month and she was "destitute." Radio personality Don Imus staged a comic demonstration on her behalf called "Gumbel Aid" outside the window of *The Early Show* set. June and Bryant Gumbel were finally divorced in 2001; Gumbel and Quinlan married the following year.

Gumbel continued to host *Real Sports with Bryant Gumbel,* a highly regarded sports journalism show on HBO that Richard Sandomir of the *New York Times* characterized as "the sporting version of CBS's *60 Minutes.*" *Real Sports* has been awarded twenty Sports Emmy awards and the 2006 duPont-Columbia University award for broadcast journalism. In 2003 Gumbel also joined Gwen Ifill on PBS as co-host of a quarterly program called *Flashpoints,* which the network described as "an innovative public affairs series from PBS that brings together both compelling examinations of critical issues and a dynamic pairing of two of the most respected names in journalism." In 2006 Gumbel was hired by the NFL Network as a play-by-play announcer, a role for which critics universally agreed that he was ill-suited. He resigned after two years of relentless criticism that he had not mastered the mechanics of play-by-play.

Underwent Cancer Surgery

In December of 2009, Gumbel announced that he had recently undergone surgery to remove a malignant tumor from his chest cavity adjacent to one of his lungs. He had kept his condition hidden from all but his family and closest friends until he mentioned it while filling in as guest host on the *Live with Regis & Kelly* show. " I'm okay for the time being," he said. "I'm hoping they greenlight me to play golf again."

Sources

Periodicals

Daily News (New York), September 19, 1992; July 5, 1996.
Entertainment Weekly, June 21, 2002.
Houston Chronicle, July 22, 1993.
Jet, August 31, 1998, p. 39; February 21, 2000, p. 16; September 10, 2001, p. 46.
New York Times, September 19, 1988; April 2, 1989; November 11, 1992, p. C1; May 5, 1999; April 4, 2000; January 24, 2001; April 5, 2002; April 10, 2005; January 1, 2007; April 12, 2008.
New York Times Magazine, June 10, 1990.
Sports Illustrated, September 26, 1988.
Time, October 6, 1997, p. 9.
UPI Newstrack, December 8, 2009.
Wall Street Journal, November 21, 1989, p. A18.

Online

"Real Sports with Bryant Gumbel," HBO, http://www.hbo.com/realsports/index.html (accessed January 10, 2010).

—Paula Pyzik Scott and Paula Kepos

Marc Lamont Hill

1978—

Professor, author, media commentator, activist

Marc Lamont Hill is a self-described "hip-hop generation intellectual." A professor of education, he has taught a wide range of classes, from literacy workshops for high school dropouts to advanced seminars in educational theory. He is best known, however, for his work as a public affairs commentator, particularly on television.

Hill was born in 1978, probably in or around Philadelphia, Pennsylvania, where he was raised. His academic success in high school won him entrance to Philadelphia's Temple University, where he received a bachelor's degree in education in 2000. He then moved across town to begin graduate studies at the University of Pennsylvania. His PhD came in 2005, after a dissertation in the growing field known variously as the anthropology or ethnography of education. His work focused, in particular, on the many ways rap and hip-hop have shaped the classroom experiences of urban high school students.

Hill's dissertation drew the attention of Temple, his alma mater, which hired him in 2005 as an assistant professor in the departments of education and American studies. Four years later, he moved to New York City to become an associate professor of English education and African-American studies at Columbia University's Teachers College, one of the nation's leading centers of education research.

Amid the growing demands of his teaching career, Hill established himself as a commentator on contemporary politics, urban culture, and the law. His views have been expressed in a variety of media, including newspapers, blogs, public lectures, and television. He is best known for his frequent appearances on the Fox News Channel (FNC), a cable station with a reputation for social and political conservatism. On Fox programs like *The O'Reilly Factor* and *Hannity,* he often found himself in impromptu debates with other guests or with the shows' hosts. His viewpoint in these discussions was generally a liberal one. A supporter of Barack Obama, he nevertheless criticized the U.S. president quite sharply on several occasions, notably for he what he viewed as Obama's failure to pursue non-military solutions to the conflicts in Afghanistan and Iraq.

In October of 2009, Hill abruptly left FNC. While the circumstances surrounding his departure were not clear, a precipitating factor seems to have been a dispute he had with fellow commentator David Horowitz, a noted conservative. According to Steve Krakauer of the blog Mediaite.com, the disagreement began when Horowitz published an online response to comments Hill made on *The O'Reilly Factor* about Iran and its controversial nuclear program. Hill then responded online to Horowitz. As the dialogue continued, tensions grew, and on September 27, 2009, Horowitz posted a blog entry in which he called his adversary "an affirmative action baby." Shortly afterwards, it was announced by FNC that Hill was leaving the network. In a Twitter message quoted in the Mediaite post, he reacted to the news with apparent equanimity, saying merely, "On to the next one."

Even without a job at FNC, Hill's position as a prominent commentator on education and current affairs was

At a Glance . . .

Born in 1978, probably in Philadelphia, PA. *Education:* Temple University, BS, education, 2000; University of Pennsylvania, PhD, education, 2005.

Career: Temple University, assistant professor of urban education and American studies, 2005–09; Columbia University, associate professor of English education and African-American studies, 2009—; Fox News Channel, commentator, 2006(?)–09; Metro Newspapers, syndicated columnist, 2006(?)—.

Memberships: My5th, founding board member; American Civil Liberties Union Drug Reform Project.

Awards: Named one of "30 Leaders of the Future," *Ebony,* 2005.

Addresses: *Office*—c/o Program in English Education, Teachers College, Columbia University, 525 W. 120th St., New York, NY 10027. *Web*—http://www.marclamonthill.com/.

likely to continue, thanks in part to his ongoing roles as a newspaper columnist and blogger. As of 2009, most of his print columns appeared in Metro Newspapers, a chain of alternative weeklies to which he contributed regularly. He has also written extensively for the blog on his Web site, MarcLamontHill.com, and for other online journals. Clips from many of his television appearances have been posted on YouTube, the popular video-sharing site. In one of these, posted in 2007, Hill commented on the use of the word "articulate" by President George W. Bush in reference to Barack Obama, then a U.S. senator. In response to a question by Bill O'Reilly, host of *The O'Reilly Factor,* Hill remarked that the word, when used by whites in reference to African Americans, is often considered patronizing. As of November of 2009, the video had been viewed more than fifty-two thousand times.

Hill has also been active for many years in a number of nonprofit outreach efforts, many of which have focused on literacy and dropout prevention. As early as 2001, he noted on his Web site, he had designed and implemented an innovative project "that use[d] hip-hop culture to increase school engagement and reading skills among high school students." Those efforts later became the basis for his dissertation.

Not all of Hill's outreach activities have been confined to the classroom. In the mid-2000s, he was a co-founder of My5th, an organization aimed at increasing young people's awareness of their legal rights, particularly the Fifth Amendment's guarantee of due process. As of 2009 he continued to serve on the group's board of trustees. Related to his work for My5th was his involvement in the American Civil Liberties Union Drug Reform Project (ACLUDRP). According to the program's Web site, ACLUDRP was established in an effort "to end punitive drug policies that cause the widespread violation of constitutional and human rights." Hill has often expressed his unease about the government's drug-enforcement efforts, arguing that they inflict a heavy and disproportionate toll on the nation's minorities, particularly African-American youth.

As of the fall of 2009, Hill had several major academic publications to his credit, including *Media, Learning, and Sites of Possibility* (co-edited with Lalitha Vasudevan, 2007) and *Beats, Rhymes, and Classroom Life: Hip-Hop Pedagogy and the Politics of Identity* (2009). The latter is "a book that helps us see the power and potential of pedagogy," Gloria Ladson-Billings of the University of Wisconsin wrote in a forward. "It is not merely what Hill decides to teach that matters. It is also how he teaches it that connects with the students."

In January of 2010 Hill was in the process of completing two new books. The first of these was tentatively titled *Knowledge of Self: Race, Masculinity, and the Politics of Reading*; the second was *You Ain't Heard It from Me: Snitching, Rumors and Other People's Business in Hip-Hop America.*

Selected writings

(Editor, with Lalitha Vasudevan) *Media, Learning, and Sites of Possibility,* Peter Lang, 2007.
Beats, Rhymes, and Classroom Life: Hip-Hop Pedagogy and the Politics of Identity, Teachers College, 2009.

Sources

Periodicals

Ebony, April 2005.

Online

"About," MarcLamontHill.com, http://www.marclamonthill.com/about (accessed November 5, 2009).
"Bill O'Reilly and Marc Lamont Hill Debate 'Articulate,'" YouTube.com, February 7, 2007, http://www.youtube.com/watch?v=fqbmcpQJwxg (accessed November 7, 2009).
"Drug Law Reform," ACLU.org, http://www.aclu.org/drug-law-reform (accessed November 7, 2009).
Horowitz, David, "Fox's Affirmative Action Baby Whines," NewsRealBlog.com, September 27, 2009,

http://newsrealblog.com/2009/09/27/foxs-affirm ative-action-baby-whines/ (accessed November 7, 2009).

Krakauer, Steve, "Liberal Analyst Marc Lamont Hill Fired from Fox News," Mediaite.com, October 16, 2009, http://www.mediaite.com/tv/confirmed-marc-lamont-hill-fired-from-fox-news/ (accessed November 5, 2009).

"Marc Lamont Hill: Educational Leadership and Policy Studies," Temple.edu, http://www.temple.edu/education/faculty/hill_m.html (accessed November 5, 2009).
"Video: Marc Lamont Hill," Philly.com, July 20, 2007, http://www.philly.com/philly/multimedia/8625952.html (accessed November 5, 2009).

—R. Anthony Kugler

Lubna Hussein

1970(?)—

Journalist, human rights activist

Hussein, Lubna, photograph. Jacques Demarthon/AFP/Getty Images.

Sudanese journalist Lubna Hussein made international headlines in 2009 when she was arrested for wearing trousers in public. Sudan's public order police detained her and several other women for violating a section of the country's criminal code that prohibits clothing considered indecent. Violators can be subject to a sentence of up to forty lashes, plus a fine. Hussein, who is an observant Muslim, fought her conviction in order to bring attention to human rights in her homeland. "Sudan has a proud and sad history of courageous men and women who have had to fight against repressive laws," she wrote in an editorial that appeared in London's *Guardian* newspaper. "They taught me that we should not hide behind privilege but that we should speak out for those who cannot find their voice."

Born in the 1970s, Hussein came of age in a country torn by civil war. Sudan's longstanding conflicts between its predominantly Muslim north and the Christian and animist south were also linked to ethnic origins; Sudanese of Arab heritage in the north found themselves in an uneasy national alliance with Nilotes of the southern regions, a union imposed by colonial British authorities when they began pulling out of this part of Africa in the years following World War II. The country's second civil war erupted in 1983 when rulers in Khartoum, the capital, began an Islamicization effort that included the imposition of sharia, or Islamic law.

In 2005 the opposing sides reached an agreement brokered by United Nations representatives that included a timetable for a referendum vote on independence for southern Sudan. Under the terms of this Comprehensive Peace Agreement, sharia law would apply only to Muslims in Sudan. The United Nations established the United Nations Mission in the Sudan (UNMIS) to oversee the agreement. Hussein worked as a public information assistant in the UNMIS media department.

Sudan's legal system operates under a penal code dating back to 1991. Islamic law applies to all residents in the north of Sudan, though the 2005 Comprehensive Peace Agreement exempted some non-Muslims in Khartoum from the sharia codes. One of those is Article 152, which covers what are termed "obscene and indecent acts" that may be construed as "contrary to public morals or causing an annoyance to public feelings." Special "public order police"—common in

At a Glance . . .

Born Lubna Ahmed Hussein in 1970(?) in Sudan; widowed. *Religion:* Muslim.

Career: United Nations Mission in the Sudan (UNMIS), public information assistant in the media department, until 2009.

Addresses: *Office*—c/o United Nations Mission in the Sudan (UNMIS), Ebeid Khatim St., Khartoum 11111, Sudan.

many Islamic nations that use sharia as the basis of their judicial systems—are given enforcement powers. Article 152 also gives sentencing guidelines that include corporal punishment. Anyone convicted under its terms may face up to forty lashes, plus a fine.

On July 3, 2009, Hussein was at Kawkab El-Sharq Hall in Khartoum, a restaurant, café, and conference hall named after the much-loved Egyptian singer Um Kalthoum, who was dubbed Kawkab El-Sharq, or the "Star of the East", and had a wide following in the Arabic world before her death in 1975. The public order police swept through and arrested Hussein and twelve other women for wearing trousers. Ten of them pled guilty and were sentenced to ten lashes and a fine of about $100. Hussein and two other defendants opted for a trial. "In practice, public order police use the vaguely worded regulations to extract bribes from women on the street," explained an anonymous writer for the Web site ForeignPolicy.com. The writer went on to note that Sudan's new interim constitution permits due process and equality between the sexes. The public order police in Khartoum continue to casually enforce Article 152. "The trouble is that usually people don't hear about this law," the writer asserted, and noted that Hussein's attempt to fight the charge was in response to this gray area. "If you tell people you have been flogged for wearing trousers, they won't believe you. This way, there will be witnesses."

Hussein's first court appearance was on July 29, 2009. Beforehand, she sent out invitation cards and an e-mail blitz. Both messages read, "Sudanese journalist Lubna Hussein invites you again to her flogging tomorrow," according to James Copnall in the London *Observer.* Scores of protesters showed up at the North Khartoum District Courthouse to support Hussein. She was adamant about fighting the charge. "Islam does not say whether a woman can wear trousers or not," she said in the *Observer* interview. "And neither does Islam flog women because of what they wear. If any Muslim in the world says Islamic law or sharia law flogs women for their clothes, let them show me what the Qur'an or Prophet Muhammad said on that issue. There is nothing. It is not about religion, it is about men treating women badly."

Technically, Hussein's job with UNMIS gave her immunity from prosecution, and the judge offered her that option, which she declined. Instead, she resigned from her United Nations post and asked to be represented by a lawyer. The judge granted that request and postponed her hearing. A week later more protesters turned up for Hussein's August 4 court date. The judge again postponed the hearing. Outside the courthouse, protesters clashed with counterdemonstrators and the police moved in to quell the violence. Some of Hussein's supporters, who wore trousers in defiance of the authorities, were dispersed with tear gas.

At her trial on September 7, Hussein wore trousers, was found guilty on the original charge, and was fined $100. The judge declined to impose the flogging sentence. Hussein announced that she would not pay the fine and was jailed. A journalists' union paid it for her and she was released a day later, but she voiced objections to the reprieve. She made plans to appeal her conviction to Sudan's Court of Appeal and asserted that she was willing to take it to the country's Constitutional Court. The flogging she had evaded was not the issue, Hussein told Copnall in the *Observer* interview. "I think that flogging does not hurt, but it is an insult. Not for me, but for women, for human beings, and also for the government of Sudan. How can you tell the world that the government flogs the people? How can you do that?"

Sources

Periodicals

Economist, August 8, 2009, p. 34EU.
Guardian (London), September 4, 2009, p. 34.
New York Times, September 7, 2009, p. A5.
Observer (London), August 2, 2009.

Online

"Lubna Ahmed Al-Hussein, Sudanese Journalist," France24.com, August 13, 2009, http://www.france24.com/en/20090813-loubna-ahmed-al-hussein-sudanese-journalist-interview-trousers-40-lashes-women-rights (accessed January 2, 2010).
"Pants Pants Revolution," ForeignPolicy.com, August 5, 2009, http://www.foreignpolicy.com/articles/2009/08/05/pants_pants_revolution (accessed January 2, 2010).
"Sudanese 'Trousers Woman' Jailed," BBC News, September 7, 2009, http://news.bbc.co.uk/2/hi/africa/8241894.stm (accessed January 2, 2010).

—Carol Brennan

Hank Johnson

1954—

Politician, attorney

Johnson, Hank, photograph. AP Images.

Georgia legislator Hank Johnson represents his state's Fourth Congressional District in the U.S. House of Representatives. A criminal defense attorney and former county commissioner, Johnson unseated a well-known legislator, Cynthia McKinney, in the 2006 Democratic primary race prior to his November election. His district encompasses a large swath of Atlanta's eastern suburbs.

Johnson was born in 1954 and grew up in the Washington, DC, area. His father was an employee of the federal Bureau of Prisons who rose to the post of director of classifications and paroles, which made him the highest-ranking African American at the Bureau. Johnson chose his career at an early age, around the time he entered kindergarten, when his cousin graduated from law school. It was his mother, Christine, who "got me interested in politics," Johnson told *Atlanta Journal-Constitution* writers Sonji Jacobs, Mae Gentry, and Ernie Suggs, also noting that she made him read the *Washington Post* every day when he was a youngster. "It has not been something that I have been obsessed with, but something I had in my mind at an early age."

Johnson moved to the Atlanta area in 1972 to attend Clark Atlanta University. He earned a bachelor's degree in political science in 1976 and went on to the Thurgood Marshall School of Law at Texas Southern University in Houston. After graduating with his law degree in 1979, he returned to Georgia, passed the bar exam, and began looking for office space in Atlanta. There he met another attorney, Dwight L. Thomas, who convinced him to move to Decatur, a city near Atlanta, where Thomas had a practice and was the only African-American lawyer in the city.

One of the first cases Johnson handled as a new attorney was a death-penalty appeal. The American Civil Liberties Union sought him out and asked him to take a look at the 1977 conviction of Howard Jones, whose trial had been marred by perjury. The matter was complicated by the fact that DeKalb County officials had lost important evidence, which made a retrial impossible. Johnson filed a writ of habeas, which initiated a review by the federal courts of Jone's death penalty conviction, and won Jones's release based on the perjured testimony of one of the prosecution's main witnesses. "I was able to drive down to the Georgia Diagnostic and Classification Center in Jackson, and he walked out of Death Row, through the bowels of the prison, and into my car," Johnson recalled in an interview with *Fulton County Daily Report* writer Greg Land. "We stopped at the first Waffle House we came to and had breakfast."

In his two decades of practicing law, Johnson earned a reputation as a skilled trial lawyer and effective persuader of juries. He and his wife, Mereda Davis Johnson, founded their own firm and handled several high-profile Atlanta-area cases. Even Johnson's courtroom adversaries gave him high marks. W. Cliff Howard, who once served as DeKalb assistant solicitor, or lawyer for the county, told Land in the *Fulton County Daily Report* article that Johnson "was a zealous advocate for his client, but he wasn't one of these lawyers who'll always try to tell you there's something wrong with your evidence. The best defense lawyers understand that, even if your client is guilty, it's your job to make the state prove their guilt. That's how he handled his cases."

Johnson's first foray into politics was in 1986, when he ran for a seat in the Georgia House of Representatives but lost. A professional colleague encouraged him to serve as an associate magistrate judge in DeKalb

County, which he did for twelve years. In 2000 he decided to run for office again when a vacancy on the DeKalb County board of commissioners opened up. He won the race and spent six years as one of seven commissioners of the county, which has a population of 737,000. He resigned his seat to run in the 2006 Congressional race.

Johnson was seeking Georgia's Fourth Congressional District seat in the U.S. House of Representatives. The district includes much of DeKalb County and parts of Gwinnett and Rockdale counties, with African Americans making up fifty-three percent of its population. Historically, it is also one of the most heavily Democratic districts in the entire southern United States. Cynthia McKinney, who was first elected to Congress in 1992, had held the seat for three consecutive terms beginning in 1996 but was beaten by a fellow Democrat in 2002 in the primary race. McKinney—the first black woman to represent Georgia in Congress, a masterly campaigner, and one of her state's most polarizing politicians—came back in 2004 and won the Fourth Congressional District seat again.

Johnson garnered a plurality of votes in the initial Democratic primary race in July of 2006, but his failure to win a majority necessitated a runoff election against the incumbent McKinney. In early August he won that race and advanced to a place on the November ballot. The upset surprised many of McKinney's supporters, but she had lost constituents in recent months following an incident involving U.S. Capitol police officers that made national headlines. In March of 2006 McKinney entered the House office building and one of the Capitol police officers stopped her. Members of Congress wear lapel pins that allow them to bypass the security checkpoints in government buildings, and McKinney was not wearing hers. As she skirted the checkpoint, an officer approached her, and there was a brief ruckus. She was initially accused of assaulting the officer, but a grand jury investigation found no cause to file charges.

In the Democratic primary runoff, Johnson won fifty-nine percent of the vote against McKinney's forty-one percent. McKinney claimed that Republican Party officials had encouraged GOP voters to cast votes for Johnson in the runoff, which is permitted, but others said that her poor legislative record was the reason for her defeat. In the final election Johnson benefited from Democratic Party campaign funding that was disbursed at the discretion of future White House Chief of Staff Rahm Emanuel. Because opposition party candidates rarely made a showing in the general election in the heavily Democratic Fourth Congressional District, Johnson was a virtual shoo-in for the seat. He beat his Republican opponent with a stunning seventy-six percent of the vote.

The father of two, Johnson is a member of the Congressional Black Caucus and serves on the House

Armed Services and Judiciary committees. In 2008 he ran unopposed for his Congressional seat. He and a House colleague from Hawaii, Mazie Hirono, are the first two Buddhists to serve in Congress.

Sources

Periodicals

Atlanta Journal-Constitution, July 20, 2006, p. A1; January 5, 2007, p. A8.
Fulton County Daily Report, July 31, 2006.

—Carol Brennan

Bill T. Jones

1952—

Dancer, choreographer

Jones, Bill T., photograph. AP Images.

Bill T. Jones is one of America's most prominent choreographers and dancers, known for the extraordinary sensuality of his work as well as for being a lightning rod for controversy on and off the stage. As the artistic director of the Bill T. Jones/Arnie Zane Dance Company, Jones has tackled such issues as race, sexuality, mythology, politics, religion, history, mortality, and loss through the lens of dance. Jones has also survived the loss of his life, business, and dance partner, Arnie Zane, to AIDS; the public revelation that he was also HIV positive; and a prominent role in the culture wars, both within and outside of the world of dance. In the late 2000s, Jones expanded his repertory to include musical theater, garnering a Tony Award for his choreography in the hit Broadway musical *Spring Awakening* and a well-received Broadway debut for his own musical, *Fela!,* based on the life of Nigerian musician and activist Fela Kuti.

Found Love and Dance While in College

William Tass Jones was the tenth of twelve children born to migrant farmers Estella and Augustus Jones. Jones was born in Florida, but when he was about twelve years old, the family left the Southeast for a nearly all-white community in upstate New York. Although they were farmers, performance ran in Jones's family. Jones's brothers and sisters sang and told stories while doing their chores, and his older sister Rhodessa grew up to be a singer, actress, and performance artist. In high school Jones sang in a rock band and acted in plays, but where he really made his mark was as a star track athlete.

Jones went to college at the State University of New York at Binghamton, where he was on the track team. In 1971 he met Arnie Zane, a photographer a few years older than he. Zane helped Jones discover that his destiny was not in singing, acting, or athletics, but rather in dance. He was also Jones's first male lover. Soon Jones left college to travel with Zane, spending time in Amsterdam and San Francisco and many places in between before returning to Binghamton in 1973. The pair joined one of their teachers, Lois Welk, to form the American Dance Asylum (ADA). The ADA, a collective that Jones wryly described to the *New York*

At a Glance . . .

Born William Tass Jones on February 15, 1952, in Bunnell, FL; parents Estella and Augustus (both migrant workers); raised in Florida and Wayland, NY; one daughter. *Education:* Attended the State University of New York at Binghamton.

Career: Dancer and choreographer, 1970—. American Dance Asylum, cofounder with Lois Welk, 1973; Bill T. Jones/Arnie Zane Dance Company, cofounder with Arnie Zane, 1982.

Awards: New York Dance and Performance "Bessie" Award, 1989 and 2001; Dorothy B. Chandler Performing Arts Award, 1991; MacArthur Fellowship, 1994; named one of America's Irreplaceable Dance Treasures, Dance Heritage Coalition, 2000; Dorothy and Lillian Gish Prize, 2003; Lifetime Achievement Award, Samuel H. Scripps American Dance Festival, 2005; Wexner Prize, 2005; Tony Award, Best Choreographer, 2007, for *Spring Awakening*; Lucille Lortel Award, Outstanding Choreographer, 2006, for *The Seven*, Outstanding Musical, Outstanding Choreographer, 2009, for *Fela!*,.

Addresses: *Office*—Bill T. Jones/Arnie Zane Dance Company, 27 West 120 Street, Suite No. 1, New York, New York 10003.

Times as "hippie types and malcontents," was experimenting with the technique known as contact improvisation. Although the group "turned up [their] noses" at the dance establishment in New York City, Jones and Zane's work with the ADA eventually led Jones to Manhattan, where he made a well-received solo debut with the Dance Theatre Workshop's Choreographers' Showcase in 1977.

During the next few years Jones and Zane performed around the world, both as soloists and as a duo. Their pairing as dance partners was an exercise in contrast—Jones was black and tall, with a more classical dance style, Zane was short and white, with non-traditional dance movements. They also found funding, partly in the form of a series of grants from the National Endowment for the Arts (NEA). In 1982 they settled in New York City, forming the Bill T. Jones/Arnie Zane Dance Company. The new group was immediately accused of selling out their avant-garde roots because they created what *New York* magazine described as "big, splashy spectacles in which outrageousness or

fashion, of social and political attitudes—melded blithely with earlier formalist concerns." However, *Interview* called the Jones/Zane troupe "one of the freshest and most innovative modern dance troupes in the world," claiming that "when they performed with jazz drummer Max Roach," at the Brooklyn Academy of Music's 1982 Next Wave Festival "[they] reinvented the language of movement."

Lost His Partner to AIDS

Although the dance troupe was a success, it was only a few years until everything Jones and Zane had built was in jeopardy. In 1984 Zane began getting sick, and the symptoms matched what was then called "gay-related immune deficiency"—later renamed Acquired Immune Deficiency Syndrome, or AIDS. In 1985 he and Jones were tested for the Human Immunodeficiency Virus (HIV), which causes AIDS. They learned that both of them were infected with HIV, but in Jones's case, the virus had not yet manifested itself as an illness. Although at that time most HIV-infected people in public life hid their status for fear of prejudice, at Zane's insistence he and Jones were open about their health.

The public did not shun Jones and Zane as performers after the news became public, but Zane's illness took a toll on their creative output. As his condition worsened, Jones became more and more preoccupied with tending to his partner's health. "We were both exhausted by his life," Jones told Jennifer Dunning of the *New York Times*. By 1988 the troupe was barely touring and on the verge of bankruptcy. According to *People* magazine, the company "was saved by a group of artist friends who sold their works to raise $100,000."

Zane died that year of AIDS-related lymphoma. Jones threw himself into work with the troupe, creating personal works through which he could express his grief. One such work, *Absence,* made its debut in 1989. In *Absence,* Jones evoked the memory of Zane by sometimes seeming out of balance on stage, as if lacking a counterweight, and then pausing forgetfully, waiting for his partner's steps. In *People,* critic Robert Jones said *Absence* had "a shimmering, ecstatic quality that was euphoric and almost unbearably moving." Tobi Tobias, dance critic for *New York,* said that the work took "its shape from Zane's special loves: still images and highly wrought, emotion-saturated vocal music."

Of course, Zane's tragic story was hardly an isolated incident. The AIDS epidemic of the 1980s took an immense toll on the world of modern dance. Everyone—choreographers, dancers, critics—knew people who had died or who were sick. In honor of Demian Acquavella, another member of his troupe who had taken ill, Jones choreographed *D-Man in the Waters,* a dance based on the metaphor of the troupe battling against a strong current.

In 1990 the troupe premiered another work inspired by Zane, *Last Supper at Uncle Tom's Cabin,* which was a juxtaposition that sprung from a joke between Zane and Jones in the last months of Zane's life. Jones brought the concept to life as a performance in four parts. One told the story of Harriet Beecher Stowe's master work, another told the stories of four women of the era, another told the biblical story of Job, with Jones portraying the man unjustly cursed by God, and a final section was called "The Promised Land." Although many critics read *Last Supper* as another work about AIDS and Zane's passing, Jones rejected that idea. To him, the performance was about isolation. In the climax of *Last Supper,* Jones's company—one of the most diverse in the business, using dancers of many ethnicities, shapes and sizes—is joined by several dozen extras, of all different ages and backgrounds, all naked. As Jones told Dunning, "[C]an we stand up as a group and not be ashamed of our nakedness? That is the promised land."

Caused Controversy with Still/Here

By 1994 Jones was one of the most celebrated dancer/choreographers in the United States. In 1989 he had received the dancing world's highest honor, the "Bessie" Award; in 1991 he had received the Dorothy B. Chandler Award; and in 1994 he was awarded a coveted "genius" grant by the McArthur Foundation. But in some circles, there were misgivings about Jones's success. Unlike most modern dancers, Jones and his troupe often spoke to their audience, in addition to moving for them. Indeed, some critics thought that there were so many non-dance elements to his work—musicians, singers, spoken word artists, and projected video—that his work could hardly be called dance at all.

An anonymous critic, speaking to Henry Louis Gates for the *New Yorker,* gave the following assessment of Jones: "Structurally, his choreography often leaves something to be desired. His work is best when he's in it. It's also true that Bill hit his stride when the dance boom was over—a lot of the talent was really decimated by AIDS.... Still, the reason he's getting so many awards so soon is that people aren't gambling on his surviving; they're giving it to him now." That critic was not alone in wondering whether Jones's body of work would have been so extensively celebrated if he was just a choreographer, not a black, gay choreographer courageously living with HIV.

Many of these critical resentments were distilled in an infamous piece written by influential *New Yorker* dance critic Arlene Croce. The reason for Croce's ire was Jones's 1994 performance entitled *Still/Here.* For a few years Jones conducted workshops in which he interviewed people with life-threatening illnesses—some with AIDS, others with cancer and other mala-

dies—using the interviewee's words, experiences, and movements as the inspiration for his choreography. In *Still/Here* the troupe performed the resulting dance, with accompaniment by such well-known musicians as guitarist Vernon Reid of the group *Living Colour* and folk singer Odetta. Audio of the interviews played throughout the performance, and video and photographs of the interviewees were projected in the background.

While she was no admirer of Jones's work in general, it was that last aspect of the performance drew Croce's ire. Using audio and video of dying people, she wrote, crossed an exploitative line, making *Still/Here* "victim art." She refused to see it, but she did not let that stop her from dismissing the performance, sight unseen, as "a kind of traveling messianic medicine show." Croce claimed that Jones and his troupe "intimidated" critics, "forcing" them to feel sorry for the performers "as dissed blacks, abused women, or disenfranchised homosexuals." Although Croce's lengthy screed had many targets, including multiculturalism, the permissive culture of the 1960s, the National Endowment for the Arts, and photographer Robert Mapplethorpe (for whom Jones had famously posed years before), her greatest venom was reserved for Jones and the late Arnie Zane, whom she identified as, respectively, the "John the Baptist" and "Christ" of victim art.

Croce's essay set off a firestorm in the dance world, and for years she and Jones exchanged verbal broadsides in the media. A decade later, Jones would still bristle at the mention of "that writer" and say that the experience had left him "scarred." Despite the controversy, *Still Here* captured the hearts of many. The work was filmed for television, and a documentary on the making of *Still/Here,* entitled "Bill T. Jones: Still/Here with Bill Moyers," aired on the Public Broadcasting Service in 1997.

Took Broadway by Storm

In 2000 Jones was honored by the Dance Heritage Foundation as an "Irreplaceable Dance Treasure." In 2002 the Bill T. Jones/Arnie Zane Dance Company celebrated its twentieth anniversary, and Jones created a retrospective of the troupe's work entitled the Phantom Project, explaining that the ever-evolving nature of his work made trying to recall a past performance like "trying to evoke a phantom." The Phantom Project made its debut in 2003, the same year Jones received the Dorothy and Lillian Gish Award for his outstanding contribution to the arts. Two years later Jones was honored with the Wexner Prize and a lifetime achievement award from the Samuel H. Scripps American Dance Festival.

The sequence of lifetime achievement awards and retrospectives often mark a career past its peak, but Jones was constantly creating new work, and his career was about to take an unexpected turn toward the Great White Way. When their dance troupe had its first prominent successes, Arnie Zane's father told Jones and Zane, "Now you guys are beginning to get somewhere. If you don't blow it, maybe you'll get to Broadway." At the time, the quote was a punch line—Zane and Jones had no plans to make it on Broadway, as they were experimental artists enjoying the type of creative freedom dancers in commercial theater could barely imagine. More than twenty years later, the first step Jones took in Broadway's direction was choreographing an Off-Broadway production called *The Seven,* an experimental hip hop reconstruction of the works Aeschylus. Despite this introduction to the ways of musical theater, his next assignment caused culture shock. *Spring Awakening,* a tale of teenage sexuality set in nineteenth century Germany, was a major production with commercial prospects. As an avant-garde choreographer with his own company, Jones had had complete creative control over his work for virtually his entire career. Going to Broadway meant working on a tighter schedule than he was accustomed to, with his choreography broken up into distinct "dance numbers." "I railed and bristled a little bit, and I said to [director Michael Mayer] 'I don't do dance numbers.'" Jones told Roslyn Sulkas of the *New York Times.* "But after a while I thought, 'O.K., they are numbers.'"

Sometimes, however, limitations are a good thing for an artist. Part of the appeal of musical theater to Jones was the opportunity to work with people chosen primarily for their acting and singing ability, often with little or no real dance training. Many of Jones's works have featured non-dancers, most prominently 2001's *The Table Project.* Jones saw working with non-dancers as an opportunity to teach untrained bodies how to express themselves with movement. In *Spring Awakening,* dances needed to evoke the powerful repressed emotions boiling just under the surface for the adolescent characters. The production was successful beyond all expectations, garnering nominations for eleven Tony Awards and winning eight, including Best Musical and Best Choreographer for Jones. The *Village Voice* praised "Jones's skill for building numbers in which the whole stage picture, rather than the dancer's feet, does the moving."

The success of *Spring Awakening* set up Jones's next Broadway venture, *Fela!,* which told the story of Nigerian musician and activist Fela Kuti. With greater responsibility for the production—he was not just the show's choreographer, but also its director and co-writer—Jones sought to introduce New York audiences to Kuti's distinctive musical genre, Afrobeat, and reproduce the energy of Kuti's elaborate performances. Opening Off-Broadway, *Fela!* was widely praised for the strong performance of leading man Sahr Ngaujah and for Jones's choreography, which, according to the *New Yorker,* improved on every aspect of the real Kuti's West African dance routines. In November of 2009 *Fela!* moved to Broadway.

Lest anyone think that Jones had abandoned modern dance for commercial theater, in 2008 he accepted a commission from the Ravinia Festival in Illinois to create a work celebrating the bicentennial of Abraham Lincoln's birth. Jones found the subject matter hard to resist. As he told Sid Smith of the *Los Angeles Times,* "Lincoln was the only white man I was allowed to love unconditionally growing up. But he was also hiding in plain sight. Sure, he's on the $5 bill. But who is he?"

November of 2009 saw the debut of Jones's answer to that question, *Fondly Do We Hope ... Fervently Do We Pray.* The work plays with time, putting echoes of current events in the Lincoln-Douglas debates and projecting reverberations of Lincoln's importance one hundred years into the future. In a 2005 interview with the *New York Times,* Jones told Edward Lewine that the worst thing about his work was "the horrible feeling that the clock is ticking and I'll run out of time." But as Bill T. Jones neared the end of his fourth decade in dance and approached the twenty-fifth anniversary of his diagnosis as HIV positive, there was no sign that he was slowing down, much less stopping.

Selected works

Dances

Pas de Deux for Two, 1973.
Absence, 1989.
D-Man in the Water, 1989.
Last Supper at Uncle Tom's Cabin/The Promised Land, 1991.
Still/Here, 1994.
The Table Project, 2001.
The Breathing Project, 2001.
The Phantom Project, 2003.
Reading, Mercy, and the Artificial Nigger, 2004.
The Blind Date, 2005.
Serenade/The Proposition, 2008.
Fondly Do We Hope ... Fervently Do We Pray, 2009.

Musicals

The Seven, 2006.
Spring Awakening, 2007.
Fela!, 2008.

Books

Last Night on Earth (memoir), Pantheon Books, 1995.
Dance (children's book), Hyperion, 1998.

Sources

Books

Body against Body: The Dance and Other Collaborations of Bill T. Jones and Arnie Zane, Station Hill Press, 1989.

Periodicals

Interview, March 1989.

Los Angeles Times, September 23, 2001; October 7, 2009.

New York, January 5, 1987; September 10, 1990; November 26, 1990.

New Yorker, November 28, 1994; December 26, 1994; December 7, 2009.

New York Times, December 31, 1989; July 22, 2000; January 27, 2002; September 18, 2005; November 20, 2005; June 7, 2007; December 30, 2007; August 5, 2008; September 5, 2008.

People, July 31, 1989.

Village Voice, August 5, 2002.

Washington Post, June 20, 2000.

Online

Bill T. Jones/Arnie Zane Dance Company, http://www.billtjones.org, (accessed January 11, 2010).

Television

Uncle Tom's Cabin/The Promised Land (Great Performances television series), PBS, 1992.

"Bill T. Jones: *Still/Here* with Bill Moyers," PBS, 1997.

"I'll Make Me a World: A Century of African American Arts," PBS, 1999.

"Free to Dance: The Presence of African-Americans in Modern Dance," PBS, 2001.

"Bill Moyers Journal, December 25, 2009," PBS, 2009.

—Derek Jacques

Teresa King

1961—

U.S. Army officer

King, Teresa, photograph. AP Images.

On September 22, 2009, Command Sergeant Major Teresa L. King made history by becoming the first woman ever to serve as commandant of the U.S. Army Drill Sergeant School at Fort Jackson, South Carolina, the army's largest training installation. A twenty-nine-year veteran, King was no stranger to leadership positions: Over the course of her career, she had worked for former U.S. Secretary of Defense Dick Cheney at the Pentagon, become the first female first sergeant to serve the 18th Airborne Corps, and held senior enlisted posts in Korea and Europe. In her new job, she took on an even bigger responsibility—overseeing the training of every enlisted solder in the army. King's appointment to head the traditionally male-dominated school was widely heralded as a sign of greater opportunities ahead for women in the military.

King was born in 1961 in Clinton, North Carolina, the eighth of twelve children. Her parents were sharecroppers who grew cucumbers and tobacco. As a girl, King eschewed her mother's attempts to get her into the kitchen, preferring instead to drive her father's tractor and play basketball. Her father was a strict disciplinarian who taught her to "give a hard day's work for

whatever I earned and to take no short cuts," she told the Associated Press, and she often was put in charge of keeping her brothers and sisters in line. As a teenager, King spent time at nearby Fort Bragg, North Carolina, a major U.S. Army installation, and it was there that she found her calling. "I saw a woman in a red beret. We looked at each other … didn't speak. But at that moment, I knew I would be a soldier," she recalled in an interview with CNN. After graduating from high school, she enlisted in the army on August 19, 1980, and departed for basic training at Fort Jackson the following day.

For her first assignment in the army, King worked as a postal clerk—a traditional job for women in the military—in Stuttgart, Germany. Within a few years, she was sent to drill sergeant school, where she was graduated as one of five women in a class of thirty. She served as a drill sergeant at Fort Dix, New Jersey, and earned the Drill Sergeant of the Cycle award, which recognizes outstanding performance and the ability to lead, teach, and motivate soldiers. As King rose up the ranks of the military, she was transferred to the Pentagon in 1988, where she was an aide to Secretary of

Defense Cheney; served the 18th Personnel Service Battalion at Fort Bragg from 1993 to 1996, supporting more than 50,000 soldiers; and held senior enlisted positions at Camp Casey, Korea, near the demilitarized zone, in 1996–97.

In March of 1997, King achieved a milestone by becoming the first female first sergeant—a title given to senior enlisted advisers—to serve the 18th Airborne Corps headquarters, the largest company at Fort Bragg and the army's largest war-fighting organization. As first sergeant, she was responsible for some 500 paratroopers, 22 sergeant majors, 22 colonels, and several general officers. For nearly two years, from 2005 to 2007, she was assigned to the U.S. Army's North Atlantic Treaty Organization headquarters in Europe, and then returned to Fort Jackson to serve as command sergeant major in the 369th Adjutant General Battalion.

In early 2009 King, then age forty-seven, was thinking about retiring from military service. But the army was not through with her yet. In June of that year, she was appointed commandant of the U.S. Army Drill Sergeant School at Fort Jackson—the first woman ever to hold the prestigious and demanding post. When she stepped into her new job that September, she took over responsibility for the army's largest training installation, which employed 78 drill instructors and turned out approximately 2,000 graduates each year.

King's appointment demonstrated the expanding role of women in the leadership ranks of the army since the 1980s. Women were first admitted to the U.S. Military Academy at West Point, the training ground for officers, in 1976. That first class included 129 women, 60 percent of whom were graduated. West Point's class of 2011 held a record number of female cadets—more than 220 out of 1,314 students—and typically 80 percent of those who enroll go on to graduate. Despite these advances, women continue to hold only a small percentage of the leadership positions in the army. Although women make up 14 percent of the armed services overall, they represent only 5 percent of active general officers in the army. Further, women are barred from serving in direct combat operations, which is the traditional path to four-star, or senior commander, rank.

Recruiting female drill sergeants has proved particularly difficult for the army. "This is a male-centric part of the army," King said of the drill sergeant school in an interview with the *Christian Science Monitor,* a result of the school's demanding schedule and tough physical requirements, as well as the difficulty of balancing military life with raising a family. But King's selection to head the school, she related in the interview, "shows that the Army is emerging ... they don't have reservations about putting the right person where they need to be." As commandant, one of her priorities would be to recruit more women drill instructors, she told the *New York Times.*

King is known among her colleagues and recruits as a tough, confident, no-nonsense drill instructor with zero tolerance for laziness or slovenliness—her nickname is "Sergeant Major No Slack." But her hard-line demeanor is tempered by a genuine concern for her soldiers and a keen sense of how to motivate people. "The difference between yelling and instructing and mentoring soldiers [is that] soldiers learn better when you coach and mentor them. And if you have trained them, why are you yelling?" she explains in an online video feature of the *New York Times.* "The drill sergeants I train will be running the army in ten years, so I gotta get it right."

In addition to her military duties, King also has made time to pursue higher education. She completed an associate's degree at Northern Virginia Community College, and then went on to earn a master's degree in business management from Almeda College. In late 2009 she was pursing a doctorate in divinity at the American Institute of Holistic Theology. She has been decorated many times for her service, receiving the National Service Medal, Army Commendation Medal, Military Outstanding Volunteer Service Medal, Adjutant General Corps Horatio Gates Medal, and the Medal of Saint Maurice, Patron Saint of the Infantry.

Sources

Books

Taylor, Robert L., William E. Rosenbach, and Eric B. Rosenbach, eds., *Military Leadership: In Pursuit of Excellence,* 6th ed., Westview Press, 2009.

Periodicals

Christian Science Monitor, July 13, 2009.
New York Times, September 22, 2009, p. A1.

Online

"Breaking through the Ranks," *New York Times,* September 21, 2009, http://www.nytimes.com/interactive/2009/09/21/us/090921-Drill-AudioSS/index.html (accessed December 8, 2009.

Brown, Crystal Lewis, "Army Picks First Female Commandant to Lead Drill Sergeant School," U.S. Army News Service, July 30, 2009, http://www.army.mil/-news/2009/07/30/25200-army-picks-first-female-commandant-to-lead-drill-sergeant-school/ (accessed December 8, 2009).

O'Neill, Julie, "First Female Commander of Army Drill Sgt. School," CNN, American Morning blog, October 20, 2009, http://amfix.blogs.cnn.com/2009/10/20/armys-top-drill-sergeant/ (accessed December 8, 2009).

Schaefer, Susanne M., "First Woman Leads Army's Drill Sergeants," Associated Press, September 18, 2009. http://news.aol.com/article/teresa-king-first-drill-sergeant-leader/675851 (accessed December 8, 2009).

U.S. Army Drill Sergeant School, http://www.jackson.army.mil/units/drill/index.html (accessed December 8, 2009).

—Deborah A. Ring

Marie Knight

1925(?)–2009

Gospel and blues singer

Marie Knight, also known as "Madame Marie Night" and "Sister Marie Knight," made a name for herself on the gospel music circuit in the late 1940s and early 1950s as part of a duo with singer-songwriter Sister Rosetta Tharpe. Together, Knight and Tharpe became one of the most popular gospel acts of the era, thrilling audiences with such hits as "Up above My Head" and "Didn't It Rain." Their unique style of gospel, tinged with the blues and rock and roll, introduced gospel music to a broader audience and made the two a crossover hit. After the duo split in the 1950s, Knight began singing rhythm and blues (R&B), touring with the Drifters and other acts. She revived her gospel career late in life after recording a solo version of "Didn't It Rain" for a Tharpe tribute album in 2003, and began touring once again. In 2007 Knight released her first full-length album in more than two decades, the critically acclaimed *Let Us Get Together,* a compilation of gospel songs written by the Reverend Gary Davis.

Born Marie Roach in Sanford, Florida, she grew up in Newark, New Jersey. Notoriously dodgy about her age, she claimed that she was born on June 1, 1925, but some gospel music scholars put her date of birth earlier,

Knight, Marie, photograph. Michael Ochs Archives/Getty Images.

at 1918, 1920, or 1923. She displayed a talent and enthusiasm for singing as a young girl. At age five, she surprised her parents' congregation at the Church of God in Christ by belting out the gospel song "Doing All the Good We Can," thrilled as the audience clapped along in response. She began singing with the church's youth choir, becoming a soloist by age nine, and taught herself to play the piano. "I used to go into the church in the daytime ... and just hit one note at a time, to hear that sound on the piano," she said, according to Gayle Wald, author of *Shout, Sister, Shout! The Untold Story of Rock-and-Rock Trailblazer Sister Rosetta Tharpe.* "It was a joy to me ... to put those notes together, on the piano, just one key at a time."

She began her professional music career in 1939, touring the revival circuit with evangelist Frances Robinson. On Christmas Day in 1941 Marie married Albert Knight, a preacher from Texas, after a courtship of less than a week—"I met him Monday and married him Thursday," she told Wald, "real quick"—and had two children. But the marriage did not last, as Marie chafed under the constraints of domestic life, more interested in performing on the road than in being a preacher's wife. She made her first recordings in the early 1940s, singing with a quartet called the Sunset Four.

In 1946 Knight met Tharpe at a concert given by gospel singer Mahalia Jackson at Harlem's Golden Gate Auditorium; during the performance, Jackson invited Knight onstage to sing with her, and Tharpe was taken with Knight's contralto voice and graceful stage presence. Not long after the concert, Tharpe visited Knight at her mother's home in Newark and offered her a contract to tour together. Two days later, the women departed for shows in Chicago and Detroit, where Knight already had been added to the bill.

Knight provided the perfect complement to Tharpe, in both voice and presentation. Her thick, expansive contralto—she sometimes sang the role of the male bass—balanced Tharpe's more feminine soprano, and Knight's simple, elegant persona contrasted with Tharpe's melodramatic style. Often, Knight played the piano while Tharpe sang, and vice versa, and sometimes both women sang while Tharpe played the guitar. Their signature performance was a "saint and sinner" act in which Knight played the sinner, donning a straw hat and playing the ukulele, while Tharpe took the role of the saint, playing the guitar and bantering with the audience. "They had a dynamic, exciting sound where they traded off vocal lines," Wald explained in Knight's obituary in the Los Angeles Times in 2009. "That was a kind of hallmark with their duet singing, and it was so vocally agile that it approximated the sounds of jazz."

The duo became one of the most popular gospel acts of their day, producing a series of hits for Decca Records. In 1948 they recorded the ballad "Precious Moments," which rose to number thirteen on the Billboard R&B singles chart. The following year, they joined with the Sam Price Trio to record "Up above My Head," their best-known song. It peaked at number six on the R&B singles chart and stayed on the chart for ten weeks, an incredible achievement for a gospel recording. In the midst of this success, however, tragedy struck in the late 1940s when Knight's two young children and her mother died in a fire.

Knight and Tharpe's crossover success was attributable to their unusual style of music, which blended the traditional call and response of gospel with bluesy rhythms—accompanied by bass, piano, and drums—and rock and roll. They introduced gospel to a broader audience, bringing the music to areas of the country that had never heard it before. In New York City, they performed at the Blue Angel nightclub, a hot spot for jazz, and at Harlem's famed Apollo Theater. A 1951 show at Griffith Stadium in Washington, DC, drew a crowd of more than 20,000 people. As Knight and Tharpe strayed further into rock and blues music, their popularity declined among gospel fans. The two split up in the early 1950s, although they continued to perform together on occasion.

Knight recorded an album with the male vocal group the Millionaires in 1956. As a solo artist, she had hits on the R&B charts with "Tell Me Why" (1957), a reworking of the gospel tune "Just a Closer Walk with Thee," and "Cry Me a River," and she toured with Brook Benton and Clyde Lensley McPhatter and the Drifters. She returned to gospel music once again in the 1970s, cutting the albums Today in 1975 and Lord, I've Tried in 1979.

As her career waned, Knight found work with the local telephone company and became a minister at the Gates of Prayer Church in Harlem. She made a comeback in 2003, however, after recording a solo version of "Didn't It Rain"—one of her early hits with Tharpe—for the album Shout, Sister, Shout! A Tribute to Rosetta Tharpe, released by M.C. Records that year. The label was so impressed with her performance that she was offered a contract to record her first full-length album in more than twenty years. Let Us Get Together, released in 2007, featured a collection of gospel songs written by Davis, including "Samson & Delilah," "I'll Fly Away," and "Death Don't Have No Mercy." Critics universally praised the album. Reviewer Lee Hildebrand of the San Francisco Chronicle, for example, noted that "her delivery is soulful enough to surely cause some nonbelievers to want to get right with God." Knight embarked on a busy tour schedule, opening for singer Madeleine Peyroux and appearing at the Chicago Blues Festival and the Lowell Folk Festival in Massachusetts.

Knight died of complications from pneumonia on August 30, 2009, in New York City.

Selected recordings

Sister Marie Knight and the Millionaires, Mercury Records, 1956.
Today, Blues Alliance, 1975.
Lord, I've Tried, Savoy Records, 1979.
Shout, Sister, Shout! A Tribute to Sister Rosetta Tharpe (includes "Didn't It Rain"), M.C. Records, 2003.

Let Us Get Together: A Tribute to Reverend Gary Davis (includes "Samson & Delilah," "I'll Fly Away," and "Death Don't Have No Mercy"), M.C. Records, 2007.

Sources

Books

Boyer, Horace Clarence, *How Sweet the Sound: The Golden Age of Gospel,* Elliott & Clark, 1995.

Carpenter, Bil, *Uncloudy Days: The Gospel Music Encyclopedia,* Backbeat Books, 2005.

Wald, Gayle, *Shout, Sister, Shout! The Untold Story of Rock-and-Roll Trailblazer Sister Rosetta Tharpe,* Beacon Press, 2007.

Periodicals

Down Beat, April 6, 1955, p. 4.
Los Angeles Times, September 2, 2009.
New York Times, September 3, 2009, p. A29.
San Francisco Chronicle, July 22, 2007.
Washington Post, September 2, 2009.

Online

"Marie Knight" (audio interview), Hear & Now, October 19, 2007, http://www.hereandnow.org/2007/10/show-rundown-for-10192007/ (accessed December 9, 2009).

Marie Knight (official Web site), http://www.marieknight.com/ (accessed December 9, 2009).

—Deborah A. Ring

Myron Lowery

1946(?)—

Politician, journalist

Lowery, Myron, photograph. AP Images.

Myron Lowery served as the sixty-sixth mayor of Memphis, Tennessee, for several weeks in 2009. As city council chair, Lowery stepped into the job when longtime Mayor Willie Herenton resigned from office. He lost a special election that November to fill out the remainder of Herenton's term but returned to his job on the city council. Richard Hackett, Memphis mayor from 1982 to 1991, told Joyce Peterson, a reporter for the city's ABC affiliate, that "Lowery has absolutely been phenomenal during the interim period. And this city owes him a great deal of gratitude for addressing the issues in such turmoil, for helping this city stay together and work together in this very rough period."

Lowery is a native of Columbus, Ohio, where he was born in the late 1940s as the first of four sons. Raised by a single mother who worked as a domestic but who was also forced to apply for government assistance to feed her family, Lowery grew up in the Poindexter Village, one of the first federally funded public housing projects in the United States. The first income he earned came from a paper route. When he graduated from East High School, he sought college guidance from the United Negro College Fund. They suggested LeMoyne College in Memphis, a historically black college that would later merge with another school, Owen College. "I got on a Greyhound bus with two pork chop sandwiches that my grandmother made for me," he told Terre Gorham in a 2009 interview for the *Memphis Downtowner*. "I stayed with a woman on Walker Avenue, and the rent I paid was $1 per day. I got a work-study job, so I paid my own tuition with that."

Lowery graduated with a bachelor's degree in sociology in 1968 and moved to the New York City area to enroll in a master's degree program in education at New York University. He also joined the National Teachers' Corps, a federal program to bring new, young qualified teachers to some of the hardest-hit urban areas of the United States. For three years he taught social studies at John S. Roberts Junior High in East Harlem. In 1971 Dr. Hollis Price, the former president of LeMoyne College, contacted him about a job. At the time, Price was the urban affairs director for Memphis's NBC affiliate, WMC-TV, which was seeking to diversify its staff. Lowery took a crash course at Columbia University designed to help train minority journalists and moved back to Memphis in late 1971. He became the station's first black full-time reporter.

In 1973 Lowery became weekend anchor at WMC, and after 1976 he served as host and producer of *Minority Report,* a current affairs program. Frustrated when coworkers were promoted to more prominent, permanent anchor slots ahead of him, he filed an employment discrimination suit against the station and its parent company, Scripps Howard Broadcasting, in 1981. Lowery's suit also contested the fact that white coworkers earned more than he did. The highly publicized trial took on a malevolent tone, as coworkers testified against Lowery, his work habits, and even his personal character. A U.S. District Court judge ruled for Lowery nonetheless, and he was awarded more than a quarter-million dollars in a settlement. The station was also ordered to increase its efforts at workplace diversity. Despite the difficulties of the trial, the ordeal was worth it, Lowery told *Commercial Appeal* journalist Marc Perrusquia years later. "That settlement was beneficial to this entire community," he said, noting that the case and the ruling set legal precedent. "It's a classic case about how not to discriminate in broadcast journalism."

Lowery had left the station in 1983 to run for a seat on the Memphis City Council. He had covered City Hall as a reporter and was often bemused by the proceedings there. "I left some of the meetings, shook my head and said, 'I can do a better job,'" he told Zack McMillin, another writer for the *Commercial Appeal.* He lost the 1983 race and a second race in 1987. During this period he returned to teaching and also worked as a press secretary for Harold Ford Sr., a black Tennessee Democrat in Congress. Lowery finally won a seat on the council in 1991, the same year that the city elected its first African-American mayor, Willie Herenton.

Though Memphis municipal elections are nonpartisan, Lowery has been involved in Democratic Party politics in the Memphis area and was a speaker at the 1996 Democratic National Convention. He was reelected to the city council four more times, and also won a seat on the Memphis Charter Commission in 2007. In June of 2009 Mayor Herenton announced that he was resigning in order to run for a seat in the U.S. Congress. The resignation was effective July 30, 2009, and as chair of the city council, Lowery automatically became mayor pro tem. He was sworn in on July 31, a chaotic day that followed severe storms and a tornado that swept through the Memphis area.

Lowery won praise for his first week in office from the editorial page of the *Commercial Appeal.* Lowery "played the kind of role during Thursday afternoon's tornado that Herenton was never comfortable with, joining a disaster response team at the Emergency Operations Center and forwarding updates on storm damage, power outages and the like," the paper declared. Lowery was also commended by local media outlets for opening up the mayor's office to the public with an open house for Memphis citizens. Renovations that had been made by the Herenton administration to the seventh floor of Memphis City Hall, with its majestic view of the Mississippi River, had been a source of public controversy.

The Memphis City Charter states that a special election must be held within ninety days of a mayoral resignation. On October 15, 2009, Lowery faced off against his main rival, Shelby County Executive A. C. Wharton. There were two dozen candidates in the entire field, and voter turnout was low. Wharton won with sixty percent of the vote, while Lowery came in second with eighteen percent. Wharton was sworn in on October 26 to serve out the remainder of Herenton's term, which expires in 2011. Lowery returned to his seat on the city council. "He had more money and a better organized campaign," Lowery said of Wharton in his concession speech. "I have run the mayor's office and the campaign the way I thought it should be done. I gave the public a chance to see what I would do."

Sources

Periodicals

Commercial Appeal (Memphis, TN), June 26, 2009; July 5, 2009; July 31, 2009; August 1, 2009; August 8, 2009; October 15, 2009.

Daily News (Memphis, TN), August 7, 2009.

Memphis Downtowner, February 2009, pp. 36–38.

Online

Brown, George, "Memphis Mayor 'Fist Bumps' Dalai Lama during Visit," Channel 3 News (WREG-TV), September 22, 2009, http://www.wreg.com/wreg-dalai-lama,0,1603231.story (accessed January 2, 2010).

"Myron Lowery," Memphis City Council, http://memphistn.gov/framework.aspx?page=712 (accessed January 2, 2010).

Peterson, Joyce, "Mayor Myron Lowery's Short But Eventful Time in Office," MyEyewitnessNews.com October 25, 2009, http://www.myeyewitnessnews.com/news/local/story/Mayor-Myron-Lowerys-Short-But-Eventful-Time-in/EAqlx6e4VkCJ-I-dpa6UMw.cspx (accessed January 2, 2010).

—Carol Brennan

Lawrence Lucie

1907–2009

Jazz guitarist, music teacher, record label founder

Lucie, Lawrence, photograph. AP Images.

Guitarist Lawrence spent more than eighty years in the music business. While most closely associated with the "big band" sounds of the 1930s and early 1940s, he handled the transition to succeeding styles adroitly. In later years he split his time between public performance, studio work, teaching, and record production.

Lucie was born December 18, 1907, in Emporia, a small town in southern Virginia. His father, a barber, was an accomplished violinist with his own band. "I started playing very early," Lucie recalled in a 2007 interview with Frank Beacham. He concentrated initially on the banjo and mandolin, but shifted his focus to the guitar in his teens. In about 1927 he moved to New York City to study at the Brooklyn-Queens Conservatory, a well-known music school. His career began shortly thereafter. Although competition was fierce, his ability to read music gave him a significant advantage over other guitarists, many of whom were self-taught. "You had to read to play with the big bands," he told Beacham.

His first break came in the 1930s, when the renowned bandleader Duke Ellington hired him to replace an ailing banjo player. Although the engagement lasted only a few nights, it brought Lucie to the attention of other bandleaders, including Benny Carter, Fletcher Henderson, and Coleman Hawkins. In all of these groups, Lucie played in the rhythm section, helping to keep the beat for the other musicians. It was a crucial job, but one that received relatively little attention from fans and critics. Lucie's peers in the music industry, however, were well aware of his talent. Trumpeter and vocalist Louis Armstrong, for example, kept the guitarist in his band for four years; he also asked Lucie to serve as best man at his wedding.

He toured frequently, particularly with Henderson, but New York was Lucie's home for his entire career. He developed particularly strong ties to two of the city's most famous music venues, the Apollo Theater and the Cotton Club. His association with the Apollo began as early as 1934, when he appeared there with Carter's band, one of the first African-American ensembles to grace its stage. Shortly thereafter, he joined the house band at the Cotton Club, arguably the best-known nightspot in the country. His healthy lifestyle, a rarity among musicians at the time, stood him in good stead at these venues, both of which held performers to

At a Glance . . .

Born December 18, 1907, in Emporia, VA; died August 14, 2009, in New York, NY; son of a barber/jazz musician; married Nora Lee King (died 1990s). Military service: U.S. Army, 1944(?)–45(?). *Education:* Studied at the Brooklyn-Queens Conservatory, 1920s.

Career: Independent musician, 1920s–2000s; Borough of Manhattan Community College, music instructor, 1974(?)–2005(?); Toy Records, co-founder, 1970s–80s.

extremely high standards of appearance and demeanor as well as technical skill.

Following his tenure with Armstrong in the early 1940s, Lucie had several years of wartime service in the U.S. Army. He returned to New York to find a slow but steady decline in the popularity of the big band style that had sustained his early career. To adapt, he switched to solo guitar in the clubs and redoubled his efforts as a studio musician. He had been working off and on in the city's recording studios since his professional debut. As the public's taste in live music began to shift in the late 1940s, however, studio work assumed a much more central role in his career. Lucie often said later that he had no idea of the number of records—both singles and full-length albums—he had helped to complete. There were certainly hundreds, many by the bandleaders with whom he remained closely associated. His guitar can be heard, for example, on several late recordings by the jazz pioneer Jelly Roll Morton. According to Peter Keepnews of the *New York Times,* Lucie was "the last living musician known to have recorded with" the famed pianist. He also worked on albums by a number of popular vocalists, including Billie Holiday and Big Joe Turner.

Lucie also turned increasingly to teaching. In the 1950s and 1960s, he offered private lessons to both children and adults. One of his young students, Jeff Tass, remembered those lessons in a post on the Web site FreddieGreen.org. In the late 1960s, Tass recalled, Lucie taught in a "funky space ... in a very cool and spooky old hotel building." The "dapper" guitarist, habitually dressed in "a vintage tuxedo jacket with creased trousers and shiny shoes," instilled in Tass a "deep appreciation and respect for the art of music." Lucie's success as a private teacher eventually drew the attention of a local educational institution, Borough of Manhattan Community College (BMCC), which added him to its music faculty about 1974. He was a fixture there for the next three decades.

The mid-1970s were a particularly busy period for Lucie. Amid preparations for his new teaching posi-

tion, he found the time to start a record label, Toy Records. Joining him in the project was his wife, vocalist and bassist Nora Lee King Lucie. Many of the label's most prominent recordings were duets the two completed together. These were generally "easy-listening" albums—melodious but relatively unexciting. Though critics and the general public would later disparage the style, it was quite popular at the time. Toy's last releases seem to have been in the 1980s.

Lucie continued to play an active role in the New York music scene until he was almost one hundred. In the 1980s he and his wife began hosting a variety program on one of the city's public access cable channels. That project came to an end with her death in the 1990s. His last major engagement was a weekly gig at Arturo's in Greenwich Village. Failing health finally forced him to stop appearing there about 2005; his work at BMCC ended about the same time.

On August 14, 2009, Lucie died in New York at the age of one hundred and one. Students, friends, and fans thronged a memorial service to pay tribute to a man BMCC's Laurence Wilson described as "a wonderful gem" to Jared T. Miller of *Downtown Express.* "I've never heard anyone say a bad word about him," Wilson added, "and for someone [who was] in the business for so long, that's not something to be taken lightly."

Selected discography

Band member

Appeared on hundreds of singles and albums by Louis Armstrong, Fletcher Henderson, and others, various labels, 1930s–2000s.

Solo/bandleader

(With Nora Lee King) *This Is It... ...The Innovator,* Toy, 1978.
(With Nora Lee King) *It Was Good..It Is Good,* Toy, 1982.

Sources

Periodicals

Downtown Express, August 28—September 3, 2009.
New York Times, December 19, 2007; August 18, 2009.

Online

Beacham, Frank, "Interview of Lawrence Lucie—Rhythm Guitarist," FreddieGreen.org, December 18, 2007, http://www.freddiegreen.org/interviews/lawrencelucie.html (accessed October 20, 2009).
Tass, Jeff, "Jeff Tass Received Guitar Lessons from Lawrence Lucie," FreddieGreen.org, March 2008,

http://www.freddiegreen.org/interviews/lawrence
lucie.html (accessed October 20, 2009).

Yanow, Scott, "Lawrence Lucie: Biography," AllMusic.
com, http://allmusic.com/cg/amg.dll?p=amg&sql
=11:wjftxq85ldfe~T1 (accessed October 20, 2009).

—R. Anthony Kugler

Jenny Lumet

1967—

Actress, screenwriter

Lumet, Jenny, photograph. AP Images.

Screenwriter Jenny Lumet made a splash in Hollywood with her 2008 film *Rachel Getting Married,* her first script ever to be produced. Directed by Jonathan Demme and starring Anne Hathaway, the film garnered rave reviews and earned scores of award nominations for Lumet, Demme, and the cast. At age forty-one, it seemed that Lumet finally had found her calling. The daughter of film director Sidney Lumet and the granddaughter of singer Lena Horne, she had begun her career in show business as an actress but found little success, and for more than a decade she had worked on scripts that went nowhere while teaching drama to middle-school students. After years of hard work, she succeeded in persuading Demme—with some help from her famous father—to direct her screenplay, and the two collaborated to make *Rachel Getting Married.* With the success of that film, Lumet has become one of the most sought-after screenwriters in Hollywood.

Lumet was born on February 2, 1967, in New York City, one of two daughters of director Sidney Lumet and journalist Gail Lumet Buckley. Jenny Lumet was raised in an affluent environment that was both interracial and interreligious: Her father is Jewish and her mother is black, and her maternal grandmother, African-American singer and actress Lena Horne, was married for more than twenty years to the Jewish composer Lennie Hayton. Jenny Lumet also grew up surrounded by her parents' many celebrity friends: Directors Bob Fosse and Mel Brooks were frequent visitors to the Lumet home, caricaturist Al Hirschfeld once sketched her portrait, and actor Sean Connery is said to have fixed Lumet her first hot toddy to help her recover from some painful dental work.

Started Out as an Actress

Following her father and grandmother into show business, Lumet initially set out to become an actress. In the 1980s she landed minor roles in the films *Deathtrap* (1982), *Running on Empty* (1988), and *Tougher Than Leather* (1988). In 1990 she starred in the police thriller *Q & A,* directed by her father, but she still struggled to get acting work.

Although she found few rewards in her career, she continued to audition. "I didn't have the confidence to try anything else," she explained to Susan King of the *Los Angeles Times* in 2008. "I thought that is what I was supposed to do. It's an excruciating profession. I don't know if I was unhappy because I couldn't get a job or I couldn't get a job because I was unhappy." Lumet made appearances in two more films—*Assassination* in 1994 and *Dodgeball* in 1995—before channeling her creative energies in new directions.

Lumet married and then gave birth to a son in the early 1990s. While pregnant, she started experimenting with screenwriting and began teaching drama to middle-school students at Manhattan Country School in New York City. For more than a decade, she worked on several scripts but none panned out. After reading one of her early efforts, Lumet's father suggested that she try writing from her own experience, and that inspiration led her to pen the script for *Rachel Getting Married*.

Struggled to Get Script Produced

Despite her famous lineage, Lumet knew that getting her script produced would be an uphill battle. She believed that Demme, whose previous films included *The Silence of the Lambs* (1991), *Philadelphia* (1993), and a remake of *The Manchurian Candidate* (2004), was just the man for the job, but she needed access to the Oscar-winning director to persuade him to take up her project. Although she was loathe to trade on her family connections, Lumet finally turned to her father and implored him to get her script into Demme's

hands. "The way it's set up in America, you have to have some kind of connection to get a movie made—unless you finance it yourself. I'm sure in my apartment building there are 14 billion screenwriters who just can't get their stuff read," she told Gaby Wood during a 2009 interview for the London *Observer*. Demme was impressed by Lumet's script and he began working with the fledgling screenwriter to turn *Rachel Getting Married* into screen-ready material.

Rachel Getting Married was released in 2008. The film's story centers on Kym (played by Hathaway), a drug and alcohol addict who returns from rehab to attend the wedding of her older sister, Rachel (Rosemarie DeWitt), and the wrenching family conflicts that she brings to the surface. Although Lumet's characters were inspired in some respects by members of her own family—a memorable scene in which the bride's father and the bridegroom engage in a dishwasher-loading competition was based on an argument between Sidney Lumet and Bob Fosse, for instance—she is quick to point out that *Rachel Getting Married* is far from an autobiographical film. Rather, it draws on the tensions found in every family. "I think families are demented, and to ignore the material God gave you is a huge mistake," she told the *Boston Globe* in 2008. To better capture these dynamics, the film was shot using only handheld cameras, giving it an intimate, home-movie feel.

Although *Rachel Getting Married* features two interracial couples—Rachel and her fiancée Sidney (Tunde Adebimpe), as well as Kym and Rachel's father and stepmother (Bill Irwin and Anna Deavere Smith)—this fact is never mentioned during the film, and indeed, it does not appear to be an issue. For Lumet, there was no message behind this choice—it simply reflected her own family experience. "Some people feel that I was attempting to make some statement about racial harmony.... No, that's kinda just what my house looks like. My mom's black and my dad's white," she told Farai Chideya in a 2008 interview for National Public Radio. "I can honestly say that I set about to make no statements at all. I just tried really hard to be brave and write honestly."

Received Critical Acclaim

Rachel Getting Married was widely praised by critics. A. O. Scott of the *New York Times* wrote in a 2008 review, "It's a small movie, and in some ways a very sad one, but it has an undeniable and authentic vitality, an exuberance of spirit, that feels welcome and rare." Wendy Ide of the London *Times* called Lumet's screenplay "smart, spiky and observant," whereas Ronnie Scheib of *Variety* described the film as "brimming with energy, elan and ... unpredictability." Lumet earned best screenplay awards from the New York Film Critics Circle, Toronto Film Critics Association, and Washington, DC, Area Film Critics Association, as well as an NAACP Image Award in 2009 for outstanding writing in a motion picture.

Buoyed by the success of *Rachel Getting Married,* Lumet has become one of Hollywood's most in-demand screenwriters. She rewrote the script for *Remember Me* (2010), a romantic drama directed by Allen Coulter and starring Robert Pattinson. By late 2009 she also had signed on as screenwriter for the Miramax film *This Strange Thing Called Prom,* based on a *New York Times* article about a group of students at an international high school who decide to organize their first prom. She was also developing a film tentatively titled *See Also: Sambo* with Jason Reitman, director of the films *Juno* (2007) and *Up in the Air* (2009).

Selected works

Films (as screenwriter)

Rachel Getting Married, Clinica Estetico, 2008.
Remember Me, Underground Films, 2010.

Films (as actress)

Deathtrap, Warner Bros., 1982.
Running on Empty, Double Play, 1988.
Tougher Than Leather, Def Pictures, 1988.
Q & A, Odyssey Distributors, 1990.

Assassination, Production Pictures, 1994.
Dodgeball, Great Jones Productions, 1995.

Sources

Periodicals

Boston Globe, October 5, 2008.
Los Angeles Times, September 28, 2008.
New York Times, October 3, 2008.
Observer (London), January 25, 2009.
Times (London), September 4, 2008.
Variety, September 3, 2008.

Online

Callaghan, Dylan, "When Truth Comes a-Callin'," Writers Guild of America, West, http://www.wga.org/content/default.aspx?id=2978 (accessed October 25, 2009).
"'Rachel Getting Married' Writer Share Creative Journey," interview with Farai Chideya, National Public Radio, October 14, 2008, http://www.npr.org/templates/story/story.php?storyId=95695107 (accessed October 25, 2009).

—Deborah A. Ring

Govan A. Mbeki

1910–2001

Political activist, journalist

Mbeki, Govan A., photograph. AP Images.

Govan A. Mbeki, known affectionately as "Oom Gov" (Uncle Gov), was a journalist and political activist who led the African National Congress (ANC) in its long struggle to end the racially oppressive apartheid system in South Africa. Under apartheid, which became official policy in 1948, a white minority controlled South Africa's government and enforced a policy of racial segregation, restricting the rights and freedoms of the majority black population. Mbeki began his activism at the grassroots level, organizing peasants in the countryside, and rose to become national chairman of the ANC. In 1963 Mbeki was charged with plotting to overthrow the government and sentenced to life in prison, together with other prominent ANC leaders such as Nelson Mandela and Walter Sisulu. A political prisoner for more than two decades, Mbeki finally was freed in 1987. When the country held its first democratic elections in 1994—marking the end of apartheid—Mbeki served in the new government under President Mandela. Mbeki lived to see his son, Thabo Mbeki, succeed Mandela as president in 1999.

Govan Mbeki (pronounced mm-BECK-ee) was born on July 9, 1910, in the Ngqamakwe district of the Transkei (present-day Eastern Cape Province) in South Africa, a member of the Xhosa ethnic group. His father, a local chief who later was deposed by the government, named him in honor of Edward Govan, a Scotsman who had established the Lovedale missionary school in the Eastern Cape during the nineteenth century to educate the native Africans. Mbeki received his early education at this school. He first became interested in politics at age fifteen, when he met a neighboring minister who was a member of the nascent ANC, a political organization formed to resist the oppression of black Africans. Mbeki soon became interested in the work of the Industrial and Commercial Workers' Union, the first mass movement of black workers in South Africa. Growing up in the Transkei, Mbeki saw firsthand the poverty of the African peasants in the countryside and he was deeply affected by their daily struggles.

Moved to Political Action

In 1929, at age nineteen, Mbeki moved to Johannesburg, where he worked as a "newspaper boy." He was

At a Glance . . .

Born Govan Archibald Mvunyelwa Mbeki on July 9, 1910, in Transkei, South Africa; died on August 30, 2001, in Port Elizabeth, South Africa; married Epainette Mamotseki; children: Linda, Thabo, Moeletsi, Jama. *Politics:* Communist. *Education:* South African Native College (now University of Fort Hare), BA, politics and psychology, 1936; University of South Africa, BA, social studies; University of Amsterdam, BA, economics.

Career: *Territorial Magazine,* editor, 1938–44; *New Age,* editor, 1954–62; African National Congress, national chairman, 1956–64; Parliament of South Africa, deputy president of the Senate, 1994–97, deputy president of the National Council of Provinces, 1997–99.

Awards: Isithwalandwe Medal, African National Congress, 1980.

struck by the plight of the African working class, and by the violence that they experienced at the hands of the white government, which tightly controlled the rights and movements of black South Africans. "I saw the poverty of the black Africans. Where I lived—in the city and in the suburbs—police raids were always taking place.... No other event up till then had provoked my anger as much as those raids and I decided definitely to join the struggle to put an end to such a system," he later wrote, according to the ANC.

As a student at South African Native College, then the intellectual hotbed of the black resistance movement, Mbeki joined the ANC and met many of the organization's future leaders. He began to form the ideological stance that would define his political life. He completed his bachelor's degree in politics and psychology and received a teaching certificate in 1936. Initially, Mbeki pursued a career as a teacher but was fired on several occasions because of his political activities. He returned to the Transkei in 1938, opening a cooperative store in Idutywa with his wife and dedicating himself to local politics and writing.

Mbeki began organizing the peasants of the Transkei into simple agricultural collectives, teaching them how to pool their resources and improve their production methods. His first publication was the *Territorial Magazine* (later renamed *Inkundla ya Bantu*), which he edited from 1938 to 1944. In 1939 he published his first collection of essays, called *The Transkei in the Making*, and in 1943 he cowrote *African Claims*, which would become the basis for ANC policy. Mbeki

was elected secretary of the Transkei Voters' Association in 1941, became a member of the Transkei General Council (known as the Bunga) in 1943, and was named general secretary of the Transkei Organized Bodies in 1945. He returned to teaching for a time in 1953 in northern Natal but once again was dismissed for his activities organizing black workers at nearby coal mines.

Led the ANC

An active organizer for the ANC since his college days, Mbeki ascended the ranks of the organization and became its national chairman in 1956, continuing in that role even after the government passed an act in 1960 that outlawed the ANC. An avowed leftist, Mbeki formally joined the South African Communist Party in 1961; the following year he was elected to its central committee.

As an editor of the left-wing weekly *New Age*, a mouthpiece for the ANC that opposed the apartheid regime, Mbeki chronicled the black resistance movement and began to advocate violence to achieve liberation, believing that all other avenues for change had been exhausted. In 1962 the government banned *New Age*. When Mbeki and his colleagues launched a successor publication, called *Spark*, the government responded by not only banning the paper but also by prohibiting its editors and writers from publishing.

Mbeki was arrested in December of 1961, charged with making explosives, and spent five months in prison at Rooi Hell (Red Hell), including three months in solitary confinement. During his imprisonment, he penned *South Africa: The Peasants' Revolt*, a history of the resistance movement, writing the text on scraps of toilet paper that were smuggled out while he awaited trial. He was acquitted on a technicality but his movements were restricted by a house arrest order. Mbeki ignored the order and went underground, joining Umkhonto we Sizwe (Spear of the Nation), the military wing of the ANC, and becoming secretary of its high command.

In July of 1963 police raided Liliesleaf Farm in the Johannesburg suburb of Rivonia, where the underground headquarters of the ANC and South African Communist Party was located, and seized a cache of incriminating documents. Mbeki, Mandela, Sisulu, and a number of other resistance leaders were arrested and charged with trying to overthrow the government. During the so-called Rivonia trial in 1963–64, Mbeki and eight others were convicted and sentenced to life in prison on Robben Island, off the coast of Cape Town.

Saw Freedom and End of Apartheid

Mbeki served twenty-three years in prison, until he was freed on November 5, 1987. Although the president of

South Africa, P. W. Botha, had previously insisted that he would not authorize the release of any of the prisoners unless they agreed to renounce violence—something that Mbeki steadfastly refused to do—his administration then reversed course, suggesting to observers that Mbeki's release was a first step toward freeing Mandela, who had become a symbol of the opposition across the world to the oppressive apartheid regime. Upon his release, Mbeki spoke with the same fervor that he had more than two decades earlier: "The ideas for which I went to jail and for which the ANC stands, I still embrace," he declared, according to *Time* magazine. Although Mbeki's release was to be unconditional, within days the government issued an order barring him from leaving the Eastern Cape district where he lived, and classified him as a "listed" person (as all communists were), meaning that he could not be quoted by the press.

South Africa's first democratic, all-race elections were held on April 27, 1994, marking the end of apartheid and the achievement of Mbeki's dream. South Africans ousted white president F. W. de Klerk and elected a majority black government, with Mandela as president. Mbeki won a seat in the Parliament and served as deputy president of the Senate from 1994 to 1997, and then held the same position in the National Council of Provinces until 1999, when he retired from politics. In that same year, Thabo Mbeki, Govan's son, succeeded Mandela as president of South Africa.

Govan Mbeki died on August 30, 2001, at his home in Port Elizabeth, at the age of ninety-one.

Selected writings

The Transkei in the Making, 1939.
(Coauthor) *African Claims,* 1943.
South Africa: The Peasants' Revolt, Penguin African Library, 1964.
Learning from Robben Island: The Prison Writings of Govan Mbeki, D. Philip, 1991.
The Struggle for Liberation in South Africa, D. Philip, 1992.
Sunset at Midday, Thorold's Africana Books, 1996.

Sources

Books

Gevisser, Mark, *A Legacy of Liberation: Thabo Mbeki and the Future of the South African Dream,* Palgrave Macmillan, 2009.

Periodicals

Guardian (London), August 31, 2001.
Independent (London), August 31, 2001.
New York Times, September 3, 1987; November 6, 1987, p. A6; August 31, 2001, p. A18.
Time, November 16, 1987, p. 53.
Times (London), December 12, 1987.

Online

"Govan Mbeki—Isithwalandwe," African National Congress, December 1980, http://www.anc.org.za/ancdocs/history/awards/isithwalandwe_gmbeki.html (accessed October 28, 2009).

—Deborah A. Ring

Tracy McGrady

1979—

Professional basketball player, philanthropist

McGrady, Tracy, photograph. AP Images.

Basketball player Tracy McGrady, often known as T-Mac, stepped into the national spotlight in 1997, when he moved directly from high school to the National Basketball Association (NBA). He has had a sterling career there, anchoring three teams (Toronto Raptors, Orlando Magic, and Houston Rockets) and leading the league in scoring twice (2002–03 and 2003–04). As of 2009, the Florida native was attracting growing attention for his philanthropy, notably on behalf of Darfuri refugees in the North African nation of Chad.

The only child of Tracy McGrady Sr. and Melanise Williford, Tracy Lamar McGrady Jr. was born on May 24, 1979, in Bartow, a small town in central Florida. His maternal grandmother, Roberta Williford, was an important influence, and her residence in Auburndale, a short drive north of Bartow, was his home for most of his childhood. In a struggling but close-knit neighborhood called "the Hill," McGrady spent his days playing a variety of sports, including baseball and football in addition to basketball. At Auburndale High School, he was an indifferent student but a star athlete. After a strong performance at a basketball camp the summer before his senior year, he was offered a scholarship to

Mount Zion Christian Academy, a North Carolina institution known for the strength of its basketball program.

Adapting quickly to his new school, McGrady worked to improve his academic performance and to impress the basketball scouts now in regular attendance at his games. A pivotal moment came toward the end of the season, when he was named Most Valuable Player at the annual Reebok Holiday Prep Classic, an annual tournament in Nevada for the nation's strongest high school teams. Several months later, he was chosen in the first round of the 1997 NBA draft by the Toronto Raptors, a relatively new expansion team. While many colleges had expressed an interest in him, he decided to accept the Raptors' offer of a three-year contract worth roughly four and a half million dollars. He also signed an even more lucrative endorsement deal with Adidas, a leading sneaker manufacturer.

McGrady's three seasons in Toronto were a mix of success and frustration. Like many rookies, he needed time to adjust to the style and pace of the professional game. The team's fans and management, however, wanted immediate results. After a disappointing rookie season (1997–98), his play grew stronger, particularly after the arrival of his friend—and distant cousin—Vince Carter in 1998–99. The following year, McGrady's final season with the team, the Raptors won forty-five games, a twenty-nine game improvement over his rookie season. Much of that success was attributable to his improved performance, particularly on offense. His points-per-game average, for example, more than doubled during his tenure with the team (7.0 in 1997–98; 15.4 in 1999–2000).

In August of 2000, Toronto traded McGrady to the Orlando Magic. The change seemed to have a positive impact on his play, and he was named the league's Most Improved Player at the end of the 2000–01 season. Two years later he led the league in scoring, a feat he repeated in 2003–04. Despite his performance, the team as a whole had only modest success, dropping out of postseason play in the first playoff round in 2000–01, 2001–02, and 2002–03. Facing growing criticism in the media for a perceived lack of motivation and leadership, McGrady struggled to maintain a positive relationship with the team's management. Few were surprised when the Magic traded him in June of 2004 to the Houston Rockets.

By the fall of 2009, he had completed five seasons in Houston and was getting ready for a sixth. His performance remained impressive, and in 2006–07 he was elected to the NBA All-Star Team for the seventh time. Injuries, however, were a growing concern, particularly after a serious knee problem kept him off the court for more than half of 2008–09. As he prepared for the next season, his thirteenth in the league, there was some speculation that it might be his last. While it was clear that his knee would not be ready by the season opener, he remained cautiously upbeat. "We'll see how I feel tomorrow," he noted in a post on his Web site in October of 2009. "This is what I expected."

While McGrady remained the subject of intense media attention, its focus in 2009 was shifting from his basketball skills to his philanthropy. His involvement in charitable work began early in his career, when he established the Tracy McGrady Foundation to oversee his donations to a variety of nonprofit organizations, most of them in the Auburndale area. He later expanded the program's scope to include Houston. Among his most prominent donations there were gifts to improve computer and library resources at two elementary schools, both in impoverished neighborhoods.

Since 2007 most of McGrady's charitable work has centered on Darfur, a vast region in the North African nation of Sudan. Years of civil war forced tens of thousands of Darfuris across the border to Chad, where they lived in overcrowded and poorly equipped camps. McGrady's determination to help began with a five-day trip to three of those facilities in the summer of 2007. His visit, inspired by reports he had heard from fellow NBA star (and Sudan native) Luol Deng, was arranged with the assistance of John Prendergast, a former White House staffer and a co-founder of the Enough Project, a Washington-based nonprofit.

In the camps, McGrady found a desperate need for educational materials. On his return, he joined Enough and other groups to form the Darfur Dream Team, an initiative designed to help American students raise money for their peers in Africa. According to a report by Prendergast on the Huffington Post, a widely read Web site, the Dream Team had raised more than two hundred thousand dollars by October of 2009. McGrady, meanwhile, had enlisted other NBA stars to help, and a documentary film of his trip had been screened for audiences nationwide. Entitled *3 Points*, it was also available online at the free site Hulu.com.

While McGrady had revealed little of his plans for life after basketball, it seemed likely in October of 2009 that his Darfur work would continue to occupy him for some time. It was "something that crept up on me," he told Michael Lee of the *Washington Post*. "It happened, I'm in it. I believe I was put here to do things like that."

Selected works

3 Points (documentary film), Double Wide Media, 2009.

Sources

Periodicals

Maclean's, April 26, 1999.
Washington Post, January 15, 2008.

Online

"About the Darfur Dream Team," DarfurDreamTeam.
org, http://www.darfurdreamteam.org/content/a
bout-darfur-dream-team (accessed October 17,
2009).

Prendergast, John, "Rachel Maddow Spotlights T-
Mac's Darfur Dream Team," HuffingtonPost.com,
September 29, 2009, http://www.huffingtonpost.
com/john-prendergast/rachel-maddow-spotlights_b
_302844.html (accessed October 17, 2009).
"T-Mac Feeling Good, Back at Practice," T-Mac.com,
October 5, 2009, http://www.t-mac.com/tmac/
blogDetail/2063 (accessed October 20, 2009).
"Tracy McGrady," NBA.com, http://www.nba.com/
playerfile/tracy_mcgrady/bio.html (accessed October 17, 2009).
"Tracy's Story," T-Mac.com, http://www.t-mac.com/
tmac/about/ (accessed October 19, 2009).

—R. Anthony Kugler

George Alexander McGuire

1866–1934

Church leader, physician, activist

In the 1920s and early 1930s, few African-American church leaders were as prominent as George Alexander McGuire. A native of the West Indies, he is best remembered as the founder of the African Orthodox Church (AOC), which he established in 1921 in response to the unremitting racism he encountered in other, more established denominations. At the time of his death in 1934, the AOC had as many as thirty thousand members worldwide.

McGuire was born on March 26, 1866, in Swetes (also spelled Sweets), a small town on the West Indian island of Antigua, then a British colony. After a distinguished career in local schools, McGuire attended the Antigua branch of Mico College, a well-known institution based in Jamaica. Upon receipt of his undergraduate degree in 1886, he traveled to the island of St. Thomas to attend Nisky Theological Seminary, earning a graduate degree there two years later.

McGuire's seminary had close ties to the Moravian church, a Protestant denomination, and it was to a Moravian congregation on the island of St. Croix that he was first posted as a pastor. After serving there for six years (1888–94), he moved with his wife, Ada Roberts McGuire, to the United States. That change coincided with a move from the Moravian church to the Episcopal. In 1897 he was ordained as an Episcopal priest and began work at a succession of African-American churches within that denomination. In 1905 he was sent to Arkansas to become what was known in that state's Episcopal diocese as the Archdeacon for Colored Work. While he achieved some success in improving vocational opportunities for African-American Arkansans, many of his efforts were thwarted by the racism of local church leaders. Deeply frustrated, he resigned in 1909 and moved to Cambridge, Massachusetts, where he established a small congregation called St. Bartholomew's Church. His attempts to win Episcopal accreditation for the new organization were rejected.

During his tenure in Cambridge, McGuire apparently had time to earn a medical degree. According to several sources, he studied at the Boston College of Physicians and Surgeons, earning a medical degree there in 1910; however, the author of his 1934 obituary in the *New York Times* omitted mention of that institution, noting instead that he was a 1910 graduate of Jefferson Medical College, a large institution in Philadelphia, Pennsylvania. He may well have studied at both schools, and he was working as a physician in 1913, when he returned to Antigua. In addition to establishing an important medical practice there, he held regular services at several local churches and championed the interests of striking sugarcane workers during a bitter labor dispute. "When the strikes led to the burning of cane fields and rioting," wrote Byron Rushing in the *Journal of Negro History*, "colonial officials asked the leading churchmen to attempt to quiet the rebels. Most of the clergy did try but to little avail. McGuire, however, refused, saying that the workers should be given a living wage."

McGuire's experience during the strikes seems to have radicalized him, and he began to immerse himself in the

At a Glance . . .

Born March 26, 1866, in Swetes (or Sweets), Antigua; died November 10, 1934, in New York City; married Ada Roberts, 1892; children: at least one daughter. *Religion:* African Orthodox. *Education:* Mico College (Antigua), undergraduate degree, 1886; Nisky Theological Seminary, graduate degree, 1888; Jefferson Medical College, MD(?), 1910.

Career: Moravian Church, pastor, 1888–94; Episcopal Church, priest and administrator, 1897–1919(?); physician and activist, 1913(?)–19(?); Universal Negro Improvement Association, chaplain-general, 1919(?)–24(?); African Orthodox Church, founder and archbishop, 1921–34.

writings of Marcus Garvey, the foremost proponent of what became known as black nationalism. Racism among whites was so intractable, Garvey believed, that people of African descent had little choice but to separate themselves, either by returning to Africa or by building their own institutions from the ground up. Inspired by what was at the time a radical message, McGuire returned to the United States in about 1919, found Garvey in New York City, and was named "chaplain general" of the latter's organization, the Universal Negro Improvement Association (UNIA). He had by that time renounced his affiliation with the Episcopal Church. Most of his efforts over the next few years focused on the creation of a new denomination to meet the spiritual needs of the African diaspora. After several false starts, the African Orthodox Church (AOC) was established in 1921.

Many of the circumstances surrounding the church's founding have been disputed over the years, particularly the precise role played by Garvey. It is known that a rift grew between the two men, and by 1924 McGuire was no longer employed by Garvey's UNIA. Until his death a decade later, he worked exclusively on building his church, eventually establishing a headquarters he called the Holy Cross Pro-Cathedral. A powerful preacher, he believed, according to Rushing, "that Black Christians should have Black religious symbols." The widespread appeal of that message was reflected in the church's rapid growth throughout the world. Affiliated congregations sprang up in other American cities, the Caribbean, and Africa.

Particularly dramatic was the AOC's growth in Uganda, then a British protectorate. Crucial to the organization's expansion into Africa was McGuire's partnership with an ecclesiastical leader in South Africa named Daniel William Alexander, who sought and obtained affiliation with the AOC in 1927. Alexander subsequently became an indefatigable representative for the church throughout southern and eastern Africa. While the reasons for the AOC's particular success in Uganda were complex, an important factor was undoubtedly the tone of the church's rituals, which were firmly in the Episcopal tradition. Because that tradition, in turn, had its roots in the Church of England, it was familiar to many Ugandans. By the 1960s, however, a variety of disputes had weakened ties between the American and African congregations, and many of the latter had left the denomination.

McGuire died in New York on November 10, 1934, after an unsuccessful operation. Seventy-five years after his death, the African Orthodox church was a fraction of the size it had once been. Of the roughly fifteen congregations still in existence in 2009, the best known by far was one dedicated to the late saxophonist John Coltrane. Founded in San Francisco in 1971, the Saint John Will-I-Am Coltrane African Orthodox Church seeks, according to its Web site, to "guide souls back to God" through the performance of Coltrane's acclaimed compositions.

Selected writings

Universal Negro Catechism, Universal Negro Improvement Association, 1921.
Universal Negro Ritual, Universal Negro Improvement Association, 1921.

Sources

Periodicals

Journal of Negro History, January 1972.
New York Times, November 12, 1934.

Online

"African Orthodox Church," Emory.edu, April 21, 2009, http://www.pitts.emory.edu/exhibit_blog/?page_id=247 (accessed October 14, 2009).
Gallaher, Rachel, "McGuire, George Alexander (1866–1934)," BlackPast.org, http://www.blackpast.org/?q=aah/mcguire-george-alexander-1866-1934 (accessed October 14, 2009).
"Welcome," ColtraneChurch.org, http://www.coltranechurch.org/ (accessed October 17, 2009).

—R. Anthony Kugler

M.C. Hammer

1963—

Rap musician, entrepreneur

M.C. Hammer, photograph. AP Images.

M.C. Hammer was one of rap music's biggest stars during the late 1980s and early 1990s. He did much to bring the music to a general American audience, and roosted atop *Billboard* magazine's sales charts for an impressive twenty-one weeks with his 1989 album, *Please Hammer Don't Hurt 'Em*. Hammer's career later went into decline, and the financial and legal problems that dogged him testified to how fleeting fame could be in the fast-moving world of hip-hop. He hit bottom in the mid-1990s when more than $13 million in debt forced him to declare bankruptcy. Hammer drew inspiration from his Christian faith to rebound into public life as a motivational speaker and entrepreneur. He participated in several successful businesses after 2000, including the Internet site DanceJam.com and the jewelry-recycling business Cash4Gold. His status as a celebrity continued through his popular Twitter postings, his self-produced recordings, and his appearances on such reality television series as *The Surreal Life* and *Hammertime*.

M.C. Hammer was born Stanley Kirk Burrell on March 30, 1963, in Oakland, California. His family was poor. The rapper recalled that six children were crammed into a three-bedroom housing-project apartment. As a boy he often went to the nearby Oakland Coliseum to watch baseball's Oakland Athletics play, and an interest in music manifested itself in attempts to copy the dance styles of such flamboyant acts of the day as James Brown and the O'Jays. The youngster's energy and flair caught the attention of Athletics owner Charles Finley, who eventually hired the future rapper as a clubhouse helper and bat boy. Athletics players detected a resemblance to the home-run king "Hammerin' Hank" Aaron and bestowed on their new assistant the nickname "Hammer."

Became Music Phenomenon during Late 1980s

Graduating from high school in Oakland, Hammer tried but failed to win a place in a professional baseball organization. Discouraged by his studies in communications at a local college, he resisted the lure of Oakland's drug trade and enlisted in the U.S. Navy, serving for three years and learning lessons that he

At a Glance . . .

Born Stanley Kirk Burrell on March 30, 1963, in Oakland, CA; son of Lewis, a gambling club manager, and Betty Burrell, a police department secretary; married Stephanie Fuller, December 21, 1985; children: A'keiba, Sarah, Stanley, Jeremiah, Samuel; also raising nephew Jamaris Knighten. *Military service:* Served three years in the U.S. Navy, early 1980s. *Religion:* Christian.

Career: Clubhouse assistant and bat boy, Oakland Athletics baseball team, 1971–80. Rap musician, c. 1985—; released debut single, "Stupid Def Yal/Ring Em," 1987; signed with Capitol Records, 1988; released debut album *Feel My Power,* revised as *Let's Get It Started,* 1989. Reality television personality, *The Surreal Life,* VH1, 2003, and *Hammertime,* A&E, 2009. Co-founder, chief strategy officer, DanceJam. com, 2008—; equity partner and spokesperson, Cash4Gold, 2009—.

Awards: Grammy Awards for best rhythm and blues song and best rap solo, both 1990, for "U Can't Touch This"; Grammy Award for best music video (long form), 1990, for *Please Hammer Don't Hurt 'Em: The Movie;* American Music Awards for best rap album and soul/R&B album, both 1991, for *Please Hammer Don't Hurt 'Em;* American Music Award for best soul/R&B single, 1991, for "U Can't Touch This"; American Music Awards for best male soul/R&B artist and best rap artist, both 1991; Living Legends of Hip Hop Award, Hip Hop International, 2008.

Addresses: *Booking agent*—Universal Attractions, 135 West 26th St., 12th Fl., New York, NY 10001.

would later apply to the musical organization he would head. Back in Oakland, he took notice of the rap music that was gaining popularity in the city's clubs and on the streets. He began rapping in small venues, and, with bigger plans on his mind, borrowed $20,000 from Athletics players Mike Davis and Dwayne Murphy to start his own label, Bust It Records, in the middle 1980s.

Hammer released a single, "Ring 'Em," and largely on the strength of tireless street marketing by Hammer and his wife, Stephanie—whom Hammer met at a church revival meeting—it achieved considerable popularity at dance clubs in the San Francisco Bay Area. After another single, "Let's Get It Started," Hammer joined with an experienced producer, Felton Pilate, who had worked with the successful vocal group Con Funk Shun. The album that resulted, *Feel My Power,* likewise had notable success. Its sales of 60,000 copies were more than respectable for a release by an unknown independent label. Heartened by his rising prospects, Hammer launched into seven-day-a-week rehearsals with the growing troupe of dancers, musicians, and backup vocalists he had hired.

It was Hammer's stage show, and his infectious stage presence, that led to his big break in 1988. Performing in an Oakland club, he impressed a Capitol Records executive who "didn't know who he was, but knew he was somebody," as she was quoted as saying in the *New Rolling Stone Encyclopedia of Rock & Roll.* "M.C. Hammer," as he was billing himself, took home a $750,000 advance and a multi-album contract, and it did not take long for Capitol to recoup its investment. *Let's Get It Started,* a revised version of *Feel My Power,* sold more than two million copies.

Hammer used some of the proceeds from the album to install a rolling recording studio in the back of his tour bus, where he recorded much of his sophomore effort, *Please Hammer Don't Hurt 'Em.* Released in 1990, this album catapulted M.C. Hammer to the top ranks of the American entertainment business. It sold more than ten million copies, took up seemingly permanent residence at the top of the charts, and spawned the hit single "U Can't Touch This." Hammer became a fixture of the television airwaves, appearing in a Pepsi commercial and starring in the children's animated series, *Hammerman.* There was even a Hammer doll. Flush with cash, he opened his own music management firm, established a children's foundation, and purchased a top-quality race horse, Lite Light. Early in 1992, *Jet* estimated that Hammer employed 200 people, with an annual payroll of $6.8 million. He purchased a $20 million mansion in the hills above San Francisco Bay.

Filed for Bankruptcy When Career Lapsed

Although some critics and hard-core rap aficionados deplored the album, the success of *Please Hammer Don't Hurt 'Em* was easy to understand. Hammer's showmanship and elaborate stage choreography, involving fifteen dancers, twelve backup singers, seven musicians, and two disc jockeys, gave him a powerful visual appeal. Hammer was the first rap artist to put together a choreographed show of this type, and his visual flair attracted heavy airplay for his videos on MTV, a music-video network with a predominantly white viewership that before Hammer had aired little rap music.

On the musical side, Hammer understood the virtues of appealing to something familiar in a genre as new and fast-changing as rap: "U Can't Touch This" was closely based on the Rick James hit "Super Freak" of a decade before. In fact, James sued Hammer for infringement of copyright, but the suit was settled out of court when Hammer agreed to credit James as co-composer, effectively cutting James in on the millions of dollars the record was earning. Some critics complained of a lack of originality in Hammer's recordings, but Hammer set the pattern, both musically and financially, for practices that became common in hip-hop music later in the 1990s in the hands of such platinum-selling performers as Puff Daddy and Will Smith.

Hammer's young empire began to collapse when his next album, 1991's *Too Legit to Quit,* failed to match the sales of its predecessor. Although three million copies were sold, the album could not sustain the massive world tour that Hammer had launched, and it was canceled midway through. Sales declined further with *The Funky Headhunter,* released in 1994, which unsuccessfully attempted to recast Hammer in the streetwise "gangsta rap" mold of the day. Hammer was sued by Pilate and by several of his former backers, and faced charges that performance troupe members endured an abusive, militaristic atmosphere.

In April of 1996 Hammer hit bottom, filing for bankruptcy in a California court. His mansion was sold for a fraction of its former price. "My priorities were out of order," he told *Ebony.* "My priorities should have always been God, family, community, and then business," he continued. Instead, he went on, they had been "business, business, and business." Hammer spoke of his renewed commitment to God, and even appeared on gospel music's Stellar Music Awards show in 1997. In the same interview Hammer discussed plans to renew his career, and by 1998 there were signs that he was making progress. He had appeared in two cable television movies, had completed a new album, *Family Affair,* and was said to be writing a book addressing the situation of African-American men.

Revived Career through Entrepreneurship

By 2000 Hammer had dropped the M.C. from his name and had devoted himself to Christian ministry. An ordained minister, he regularly conducted Gospel hip-hop events and hosted a radio show on the Trinity Broadcasting Network. He had adjusted to a more modest lifestyle in a four-bedroom home in northern California that he shared with his wife and growing family. Hammer traced the transformation in his life to a surgery in 1996 that corrected a leg injury. He told Julie K. L. Dam and Ken Baker in *People,* "I remember God speaking to me and saying that the breaking of my leg was symbolic of the breaking of all the old ties, old habits—all the things that had stopped me from focusing on the man he made me to be…. I thought it was time to get back to being a man of God."

In 2006 Hammer released a new album, *Look Look Look,* and marketed it himself using social networking Internet sites, including Club Look, an online site he established for fans to upload videos of themselves performing or lip-synching his songs. Unlike many music industry companies that disapprove of fan videos as an infringement of copyright laws, Hammer told Kevin Maney in *USA Today* that he encourages uploads. "If some kid is taking my song and dancing to it and uploading the video, he's saying that's part of his life…. How can that not be good?" Expanding on the Club Look idea, in early 2008 Hammer launched the dance-oriented site DanceJam.com with partners Geoffrey Arone and Anthony Young. The site includes competition videos, dance lessons, fan performances, and contests in which site users upload and rate videos.

An early user and advocate of social networking online, by 2009 Hammer had more than 1.7 million followers on Twitter. He made public appearances at technology forums, including conferences at the Harvard Faculty Club and Stanford University, to discuss the impact and use of Internet marketing tools. He continued to perform and did not try to distance himself from his early hits. In early 2009 he reunited in Utah for a show with former rival rapper Vanilla Ice (Robert Van Winkle). Reviewing the show in *Newsweek,* Joshua Alston concluded: "The harsh truth is, these songs are giddy and infectious, just as much now as then."

Drawing on his sustained popularity and marketing appeal, Hammer became a spokesperson for the gold refining company Cash4Gold and appeared in a popular commercial for the company that first aired during Super Bowl XLIII in February of 2009. The relationship between Hammer and the company strengthened late in that year when Hammer became an equity partner in the gold-recycling firm.

In summer 2009 A&E began airing episodes of *Hammertime,* a reality show starring Hammer, his wife, Stephanie, and their children, A'keiba, Sarah, Stanley, Jeremiah, Sammy, and nephew Jamaris Knighten. Following his participation in the VH1 series *The Surreal Life* in 2003, Hammer had received numerous offers to star in a reality series of his own. He turned them down, however, until he believed a show based on his family would have something unique to offer. In *USA Today* Gary Strauss described Hammer's life as a "rags-to-riches-to-rags-and-back saga." Hammer told Strauss he believed his story could offer inspiration to many families struggling through difficult economic times. "We're in a recession, but there are a great number of people who haven't experienced adversity and aren't able to adjust…. I can tell you that even through hardships, you can rear a family you can be proud of."

Selected works

Albums

Let's Get It Started, Capitol (revised version of *Feel My Power*), 1989.
Please Hammer Don't Hurt 'Em, Capitol, 1990.
Too Legit to Quit, Capitol, 1991.
The Funky Headhunter, Giant, 1994.
Inside Out, Giant, 1995.
Family Affair, EMI, 1998.
Active Duty, World Hit Records, 2001.
Full Blast, Full Blast Digital Music, 2004.
Look Look Look, Full Blast Digital Music, 2006.

Television

The Surreal Life, VH1, 2003.
Hammertime, A&E, 2009.

Sources

Books

Romanowski, Patricia, and Holly George-Warren, eds., *The New Rolling Stone Encyclopedia of Rock & Roll,* Fireside, 1995.

Periodicals

Billboard, February 19, 1994, p. 20; January 28, 1995, p. 29.
Ebony, April 1994, p. 22; August 1997, p. 30.
Entertainment Weekly, December 28, 1990; March 18, 1994, p. 102.
Hollywood Reporter, November 1, 2005.
Jet, April 6, 1992, p. 60; August 28, 1995, p.38; June 24, 1996, p. 38; September 8, 1997, p. 64; January 21, 2008, p. 12.
Los Angeles Times, June 14, 2009.
Newsweek, March 16, 2009, p. 52.
People, June 19, 2000, p. 135.
USA Today, July 5, 2006, p.B3; June 12, 2009, p. D13.

Online

Hammer, M.C., Twitter, http://twitter.com/Mchammer, December 18, 2009 (accessed December 18, 2009).
Hempel, Jessi, "MC Hammer Goes for the Gold," CNNMoney.com, December 7, 2009 (accessed December 18, 2009).

—James M. Manheim and Laurie DiMauro

Leatrice McKissack

1930—

CEO, educator

Leatrice B. McKissack, a teacher by training, came to national prominence in the mid-1980s when she became CEO of the architecture firm McKissack & McKissack, the oldest African-American company in that field. During her seventeen-year tenure there, the Missouri native won dozens of new contracts and expanded the business far beyond its Southern roots.

McKissack was born Leatrice Buchanan on July 27, 1930, in Keytesville, Missouri, a small community in the north-central region of the state. Her father, Archie Buchanan, was a farmer; her mother, Catherine Brummell Buchanan, maintained the family home and looked after the couple's five children, of whom Leatrice was the second. Like most families in the nation's agricultural heartland, her family struggled financially in the Depression of the 1930s, particularly in the period following her father's death in 1937. Catherine Buchanan moved with her children to the growing city of Nashville, Tennessee. There she met Alrutheus A. Taylor, an administrator at Fisk University, one of the most prominent African-American schools in the country. Her marriage to Taylor some months later brought Leatrice and her siblings onto the Fisk campus, where they regularly encountered the poet Langston Hughes, the artist Aaron Douglas, and other major figures.

At Pearl High School, a segregated institution, McKissack showed a marked aptitude for the sciences. Upon graduation, she matriculated at Fisk, where she focused on chemistry and math, receiving a bachelor's degree in the latter in 1951. She completed her education six years later with a master's degree in psychology from Tennessee Agricultural and Industrial State University (later known as Tennessee State University).

McKissack's teaching career began in 1952, when she joined the Nashville public school system. She remained there for the next seventeen years, teaching math and science at the elementary and junior-high levels. She also served as an informal advisor to the school system's administrators, particularly on the pressing issue of desegregation. Health problems, however, forced her retirement in 1969. For roughly the next decade and a half, she focused on her family, which included her husband, William DeBerry McKissack, whom she had married while at Fisk, and three daughters.

William McKissack, an architect, was the son of Moses McKissack III, who had founded the firm later known as McKissack & McKissack in 1905. The family's roots in the building trades had begun with the first Moses McKissack, a skilled slave in North Carolina in the first decades of the nineteenth century. By the time William took over as the firm's CEO in 1968, it had built hundreds of structures throughout the South, including churches, schools, and government buildings. That growth accelerated under his tenure. In 1983, however, William McKissack had to step down after suffering a serious stroke. His illness sparked a crisis at the firm, for there were few internal candidates suitable for the post. A larger company in that situation might have looked elsewhere for an experienced executive, but McKissack & McKissack was family-owned and family-run. Leatrice saw little choice but to take charge herself. Two days after her husband's stroke, she succeeded him as CEO. At the time, she recalled to a Tennessee newspaper some years later, "all I knew about architecture was how to spell it."

McKissack knew she needed help. One of her first acts was to hire a number of consultants, who walked her through the complex legal and financial arrangements required for the design and construction of even a modest building. She also sold off a number of subsidiary businesses, including a contracting company and an apartment complex, in order to focus on the firm's core mission: building solid, aesthetically pleasing structures at a fair price. As she immersed herself in the company's day-to-day operations, her confidence grew, and within months she was taking decisive steps to strengthen its position. In 1984, for example, she sued the city of Nashville on the grounds that it was not giving full consideration to McKissack & McKissack's bids for several major public-works projects. Her aggressive approach soon brought a number of new contracts for work in and around the city. One of the most prominent of these came in 1987, when the state of Tennessee hired the firm to build a National Civil Rights Museum (NCRM) on the site of Nashville's Lorraine Motel, where Dr. Martin Luther King Jr. was

murdered in 1968. According to its Web site, the museum had reached an annual attendance of more than a hundred thousand within four years of its 1991 opening.

McKissack also sought to expand the firm's presence beyond the South. In one important project in the late 1980s, the firm conducted a thorough renovation of the dormitories at Howard University in Washington, DC. McKissack also began an ambitious effort to build affordable housing, an area architecture firms had largely eschewed. Branch offices, meanwhile, were established in several northern cities. Two of these were run by McKissack's twin daughters, Cheryl and Deryl, both engineers by training. Cheryl succeeded her mother as CEO in 2000. Under the name The McKissack Group, the firm continued to grow under the younger McKissack's direction. In 2007 it won the largest contract in its history when Forest City Ratner Companies hired McKissack to provide construction management services for the redevelopment of Brooklyn's Atlantic rail yards. According to a press release posted on its Web site, the work allocated to the firm was worth one hundred and eighty-two million dollars.

McKissack remained active in her retirement, regularly addressing a variety of business and community groups. She also maintained close relationships with several Nashville-area organizations, notably her alma mater, Fisk University, and Capers Memorial CME Church. In honor of her accomplishments and of her long service on its board of trustees, Fisk presented her with an honorary doctorate in the spring of 2009. Other awards have included the U.S. Department of Commerce's National Female Entrepreneur Award in 1990 and the 1996 Human Relations Award from the Nashville chapter of the National Conference of Christians and Jews.

Sources

Online

"About Us: Fact Sheet," CivilRightsMuseum.org, http://www.civilrightsmuseum.org/factsheet.htm (accessed October 28, 2009).

"Fisk University Celebrates 135th Commencement with Renowned Judge Glenda A. Hatchett," FiskUniversity.WordPress.com, April 29, 2009, http://fiskuniversity.wordpress.com/2009/04/29/fisk-university-celebrates-135th-commencement-with-renowned-judge-glenda-a-hatchett/ (accessed October 28, 2009).

"Leatrice McKissack," VisionaryProject.org, http://www.visionaryproject.org/mckissackleatrice/ (accessed Ocotber 26, 2009).

"Leatrice McKissack Biography," TheHistoryMakers.com, March 13, 2007, http://www.thehistorymakers.com/biography/biography.asp?bioindex=1656&category=Businessmakers (accessed October 27, 2009).

"The McKissack Legacy," McKissack.com, http://www.mckissack.com/ (accessed October 26, 2009).
"Preliminary Work to Begin on Atlantic Yards Development," McKissack.com, http://mckissack.com/pdf/ay2.pdf (accessed October 28, 2009).

—R. Anthony Kugler

Zakes Mokae

1934–2009

Actor

South African actor Zakes Mokae is best known for his collaboration with countryman Athol Fugard, a white playwright who dramatized the brutality of life under apartheid for an international audience in such works as *The Blood Knot, Boesman and Lena,* and *"Master Harold" … and the Boys.* In 1960 Mokae and Fugard defied a national taboo by appearing together on the same stage—the first black and white performers to do so in South Africa. In the United States, where he made his home after being barred from returning to South Africa, Mokae appeared in many of Fugard's plays, both on and off Broadway and at regional theaters. He won a Tony Award for his performance in Fugard's *"Master Harold" … and the Boys* in 1982, and earned a second nomination in 1993 for his role in *The Song of Jacob Zulu.* In his career, Mokae appeared in more than forty films, including *Cry Freedom* (1987) and *A Dry White Season* (1989), both of which dealt with apartheid, as well as many television series.

Began Working with Fugard

Mokae (pronounced mo-KYE) was born on August 5, 1934, in the Sophiatown neighborhood of Johannesburg, South Africa, a member of the Xhosa ethnic group. When he met Fugard in 1958, Mokae was a saxophone player who wanted to become an actor; Fugard was a journalist who wanted to become a playwright. The two men hung out in clubs such as the Dorkay House, where whites and blacks mingled—a risky social enterprise, as South Africa was then under the thumb of the racially oppressive apartheid system.

Under apartheid, a policy of racial segregation was strictly enforced by the white minority, restricting the rights and freedoms of the majority black population. "The club was pretty close to the wind," Fugard explained to Michael Kuchwara of the Toronto *Globe & Mail* in 1985. "The authorities busted in on occasion to find out what was going on. All they found were a lot of musicians and would-be actors hanging out, talking and trying to do some work."

Mokae had no formal training in theater before he met Fugard. "You don't have that in South Africa; it's for white folk," he said, according to the *Herald* of Scotland. Nonetheless, in 1958 he and Fugard formed a theater workshop called the Rehearsal Room, which they intended as a forum for producing plays that depicted the realities of South African life under apartheid. In September of 1960 they performed in Fugard's *The Blood Knot,* a play about two brothers, one light skinned (Morris, played by Fugard) and the other dark skinned (Zachariah, played by Mokae). The performance was groundbreaking in that it marked the first time a white and a black performer appeared together on a South African stage.

Initially planned as a one-night performance, the play was so well received that it went on to a six-month engagement at the Intimate Theatre—an all-white venue—and then toured the country. While on tour, Fugard saw firsthand the injustices that his black countrymen had to endure. Mokae was harassed by the authorities and arrested for refusing to carry a passbook, the identification required for black South Africans. Whereas Fugard traveled first class on the train, Mokae had to ride in third class. "I didn't know it then but Zakes had the word 'survivor' written all over him. Not just 'survivor' but 'magnificent survivor,'" Fugard said, according to the *Herald.* "I saw Zakes at the receiving end of a terrible system, and we shared some pretty dark moments."

Barred from South Africa

After concluding its South African tour, *The Blood Knot* was staged at the Arts Theatre in the West End of London, where Mokae continued his role and received positive reviews. Although the play launched Mokae's career as an actor, he was barred from returning to South Africa thereafter. He studied acting at the Royal Academy of Dramatic Art in London (where such actors as Sean Connery, Anthony Hopkins, and Peter O'Toole have trained), and in 1969 he relocated to the United States, settling in Las Vegas, Nevada. The following year, Mokae appeared in the American premiere of Fugard's *Boesman and Lena,* starring James Earl Jones and Ruby Dee in the title roles, at the Circle in the Square Theatre in New York. He later performed in *A Lesson from Aloes* in regional theater.

Mokae and Fugard collaborated once again on *"Master Harold" … and the Boys,* the first of the playwright's works to have its world premiere outside South Africa. The drama centers on a white South African student and his relationship with two black men who work in his father's tearoom; Mokae originated the role of Sam, the elder worker. The production began at the Yale Repertory Theatre in 1981 and ran for 344 performances the following year at the Lyceum Theatre on Broadway. The script later was filmed for television, starring Mokae and Matthew Broderick. Mokae won a Tony Award for his performance in 1982. His professional success, however, was marred by personal tragedy: On the same night as he received his Tony, he learned that his brother, James, had been sentenced to death for murders committed during a robbery. Mokae was permitted to return to South Africa—his first trip

home in more than two decades—and arrived in time to witness his brother's execution.

A 1985 revival of *The Blood Knot* at Yale Repertory Theatre reunited Mokae and Fugard onstage in their original roles, and in December of that year it had its Broadway premiere at the John Golden Theatre, running for ninety-five performances. Writing a review in the December 11, 1985, *New York Times,* Frank Rich described the relationship between the actor and playwright: "In a sense the men have been playing their parts, spiritually if not literally, ever since that premiere. There is an arc to the Fugard-Mokae collaboration that runs from 1961 to their last joint effort, as writer and co-star of *'Master Harold' … and the Boys* in 1982— just as there is a continuum to the South African history to which they have devoted their creative lives." In 1993 Mokae earned a second Tony nomination for his performance in *The Song of Jacob Zulu,* by the white South African playwright Tug Yourgrau, at the Plymouth Theater on Broadway.

Mokae also acted in more than forty films during his career. In addition to *Cry Freedom* and *A Dry White Season,* he appeared in *The Comedians* (1967), *The Serpent and the Rainbow* (1988), *A Rage in Harlem* (1991), and *Outbreak* (1995). He also made guest appearances on scores of television shows, including *The X-Files, Law & Order, Oz, The West Wing,* and *Monk.* In his later years, Mokae turned to directing, working with the Nevada Shakespeare Company.

Returned to South Africa to Live

Mokae moved back to South Africa in 2005, more than a decade after the end of apartheid, "so he could live under freedom there and have some memory of it," according to his obituary in the September 15, 2009, *New York Times.* He was diagnosed with Alzheimer's disease and Parkinson's disease, and died of complications from a stroke on September 11, 2009, in Las Vegas, where he kept a second home, at the age of seventy-five.

Selected works

Theater

Blood Knot, Arts Theatre, London, 1961.
Boesman and Lena, Circle in the Square Theatre, New York, 1970.
Fingernails as Blue as Flowers, American Place Theatre, New York, 1971.
The Cherry Orchard, New York Shakespeare Festival, Public Theatre, New York, 1973.
Boesman and Lena, Trinity Square Repertory Company, Providence, RI, 1978.
Boesman and Lena, Yale Repertory Theatre, New Haven, CT, 1980.
An Attempt at Flying, Yale Repertory Theatre, 1980.

A Lesson from Aloes, Playhouse Theatre, New York, 1980–81.

"Master Harold" ... and the Boys, Yale Repertory Theatre, 1981; Lyceum Theatre, New York, 1982–83.

The Blood Knot, Yale Repertory Theatre, 1985; John Golden Theatre, New York, 1985–86.

The Count of Monte Cristo, John F. Kennedy Center for the Performing Arts, Washington, DC, 1986.

The Song of Jacob Zulu, Plymouth Theater, New York, 1993.

Films

The Comedians, Maximillian Productions, 1967.
Fragment of Fear, Columbia Pictures, 1970.
The River Niger, River Niger Company, 1976.
The Island, Universal Pictures, 1980.
Roar, Alpha, 1981.
Cry Freedom, Universal Pictures, 1987.
The Serpent and the Rainbow, Universal Pictures, 1988.
A Dry White Season, Davros Films, 1989.
Gross Anatomy, Hill/Rosenman, 1989.
Dad, Amblin Entertainment, 1989.
A Rage in Harlem, Miramax, 1991.
Dust Devil, British Screen Productions, 1992.
Outbreak, Punch Productions, 1995.
Vampire in Brooklyn, Eddie Murphy Productions, 1995.

Waterworld, Universal Pictures, 1995.
Krippendorf's Tribe, Touchstone Pictures, 1998.

Television

One in a Million: The Ron LeFlore Story, EMI Films, 1978.
Roots: The Next Generations, ABC, 1979.
"Master Harold" ... and the Boys, Lorimar Pictures, 1985.
Rise and Walk: The Dennis Byrd Story, Fox, 1994.

Sources

Books

Kruger, Loren, *The Drama of South Africa: Plays, Pageants, and Publics since 1910,* Routledge, 1999.

Periodicals

Globe & Mail (Toronto), December 26, 1985.
Herald (Scotland), September 28, 2009.
Mail & Guardian (South Africa), September 17, 2009.
New York Times, May 6, 1982; December 11, 1985; September 15, 2009.
Playbill, September 15, 2009.

—Deborah A. Ring

J. O. Patterson Jr.

1935—

Religious leader, politician

The rise of the first African American to lead a U.S. city is always a pivotal and noteworthy event, but perhaps nowhere more so than in Memphis, Tennessee, in 1982. Fourteen years after the death of Rev. Martin Luther King Jr., attorney and veteran Democratic activist J. O. Patterson Jr. became the city's first black mayor pro tem when the elected mayor resigned. Patterson served for twenty days before running in the special mayoral election and losing to a white challenger.

Patterson comes from one of Memphis's leading black families. Born in 1935, he was the namesake of his father, James Oglethorpe Patterson Sr., a leading figure in the Church of God in Christ (COGIC). Patterson's mother, Deborah Mason Patterson, was the daughter of the Protestant group's founder, Charles Harrison Mason. The church was based in Memphis but grew enormously during the early decades of the twentieth century to become the largest black Pentecostal denomination in the United States.

Elected to City Council

As a young man, Patterson earned an undergraduate degree in business administration from Fisk University in Nashville, then went on to law school at DePaul University in Chicago. He returned to Memphis and became active in local Democratic politics. In 1967 he made a run for the Tennessee State Senate and became the first African American from Shelby County—of which Memphis is the county seat—elected to that body since the end of Reconstruction in the 1870s.

That same year he became one of three blacks to win seats on the Memphis City Council for the first time in city history. He held both his seats simultaneously.

Memphis was a battleground in the first years of the post–civil rights era. In the early twentieth century it had become a major black metropolis, but gaining black representation in municipal politics had been a hard-won struggle. "Under a 1967 plan, Memphis voters chose seven district council members and six at-large members," explained *Commercial Appeal* writer Jerome Wright. "The effect was to guarantee that only a handful of African-Americans would be elected to the council." Fred Davis, an insurance agent, and minister James Netters were the other two African Americans colleagues elected to the city council in 1967, the year the plan took effect.

A staunch white conservative, Henry Loeb, had been elected in 1967 to a second term as mayor of Memphis after running with the campaign slogan "Be Proud Again," a somewhat incendiary call to arms in a city that was already riven by long-simmering racial tensions. In his first months in office in 1968 Loeb refused to address demands of the city's garbage workers. These were 1,300 members of Local 1733 of the American Federation of State, County and Municipal Employees (AFSCME); ninety-eight percent of the local were black. They walked out in February after two work-related deaths tied to safety issues, striking for union recognition and improved wages and working conditions. Loeb and his allies on the council refused to consider their demands, and the strike evolved into a

At a Glance . . .

Born James Oglethorpe Patterson Jr. on May 28, 1935, in Memphis, TN; son of James Oglethorpe Sr. (a minister) and Deborah Indiana Mason Patterson; married Rose E. Kelly; children: James O. III, Aaron Lamont, Jennifer Rose, Charles Harrison Mason. *Politics:* Democrat. *Religion:* Pentecostal (Church of God in Christ). *Education:* Fisk University, BA, business administration, 1958; DePaul University School of Law, JD, 1963; Memphis Theological Seminary, MA, 1985.

Career: Elected to the Tennessee State Senate, 1967, reelected, 1971; also served two years in the Tennessee House of Representatives; elected to the Memphis City Council, 1967, and served for twenty years; delegate to the 1972, 1976, and 1980 Democratic National Conventions; Pentecostal Temple Church of God in Christ, senior pastor, 1989—; within the Church of God in Christ has served as elder, district superintendent, auxiliary bishop, and legal counsel; consecrated a bishop in the Church of God in Christ, 1988; Church of God in Christ General Assembly, elected vice chair, 1998, became chair, 2000.

Addresses: *Office*—Church of God in Christ, PO Box 320, Memphis, TN 38101-0320.

civil rights matter when the African-American community began to rally, with discussion of a boycott of downtown businesses. Rev. Martin Luther King Jr. came to Memphis to march with the striking workers and to seek a negotiable solution between them, their union officials, and the city, and he was shot to death from the balcony of the Lorraine Motel on April 4.

Excoriated Council and Mayor

Several days after King's assassination, the city council voted to accept a revised labor contract submitted by the striking sanitation workers' union. Patterson chastised the council, according to the *Daily Collegian*, the student newspaper of Pennsylvania State University. "Seven weeks ago we agreed to the main issues almost identical to those brought before us today and then a majority of the council changes its mind," the paper quoted Patterson as saying. "[The council] refuse[d] to take any action on the matter and a lot of hell broke out across the city and across the nation."

Racial tensions remained high in Memphis into the 1970s. Patterson took up several important causes, with police brutality at the top of that list. In May of 1970 the Memphis Police Department began using so-called "dumdum bullets," which were outlawed in most nations under international warfare agreements. These non-ricocheting bullets expanded when they hit their target, and by July there had been a spate of deaths. Eight citizens died after encounters with the police, and six of the fatalities were African American. Members of the community again rallied in protest. "It's time battle lines were drawn between the Council and Police Department," Patterson said, according to a *New York Times* report.

In August of 1972 Patterson entered the Democratic primary for a seat representing Tennessee's Ninth Congressional District. He beat out three white contenders hoping to unseat the Republican, Dan Kuykendall, but lost the November race in a nationally historic election that featured forty-four African Americans in congressional races across the country. Among those who won House seats were Barbara Jordan of Texas and Andrew Young of Georgia. In 1974 another black Memphis Democrat, Harold Ford Sr., finally unseated Kuykendall. The political fortunes of the Patterson and Ford families had long been intertwined; Ford, his brothers, and his sons were perennial challengers in the races for city council, the state senate, and the state house of representatives. Both families also owned successful funeral home businesses that drew many of their clientele from Memphis's African-American community.

Made Memphis History

By 1982, after fourteen years on the city council, Patterson had risen to the post of council chair. When Mayor J. Wyeth Chandler resigned in early October, after ten years in office, to take a judicial appointment, Patterson automatically became the mayor pro tem. He was the first African American ever to hold the job but served for only twenty days. As specified by the city charter, the question of a permanent replacement went to the council, which voted to replace Patterson with Chandler's chief of staff, Wallace Madewell.

A lawsuit was filed to force a special election to fill the mayor's post for the remainder of Wyeth's term. The election was held in November of 1982, with Patterson running as the sole African-American candidate among the four contenders; he won forty percent of the vote. Because the Memphis City Charter specified that a runoff election must be held if no candidate wins a fifty-one percent majority, Patterson faced off against Richard C. "Dick" Hackett, court clerk of Shelby County, who had polled twenty-nine percent of the vote. Hackett received fifty-four percent of the vote in the runoff against Patterson's forty-five percent to be elected mayor of Memphis.

Hackett was to be the last white mayor of Memphis. Patterson returned to his council seat, but his defeat "was an exclamation point for African-Americans," noted Wright in the *Commercial Appeal,* which seemed to affirm "that the city's electoral process was designed to keep black people from winning citywide office." Community activists filed a lawsuit challenging Memphis electoral laws, and a federal district court eventually concurred with the reformers. That paved the way for the 1991 election of Willie Herenton, the first African American to be elected mayor of Memphis. Herenton had run against Hackett and won by only 142 votes.

Patterson retired from politics a few years after his brief stint as mayor. His father, head of the Church of God in Christ since the early 1970s, died in 1989. After returning to school for a graduate degree from the Memphis Theological Seminary, Patterson was consecrated a bishop in the church. In 1998 he was elected vice chair of the COGIC General Assembly, and became chair two years later. In 2009 the presiding bishop of the church was Gilbert E. Patterson, Patterson's nephew. Patterson has four children with his wife Rose Kelly Patterson. His youngest son, Charles Harrison Mason Patterson, is an elder in the COGIC church.

Sources

Books

Wright, Sharon D., *Race, Power, and Political Emergence in Memphis,* Taylor & Francis, 2000, pp. 104, 105.

Periodicals

Commercial Appeal (Memphis, TN), July 12, 2009; July 26, 2009.

Daily Collegian (Pennsylvania State University), April 17, 1968.

Jet, October 4, 1982, p. 5.

New York Times, July 5, 1970, p. 34; October 24, 1971, p. 24.

Online

"J. O. Patterson, Jr.," MemphisHistory.org, http://www.memphishistory.org/TheChurch/TheChurch ofGodinChrist/JOPattersonJr/tabid/146/Default. aspx (accessed January 2, 2010).

—Carol Brennan

Fayette Pinkney

1948–2009

Singer, health professional

Fayette Pinkney was an original member of the Philadelphia, Pennsylvania–based vocal trio the Three Degrees, remembered for their soulful hits in the 1970s, including "When Will I See You Again?" and "T.S.O.P. (The Sound of Philadelphia)," the theme song for the television show *Soul Train*. In a group whose lineup was constantly changing, Pinkney was the mainstay of the Three Degrees from 1963 to 1976, joined by Sheila Ferguson and Valerie Holiday in the group's best-known incarnation. The Three Degrees reached the

Pinkney, Fayette, photograph. RB/Redferns/Getty Images.

height of their popularity in the mid-1970s after partnering with legendary producers Kenny Gamble and Leon Huff, pioneers of "Philly soul" (also called the Philadelphia Sound), a stylish brand of soul music infused with funk rhythms. Pinkney left the group in 1976 and retired from public life, going on to pursue higher education and a career in the medical health profession, although she continued to sing on occasion.

Pinkney was born on January 10, 1948, in Philadelphia. As a teenager at Overlook High School, she was one of three girls brought together in 1963 by record producer Richard Barrett to form a vocal group called

the Three Degrees. Barrett had been the lead singer of the doo-wop group the Valentines in the 1950s; as a producer he had made successes of the Chantels, Little Anthony and the Imperials, and Frankie Lymon and the Teenagers. He signed the trio, whose original lineup include Pinkney, Linda Turner, and Shirley Porter Poole, to a deal with Swan Records. Pinkney sang lead vocals on the Three Degrees' debut single, "Gee Baby (I'm Sorry)," released in 1963. Before long, however, Turner and Poole left the group, replaced by Helen Scott and Janet Jones Harmon. More personnel changes brought Ferguson and Holiday in alongside Pinkney, cementing the group's lineup.

In 1970 the Three Degrees switched to Roulette Records and had their first hit with "Maybe," a remake of the Chantels' song of the same name, which reached number four on the R&B chart. They followed up with "I Do Take You" and "You're the One," both modest successes. Pinkney and the Three Degrees became a popular nightclub act in the early 1970s, adding to their tight three-part harmonies choreographed dance moves, flashy dresses, and towering hairdos. The group toured with Engelbert Humperdinck, performing

At a Glance . . .

Born Fayette Regina Pinkney on January 10, 1948, in Philadelphia, PA; died on June 27, 2009, in Lansdale, PA; children: Ayana Alexandria. *Education:* Temple University, coursework in psychology; Lincoln University, MA, human services, 1985.

Career: The Three Degrees, singer, 1963–76; Opportunities Industrialization Center, project coordinator, 1979–83; Women's Medical College of Pennsylvania, administrative assistant, education coordinator, 1989–94; United Behavioral Health, intake coordinator, 2001–09.

at the Riviera Hotel in Las Vegas, and they appeared at the famous Copacabana in Manhattan, where they snagged the attention of film director William Friedkin. In 1971 Friedkin gave the group a cameo appearance in *The French Connection.*

After shopping the group around to several labels, Barrett struck a deal in 1973 with producers Gamble and Huff to sign the Three Degrees to their record company, Philadelphia International Records. Together, Gamble and Huff had pioneered the genre that became known as Philly soul, a smooth, stylish blend of soul and funk music that was characterized by lush instrumental arrangements of strings and horns. The sound had been popularized by groups such as the O'Jays, the Spinners, and Harold Melvin and the Blue Notes.

The Three Degrees' first Philadelphia International single, "Dirty Ol' Man," was a disco hit. Next, Gamble and Huff teamed the three women with their studio band, MFSB (which stood for Mother Father Sister Brother), to record "T.S.O.P. (The Sound of Philadelphia)," a mostly instrumental piece that included the Three Degrees' vocals at the end. The song was chosen as the theme for the popular television show *Soul Train* and rose to the top of the Billboard Hot 100 chart, staying there for two weeks. In the summer of 1974, the group had their biggest hit with the soulful ballad "When Will I See You Again?" which became their signature song. The single went platinum, selling more than two million copies, and rose to number four on the R&B chart and number two on the pop chart that fall. The album *The Three Degrees* was released at the end of 1974, featuring "Dirty Ol' Man" and "When Will I See You Again?," as well as "A Woman Needs a Good Man," "I Like Being a Woman," and "If and When."

Pinkney and the Three Degrees followed up with the album *Take Good Care of Yourself,* whose title track

was their last charting single, reaching number sixty-four on the R&B chart in the summer of 1975, and they recorded live albums at Bailey's in Leicester, England, and in Japan. The group achieved enormous popularity in the United Kingdom and continental Europe—even more so than in the United States—and were a particular favorite of England's Prince Charles, who later invited the trio to perform for his thirtieth birthday at Buckingham Palace.

In 1976 the Three Degrees left Philadelphia International, at Barrett's urging, to sign with CBS Sony. Pinkney took the move as her cue to leave the group and pursue a career outside the entertainment industry. She was replaced by Scott, who had sung with the group in its early years. Pinkney recorded her only solo album, *One Degree,* in 1979.

Pinkney studied psychology at Temple University and went on to complete a master's degree in human services at Lincoln University in 1985. She served as a project coordinator at the Opportunities Industrialization Center in North Philadelphia from 1979 to 1983, and then worked at the Women's Medical College of Pennsylvania from 1989 to 1994, first as an administrative assistant and then as an education coordinator. In 1994 she gave birth to a daughter, who died after only few days as a result of sudden infant death syndrome. From 2001 until a month before her death, she was an intake coordinator for United Behavioral Health in Philadelphia. Although Pinkney no longer recorded, she gave lessons as a vocal coach and traveled with the Intermezzo Choir Ministry.

Pinkney died of acute respiratory failure on June 27, 2009, in Lansdale, Pennsylvania, at the age of sixty-one. Upon her death, producers Gamble and Huff released a statement in which they called the Three Degrees "our Philly sound version of Motown's Supremes—but bigger and stronger and more melodic," according to the June 30, 2009, *Philadelphia Inquirer.*

Selected recordings

Albums with the Three Degrees

Maybe (includes "Maybe"), Roulette, 1970.
The Three Degrees (includes "Dirty Ol' Man," "When Will I See You Again?," "A Woman Needs a Good Man," "I Like Being a Woman," and "If and When"), Philadelphia International, 1974.
The Three Degrees International Philadelphia International, 1975.
The Three Degrees Live, Philadelphia International, 1975.
Take Good Care of Yourself, Philadelphia International, 1975.

Solo albums

One Degree, Chopper Records, 1979.

Sources

Books

Jackson, John A., *A House on Fire: The Rise and Fall of Philadelphia Soul,* Oxford University Press, 2004.

Periodicals

Guardian (London), July 7, 2009.
Independent (London), July 8, 2009.
New York Times, July 1, 2009.
Philadelphia Inquirer, June 30, 2009.

Online

Hogan, Ed, "The Three Degrees," allmusic, http://www.allmusic.com/cg/amg.dll?p=amg&sql=11:0ifrxqr5ldse~T1 (accessed October 19, 2009).
Three Degrees (official Web site), http://www.thethreedegrees.com/ (accessed October 19, 2009).

—Deborah A. Ring

Sol T. Plaatje

1876–1932

Journalist, linguist, political activist

Sol T. Plaatje was one of the leading journalists and newspaper editors in South Africa during the early twentieth century, remembered as a passionate advocate for the rights of his black countrymen and a vocal critic of the government's racial segregation policies. He was a founder of the South African Native National Congress (which later would become the African National Congress) in 1912, and he served as that organization's first secretary general. His major works include *Native Life in South Africa before and since the European War and the Boer Rebellion* (1916), a rebuke of the South African government's Natives Land Act of 1913, and *Mhudi: An Epic of South African Native Life a Hundred Years Ago* (1930), the first novel ever written in English by a black South African. Plaatje was an accomplished linguistic scholar as well, fluent in at least seven languages, who devoted himself to the preservation of his native Tswana language.

Plaatje (pronounced ply-KEY) was born on October 9, 1876, in the Boshof District of the Orange Free State (present-day Free State Province) in South Africa, the son of Johannes and Martha Plaatje. He was raised in a large family that belonged to the Barolong ethnic group and spoke the Tswana (also spelled Sechuana or Setswana) language; his ancestors were among the first African converts to Christianity in southern Africa. Plaatje was educated at the Berlin Missionary Society (a Lutheran mission) at its station in Pniel, near the town of Kimberley, which was then the center of the nascent diamond-mining industry. He benefited from the kindness and support of the Reverend Ernst Westphal and

his wife Elizabeth, who took an interest in his education. Plaatje was an exceptionally bright student, and he displayed a remarkable talent for languages, both African and European. Though he completed only a few years of formal education, he stayed on at Pniel for some time, acting as a teaching assistant and studying German, English, and music with Elizabeth Westphal.

Recorded the Siege of Mafeking

In 1894 Plaatje left the mission to take a job as a postal messenger in Kimberley. In his spare time, he undertook to master the English language, one of the two official languages (Dutch being the other) in the Cape Colony. In 1898 he married Elizabeth M'belle, the sister of a prominent court interpreter, and the couple moved north to Mafeking (present-day Mafikeng). There, Plaatje joined the Cape civil service as a court interpreter as well, distinguishing himself by his extensive knowledge of English, Dutch, German, and the major African dialects.

During the siege of Mafeking (October 1899–May 1900), one of the key episodes of the Second Anglo-Boer War, Plaatje, like many residents of the city, kept a detailed personal diary. Writing entirely in English, he provided a vivid day-by-day account of events during the war, with particular attention to the contributions that Africans made to the British victory, which went largely unrecognized at the time. Though many white diarists had their writings printed and distributed in the aftermath of the war, Plaatje seems to have made no attempt to publish his account. The diary remained

At a Glance . . .

Born Solomon Tshekisho Plaatje on October 9, 1876, in the Boshof District, Orange Free State, South Africa; died on June 19, 1932, in Johannesburg, South Africa; son of Johannes and Martha Plaatje; married Elizabeth M'belle, 1898; children: Sainty, Richard, Olive, Violet, Halley. *Religion:* Christian.

Career: Cape Colony, postal clerk, 1894–98; Cape Civil Service, court interpreter, 1899–1902; *Koranta ea Becoana,* editor, 1902–10; *Tsala ea Becoana* (renamed *Tsala ea Batho*), editor, 1910–17; South African Native National Congress, general secretary, 1912–15.

unknown until 1969, when his great-grandson, Victor Molema, discovered an old scrapbook that had not been opened since Plaatje's death, which Molema turned over to anthropologist John Lionel Comaroff. The diary was found inside and published in 1973.

Lacking opportunities for advancement in the civil service because of his race, Plaatje resigned his post in 1902 and began a career in journalism. He took over the editorship of the Tswana-English newspaper *Koranta ea Becoana* (Tswana gazette), which was financed by a local chief. In 1910, the same year in which the Union of South Africa was formed, he moved back to Kimberley to take a job as editor of the weekly *Tsala ea Becoana* (Friend of the Tswana), which later was renamed *Tsala ea Batho* (Friend of the people). Both newspapers had circulations in the thousands. During this time, Plaatje became one of the leading journalists and newspaper editors in Africa, and he used his position to advocate for the rights of black South Africans under the new British regime.

Became Involved in South African Politics

Plaatje's work involved him in national politics. In 1912 he was one of the founders of the South African Native National Congress (SANNC)—renamed the African National Congress in 1926—which was formed to protect the rights of black South Africans and to see that they were represented in the institutions of government. Plaatje served as the organization's first secretary general. The following year, the South African legislature passed the Natives Land Act, which significantly restricted the rights of nonwhite "natives" to own or occupy land. In effect until 1990, the act would become a cornerstone of South Africa's racially oppressive apartheid system.

An outspoken opponent of the legislation, Plaatje traveled to Great Britain in 1914 as part of an SANNC delegation sent to implore the British government to repeal the act. Although the delegation failed to make any headway with the British, Plaatje earned notice for his impassioned pleas on behalf of black South Africans. His obituary in the London *Times* in 1932 noted that "his sincere, heart-felt longing to uplift his people touched all who heard him." When the delegation returned to South Africa at the outbreak of World War I, Plaatje chose to remain in Britain.

Plaatje produced three books during his time in Britain, all published in 1916. The first, *Native Life in South Africa*—considered his most important work—was a thoughtful, well-reasoned indictment of the Natives Land Act and a defense of South Africans' political rights. In it, Plaatje sought to debunk the common belief among whites that blacks were uncivilized, and to expose the injustices of the South African system of land distribution and of racial segregation more generally.

He also wrote two books on his native language. *A Sechuana Reader,* cowritten with linguist Daniel Jones of University College London, attempted to set down the exact sounds of the language—which Plaatje feared was being eclipsed by other African tongues—by applying the international phonetic alphabet, something that had never been done with an African language. *Sechuana Proverbs* collected more than 700 Tswana proverbs and folktales, together with their literal English translations and English- or European-language equivalents where they existed. Although the two books did not gain a wide readership, they are considered among the finest works on the Tswana language to this day.

In 1917 Plaatje returned to South Africa; two years later he joined a second SANNC delegation to London in its effort to appeal to the British government to intervene on behalf of black South Africans. Despite an audience with Prime Minister David Lloyd George, this visit was no more successful than the first. In 1920 Plaatje traveled to Canada and the United States, where he lectured on the plight of his countrymen. There he met several prominent African-American leaders, including Marcus Garvey of the Universal Negro Improvement Association and W. E. B. Du Bois of the National Association for the Advancement of Colored People. Du Bois arranged for the American publication of Plaatje's *Native Life.*

Devoted to Literary and Linguistic Work

Plaatje rejoined his family in Kimberley in 1923, discouraged that he had failed to effect change in South Africa's political situation. He devoted the rest of his life to journalism, literary work, and the preservation of the Tswana language. He wrote articles for most of the

English-language newspapers in South Africa, as well as for *Umteteli wan Bantu* (The mouthpiece of the people). Long preoccupied with the works of William Shakespeare, he translated at least six of the bard's plays into Tswana, although only two survive: *Diphosho-phosho* (*A Comedy of Errors*), published around 1930, and *Dintshontsho tsa bo-Juliuse Kesara* (*Julius Caesar*), published posthumously in 1937. Plaatje compiled a new Tswana-English dictionary and prepared a second edition of his *Sechuana Proverbs*. He also compiled a new collection of Tswana folktales and poems. None of these works, however, was published.

In 1930 Plaatje saw the publication of his only work of fiction, *Mhudi: An Epic of South African Native Life a Hundred Years Ago*. He had begun writing the novel in 1919–20 in London but had been unable to find a publisher for almost a decade. Set in South Africa during the 1830s, *Mhudi* chronicles two characters, Ra-Thaga and Mhudi, living amid tribal warfare following the forced migrations that resulted from the expansion of the Zulu Empire. The novel combines both African and Western literary elements, incorporating the oral traditions of African stories into the narrative structure of European works. It is notable as the first novel ever written in English by a black South African. *Mhudi* was not widely read in its time but was rediscovered after it was reissued as part of the Heinemann African Writers Series in 1978.

Plaatje died of pneumonia on June 19, 1932, while on a trip to Johannesburg. His home in Kimberley was designated a national monument in 1992, and today houses the Sol Plaatje Museum and Library.

Selected writings

Books

Native Life in South Africa before and since the European War and the Boer Rebellion, King, 1916.
(With Daniel Jones) *A Sechuana Reader,* University Press of London, 1916.

Mhudi: An Epic of South African Native Life a Hundred Years Ago, Lovedale, 1930.
The Boer War Diary of Sol T. Plaatje, edited by John L. Comaroff, Macmillan, 1973.

Translations

Sechuana Proverbs with Literal Translations and Their European Equivalents, Kegan Paul, Trench, Trubner, 1916.
Diphosho-phosho (*A Comedy of Errors*), by William Shakespeare, Morija, c. 1930.
Dintshontsho tsa bo-Juliuse Kesara (*Julius Caesar*), by William Shakespeare, University of the Witwatersrand Press, 1937.

Sources

Books

Rall, Maureen, *Peaceable Warrior: The Life and Times of Sol T. Plaatje,* Sol Plaatje Educational Trust, 2003.
Willan, Brian, *Sol Plaatje: South African Nationalist, 1876–1932,* University of California Press, 1984.

Periodicals

Critical Arts, vol. 16, no. 1, 2002, p. 23.
Journal of Commonwealth & Comparative Politics, November 2000, pp. 194–195.
Research in African Literatures, Spring 2000, pp. 189–191.
Times (London), July 28, 1932.

Online

"Plaatje, Solomon Tshekisho (1876–1932)" African National Congress, http://www.anc.org.za/anc docs/history/people/plaatje/plaatje.html (accessed October 29, 2009).
"Solomon Tshekisho Plaatje," South African History Online, http://www.sahistory.org.za/pages/people /bios/plaatjie.htm (accessed October 29, 2009).

—Deborah A. Ring

Trevor Rhone

1940–2009

Playwright, screenwriter, actor

Playwright, screenwriter, and actor Trevor Rhone was one of Jamaica's most celebrated dramatists. In the Caribbean he was best known for his stage plays, including *Smile Orange* (1971), *School's Out,* and *Old Story Time* (1979), which helped establish an indigenous Jamaican theater in the 1970s and gave a voice to Jamaicans as they forged their own identity after independence from Great Britain. Internationally, Rhone earned acclaim for his screenplay for the 1972 film *The Harder They Come,* which introduced reggae music and Jamaican culture to a world audience. Critics both at home and abroad praised Rhone for his sensitive, authentic representations of the common man.

Rhone was born on March 24, 1940, in Kingston, Jamaica, the youngest son of Hezekiah Rhone and Rosamond McCalla-Rhone. He was raised in a large family—his father had twenty-three children—in the rural village of Bellas Gate, located in the St. Catherine region of eastern Jamaica. He received his education at Beckford and Smith High School in Spanish Town. After graduation, Rhone wrote radio plays for the nascent Jamaican Broadcasting Corporation for a time before going to London in 1959 to study acting on scholarship at the Rose Bruford College of Speech and Drama, where he was graduated in 1963 at the top of his class.

Rhone stayed in England to pursue a career in acting but soon found that roles for black actors were few and far between, and that black characters often were portrayed in a negative light. "It was like a rude

awakening when one discovered in England that there were very few parts for black people. In the 60's … you played Othello, the Prince of Morocco, in the 'Merchant of Venice,' and that was it," he told the *New York Times* in a 1985 interview. "A lot of the parts one had to play were things which didn't necessarily make me feel good about myself, or even represent accurately a positive image of myself, the way I saw myself…. I thought, 'Do I really want to spend my life perpetuating false images of myself?' And I thought not, and one day I just got up and left England and went home."

Returning to Jamaica, Rhone taught drama for a year and then teamed up with friend Yvonne Jones-Brewster to form a drama group called Theatre 77 in 1967. Their goal was to establish a distinctly Jamaican style of theater and a venue for doing so. The two converted a garage in Jones-Brewster's family home into a performance space that seated 150 people, calling it the Barn Theatre. It became the model for the small, professional theaters that began to spring up around Kingston. Rhone supported himself as a teacher while he turned to playwriting. Initially, his goal was to create plays that would reflect Jamaican life on the stage; secondarily, he hoped to provide better roles for himself. "I always saved the best role for myself," *America's Intelligence Wire* quoted him in 2003 as having said. His first play, *The Gadget* (1969), explored the tensions between an illiterate woman from the countryside and her educated, urbanized son. The work earned Rhone the Silver Medal at the Jamaican Arts Festival.

In 1970–71 Rhone collaborated with Jamaican filmmaker Perry Henzell to write the script for *The Harder They Come,* the story of an aspiring singer who turns to a life of crime; the character was based on a real-life Jamaican criminal who achieved notoriety in the 1940s. The film starred reggae singer Jimmy Cliff, who sang the title song, and featured music by Desmond Dekker and Toots and the Maytals. The movie provided a first glimpse of Jamaican culture and an introduction to reggae music for many international audiences. *The Harder They Come* broke box-office records in Jamaica and remained an art-house classic in the United States for many years.

By the time the film was released in 1972, Rhone had already achieved success on the stage in Jamaica. In 1971 he produced *Smile Orange,* a satirical work written in the Jamaican dialect that depicts the local tourism industry through the eyes of underpaid hotel clerks and waiters at a resort in Montego Bay. The play was a huge success, running for 245 performances at the Barn—a record at the time—and establishing Rhone as a national playwright. He followed with a series of popular plays, including *Sleeper* (1972), *Comic Strip* (1973), and *School's Out* (1975). *School's Out* was based on Rhone's experiences as a teacher in the 1960s, and offered a stinging rebuke of the dysfunctional education system in Jamaica.

Rhone had another success with *Old Story Time* (1979), which delved into Jamaicans' changing attitudes toward race and class in the aftermath of independence from Great Britain. The play enjoyed a long run in Jamaica, and then toured throughout the Caribbean and North America. In 1983 he penned *Two Can Play,* in which a couple flee the political turmoil of Jamaica and settle in the United States. Rhone's script for the film *Milk and Honey,* about a Jamaican immigrant in Toronto, earned him a Genie Award for best original screenplay in Canada, that country's highest film honor.

The use of humor to deliver biting social commentary was a hallmark of Rhone's dramatic works. So, too, was his keen sense of the beauty and rhythm of the Jamaican language, and a deep sensitivity to the plight of Jamaicans as they struggled to forge a new identity in a postcolonial world. In his obituary in the *Jamaica Gleaner,* he was quoted as having said that he wrote his scripts so as "to mirror the lives of the ordinary man, and to reaffirm his strengths in such a way that he learns to diminish his weaknesses and to believe that he can make a positive difference in his society." Rhone's success on the stage was instrumental in fueling the development of a Jamaican theater scene, and laid the groundwork for the next generation of actors, directors, and playwrights.

In 2002 Rhone wrote the autobiographical play *Bellas Gate Boy* for the Calabash International Literary Festival; he later turned the work into a book and toured as a one-man show, to much acclaim. His last screenplay, *One Love,* was produced in 2003, starring Bob Marley's son Ky-Mani as a Rastafarian who falls in love with a Christian girl, in spite of their religious differences. Rhone received numerous accolades for his creative works, including the Institute of Jamaica's Musgrave Gold Medal, the Prime Minister's Award for Lifetime Achievement, and the Commander of the Order of Distinction, Jamaica's highest civilian honor.

Rhone died of a heart attack on September 15, 2009, in Kingston at the age of sixty-nine.

Selected works

Plays (as playwright)

The Gadget, 1969.
Smile Orange, 1971.
Sleeper, 1972.
The Web, 1972.
Comic Strip, 1973.
School's Out, 1975.

Old Story Time, 1979.
Two Can Play, 1983.
One Stop Driver, 1989.
Bellas Gate Boy, 2002.

Screenplays

(With Perry Henzell) *The Harder They Come,* International Films, 1972.
Smile Orange, Knuts, 1976.
Milk and Honey, Castle Hill, 1988.
One Love, One Love Films, 2003.

Sources

Periodicals

America's Intelligence Wire, January 19, 2003.
Guardian (London), September 29, 2009.
Jamaica Gleaner, September 20, 2009.
New York Times, August 7, 1985; September 21, 2009.
Stabroek News (Guyana), September 27, 2009.
Times (London), September 24, 2009.

—Deborah A. Ring

Dovey Roundtree

1914—

Attorney, civil rights activist

Dovey Roundtree is a little-known heroine of the civil rights movement who attained several notable firsts during her long career. An attorney, ordained minister, and member of the first group of female African-American officers in the U.S. military, Roundtree's principal contribution to the historical record came with her successful argument of a 1955 antidiscrimination lawsuit involving interstate transportation. That legal victory ultimately became one of the linchpins in the series of challenges to end restrictive segregation laws in the southern United States.

Roundtree was born in 1914 in Charlotte, North Carolina, one of four daughters of James, who worked as a printer for the African Methodist Episcopal (A.M. E.) Church, and Lela, a seamstress and domestic. Roundtree's father died in the 1919 influenza epidemic, and Lela moved her daughters into the home of Roundtree's formidable grandmother, Rachel Bryant Graham. Rachel had also been widowed at a young age but married again, this time to a minister, Clyde Graham, who was the pastor of East Stonewall A.M.E. Zion church in Charlotte and whom Roundtree and her sisters considered their beloved grandfather.

Through her work with various Charlotte charities, Rachel Graham was friends with Mary McLeod Bethune, founder of Bethune-Cookman College in Florida and one of the most famous African-American women of her era. A respected educator, activist, and advocate for the disadvantaged, Bethune headed the National Association of Colored Women's Clubs and would play an important role in Roundtree's life. But it was

Roundtree's eighth-grade Sunday-school teacher who suggested she set her sights on Spelman College in Atlanta. The sister school to the all-male Morehouse College, Spelman educated the daughters of the South's African-American elite and was quite expensive: At the time, tuition and board ran to $300 per year. Roundtree's grandmother wanted her to attend a teacher's college for blacks in Winston-Salem that was much more affordable. There was a second factor to her grandmother's wish, as Roundtree recalled in her 2009 autobiography, *Justice Older Than the Law: The Life of Dovey florida Roundtree*. "Spelman was in Atlanta, the heart of [Ku Klux] Klan country.... To send her 'chillun' 250 miles into the Deep South, to a city where blacks feared to walk the streets, even in the daytime, was more than my grandmother could contemplate." Fortunately for Roundtree, her mother worked in the household of a white family in Charlotte that was moving to Atlanta because of the husband's job, and they suggested that Lela come with them.

Made Military History

Roundtree excelled at Spelman and graduated in 1938. She took a teaching job in South Carolina, but moved to Washington, DC, in the summer of 1941 as the United States was on the verge of war. Already the nation's industries were preparing for the shift from manufacturing to defense, and a new law banning employment discrimination on the basis of race at worksites that won government defense-related contracts was about to go into effect. Hoping to make

At a Glance . . .

Born Dovey Mae Johnson on April 17, 1914, in Charlotte, NC; daughter of James Eliot (a printer) and Lela (a seamstress and domestic; maiden name, Bryant) Johnson; married William Roundtree, 1945. *Military service:* Women's Army Auxiliary Corps, 1942–45; commissioned a captain. *Religion:* African Methodist Episcopal (A.M.E.). *Education:* Spelman College, BA, 1938; Howard University School of Law, JD, 1950.

Career: Teacher in South Carolina, 1938–41; assistant to Mary McLeod Bethune at the National Council of Negro Women, 1941; admitted to the bar of the District of Columbia, 1950; Robertson & Roundtree (law firm), founding partner, 1952, and attorney, 1952–61; attorney in private practice, 1961–70; Roundtree, Knox, Hunter & Parker, founding partner, 1970, and attorney, until 1996; ordained a minister in the African Methodist Episcopal Church, 1961; Allen Chapel A.M.E. Church, Washington, DC, minister, 1964–96.

Awards: Margaret Brent Women Lawyers of Achievement Award, American Bar Association, 2000; Letitia Woods Brown Memorial Book Prize (with Katie McCabe), Association of Black Women Historians, 2009.

Addresses: *Office*—c/o Women in Military Service for America Memorial Foundation, Dept. 560, Washington, DC 20042-0560.

more money than her meager teacher's salary in order to support her mother and now widowed grandmother, Roundtree moved to the nation's capital to find a job. She went to see Bethune, who was president of the National Council of Negro Women, at her home and council offices at Ninth and Westminster streets. Bethune gave her a job as a researcher, clipping articles from black newspapers around the nation, and then recommended her as one of the first class of forty black women who would enter officer-candidate training school in the newly created Women's Army Auxiliary Corps. The historic first was the result of Bethune's friendship with First Lady Eleanor Roosevelt, who was also seeking strategies to end racial segregation in America.

Roundtree completed the officer training course and was commissioned on August 29, 1942. Rising to the

rank of captain, she became a recruiter for the WACs, as the renamed Women's Army Corps became known, and traveled throughout the South speaking to young women at high schools and historically black colleges and urging them to join the war effort. She wore her WAC uniform while using the private bus lines that served as the mainstay of interstate travel in an era before automobile ownership became commonplace. In 1943 she boarded a bus in Miami but was instructed by the driver to stand at the end of the line, where other African-American travelers waited. "The black passengers in the rear went quiet. They knew, as I did, that this was how 'incidents' started," she wrote in her autobiography, noting that there were already reports of black service personnel being court-martialed for disobeying the Jim Crow laws in the South. "Rumor had it that black soldiers had been shot on city streets by southern 'peace officers' and even lynched on the bases.... The army, it was said, simply turned its back." White military personnel—many of them lower ranking than Roundtree—boarded the bus, and she was left stranded at the bus station at midnight.

With the end of World War II Roundtree went to work for A. Philip Randolph, the pioneering black labor leader who was seeking to turn the 1941 executive order barring employment discrimination in defense industries into permanent federal law. She met another young woman, Pauli Murray, who had earned a law degree from the University of California at Berkeley, and decided to enter law school using her G.I. Bill education benefits. She entered Howard University School of Law in the fall of 1947 as one of five women in her class. At the time, two of her professors there were working with Thurgood Marshall, the lead attorney for the school desegregation cases undertaken by the National Association for the Advancement of Colored People (NAACP) and its Legal Defense Fund. The cases were later combined into one, *Brown v. Board of Education,* which went before the U.S. Supreme Court in 1954. Roundtree graduated with her law degree in 1950 and was one of several recent black law-school graduates who assisted in the legal work on these cases.

Won Important Judgment from Federal Agency

Roundtree stayed in Washington and in 1952 went into partnership with another Howard Law School graduate, Julius Winfield Robertson. Their firm took on the case of Sarah Keys, a WAC who was stationed at Fort Dix, New Jersey, in August of 1952 when she boarded a bus to visit her parents in North Carolina. In North Carolina a new bus driver took over the journey and ordered her to sit in the rear of the Carolina Trailways bus. Keys refused, and the bus driver ordered the rest of the passengers onto another bus, which then departed the station. Keys was arrested and jailed overnight. She and her father sought help from the NAACP, who put her in contact with Roundtree and Robertson's firm in Washington.

That case became *Sarah Keys v. Carolina Coach Company.* Roundtree and Robertson's legal defense centered on the question of whether a private carrier was allowed to enforce segregation laws. The case dealt with the realm of interstate commerce, which had historically been a tricky area for courts to navigate. A U.S. District Court for the District of Columbia dismissed the case, but Roundtree and Robertson appealed the decision to the Interstate Commerce Commission (ICC). It was the first bus desegregation case to be heard by the ICC, which had been created in 1887 by the Interstate Commerce Act, whose language stated that "it shall be unlawful for any common carrier... to subject any particular person, company, firm, corporation, or locality, or any particular description of traffic, to any undue or unreasonable prejudice or disadvantage in any respect whatsoever." The ICC court initially dismissed the case, but Roundtree and Robertson filed exceptions based on the *Brown v. Board of Education* ruling. On November 7, 1955, the ICC ruled that Carolina Trailways and its employees had violated the terms of the Interstate Commerce Act.

The ICC ruling had little effect in the immediate aftermath. The discriminatory boarding and seating practices on interstate bus lines and in transportation terminals in the South continued until the summer of 1961, when civil rights workers began the first of the so-called "Freedom Rides." Groups of activists, both black and white, boarded buses bound for southern destinations and refused to comply with the segregated seating rules once past the Mason-Dixon Line. The campaign provoked an intense response from law-enforcement authorities and white mobs in southern states until U.S. Attorney General Robert F. Kennedy stepped in. Invoking the ICC court judgment from Roundtree's victorious case in 1955, his directive to the ICC ordered it to begin enforcing its court's own ruling.

Won Reprieve in Socialite Murder Case

Roundtree's law partner, Julius Robertson, died suddenly in November of 1961. Though she continued to practice law for many years, Roundtree was already moving into a second career as a minister in the A.M.E. church. She was one of the first women to be granted full minister status after reforms within the denomination.

In 1963 Roundtree became the first African-American woman admitted to the Women's Bar of the District of Columbia. A year later she took on one of Washington's most notorious murder cases, involving a forty-three-year-old Georgetown socialite named Mary Pinchot Meyer who was found shot to death in October of 1964. Meyer was the ex-wife of a Central Intelligence Agency (CIA) official and was rumored to have had an affair with President John F. Kennedy prior to his assassination in 1963. Meyer's body was found near a towpath of the Chesapeake and Ohio Canal, where she walked daily. An African-American man named Raymond Crump was taken into custody after a witness claimed that he had heard Meyer's cries for help and had seen an African-American man standing over her body. The suspect had been described as about five feet, eight inches tall and weighing 180 pounds, while the twenty-six-year-old Crump was several inches shorter and of slight build. No weapon was found, nor was Crump linked to the possession of any firearm. Roundtree won an acquittal for Crump in July of 1965. Ten years later reports surfaced again about Meyer's alleged affair with Kennedy and allegations were made that a top CIA official had attempted to enter her home following her murder. Because of Meyer's CIA connections and the railroading of the hapless Crump, the never-solved murder has become part of the web of conspiracy theories involving the Kennedy assassination.

In 1970 Roundtree and three partners founded a law firm in Washington, DC Roundtree, Knox, Hunter & Parker handled several notable cases over the next quarter-century. Roundtree retired from legal practice in 1996, the same year that she retired from the pulpit at Allen Chapel A.M.E. Church in Washington, where she had served as a minister since 1964. In 1997 she and Sarah Keys were honored with a plaque at the newly opened Women in Military Service for America Memorial at Arlington National Cemetery. Roundtree was not able to attend the dedication but sent a letter of thanks to the Women in Military Service Memorial board of directors. Her words were quoted in an article for the Memorial's Web page by curator Judith Bellafaire. Referring to the historic ICC ruling in the case of Sarah Keys, now Sarah Keys Evans, Roundtree reflected that it hit "the very heart of what we as Americans have always fought for in battlegrounds around the world: freedom and justice. Mrs. Evans and I wish the plaque to stand as tribute to all women who, while serving their country in the armed forces, also fought in America's 'other war'—the war for civil rights."

Selected works

(With Katie McCabe) *Justice Older Than the Law: The Life of Dovey Johnson Roundtree,* University Press of Mississippi, 2009.

Sources

Books

Roundtree, Dovey Johnson, and Katie McCabe, *Justice Older Than the Law: The Life of Dovey Johnson Roundtree,* University Press of Mississippi, 2009, p. 19.

Online

Bellafaire, Judith, "Challenging the System: Two Army Women Fight for Equality," Women in Military Service for America Memorial Foundation, http://www.womensmemorial.org/Education/BHMSys.html (accessed January 2, 2010).

"Dovey Roundtree," National Visionary Leadership Project, www.visionaryproject.org/roundtreedovey/ (accessed January 2, 2010).

"Profile: Dovey Roundtree," Religion and Ethics Newsweekly, February 19, 1999, http://www.pbs.org/wnet/religionandethics/week225/profile.html (accessed January 2, 2010).

—Carol Brennan

RZA

1969—

Rap musician, composer

RZA, photograph. AP Images.

Hip-hop artist RZA banded together with a group of childhood pals and cousins to form the Wu-Tang Clan, one of the top-selling rap acts of the 1990s. RZA and several other members of the group have gone on to equally profitable solo careers but occasionally reunite for new Wu projects. An astute negotiator and disciple of the Shaolin kung-fu martial art and its philosophy, the musician and producer played a key role in the creation of a multifaceted Wu-Tang multimedia empire and then became an acclaimed composer of film scores for directors such as Quentin Tarantino and Jim Jarmusch. "Sometimes I wake up and say, 'Man, we came from nothing and look at what we've got,'" RZA once told *Time* magazine reporter Mike Eskenazi. "I just wish America one day can take a look and realize the prodigal children it has. All the potential released from its hells."

RZA was born Robert Fitzgerald Diggs in 1969 in Brooklyn, New York, and spent time in several places, including the Brownsville section of his home borough; North Carolina, where an aunt lived; and Pittsburgh, where his father owned a convenience store. By his teen years he was living in the Staten Island housing project of Park Hill, which became known as "Killer Hill" in the 1980s during the crack epidemic. For a time he sang in the choir at Curtis High School on Staten Island.

Discovered Parallels in Kung-fu Films

From a young age, RZA was devoted to martial-arts films from Asia. His interest was sparked in the late 1970s and early 1980s when he went along with his older brothers and cousins to the rundown theaters in Manhattan's Times Square to see triple features from the genre. Later, when VCRs became more affordable, he and his friends began collecting VHS tapes of their favorite action films. RZA quickly perceived that the challenges faced by the movies' heroes in troubled realms mirrored his own experience, and he and his friends even reimagined their gritty New York City world and its boroughs as the faraway lands and mythical kingdoms in the martial-arts universe.

RZA began making his first recordings in the late 1980s with a four-track recorder that he and some friends jointly purchased. With cousins Gary Grice (who called himself "GZA") and Russell Jones (who adopted

At a Glance . . .

Born Robert Fitzgerald Diggs on July 5, 1969, in Brooklyn, NY; several children.

Career: Worked as a disc jockey in the New York City area, late 1980s and early 1990s; formed first group, Force of the Imperial Master, with GZA and Ol' Dirty Bastard; group became All in Together Now Crew; cofounder of the Wu-Tang Clan, 1992; group signed by RCA/Loud Records, 1993; has written and produced several Wu-Tang Clan releases, plus solo projects for other members; released first solo record, *Bobby Digital in Stereo*, 1998; has also composed film scores, acted in films, and written two books.

Addresses: *Office*—SRC Records, 1755 Broadway, 7th Fl., Ste. 7, New York, NY, 10019.

the name Ol' Dirty Bastard), RZA formed the act Force of the Imperial Master, then changed its name to All in Together Now Crew after some success with a self-released cassette single of the same name. This group formed the core that evolved into the Wu-Tang Clan. Failing to get a record deal as the All in Together Now Crew, the cousins pursued independent solo contracts instead. GZA was signed to the Cold Chillin' label as The Genius and released the 1991 recording *Words from the Genius*, which did not do very well. RZA meanwhile styled himself as "Prince Rakeem" and landed on Tommy Boy Records. He cut some tracks for his own 1991 record, an EP entitled *Ooh I Love You Rakeem*.

In 1991 RZA was arrested on a charge of attempted murder. He claimed he had fired in self-defense, and the case went to trial in 1992. The jury voted for acquittal, and RZA walked away a free man. Grateful for his second chance, he approached Cliff Smith, a friend from Park Hill. "I went to Method Man [Smith's professional name]," RZA recalled in an interview with Jon Pareles in the *New York Times*, "and I said: 'Are you with me? I'm ready to do this. I want to get off these streets. If we don't get out of here, we're going to be dead.'" Four months after the trial ended, RZA formed a company, Wu Tang Productions, named after the Chinese region associated with his heroes of martial art, the disciplined Shaolin fighting monks.

Devised Savvy Business Plan

The Wu-Tang Clan included RZA, GZA, Ol' Dirty Bastard, Method Man, and four other musicians from Staten Island: Jason Hunter, also known as Inspectah

Deck; Raekwon the Chef, born Corey Woods; Lamont Hawkins, who went by the name U-God; and Dennis Coles, the Ghostface Killah. Masta Killa, a Brooklynite born Elgin Turner, was the last to join the group and did not appear on its first single, "Protect Ya Neck." They approached Tommy Boy Records, which briefly considered signing the group but chose a trio of white rappers from Long Island called House of Pain instead.

"Protect Ya Neck" was released as a single in early 1993 and was soon picked up by RCA. By the time the group signed its major-label deal, RZA had worked out an entire five-year plan: Like a martial arts guru, he asked Clan members for absolute authority and five years of their lives. With the input of their individual talents, he promised to make them the biggest hip-hop act of the 1990s. He read business books and studied the record-industry trade journals, devising from them a multifaceted strategy to conquer the charts. The Wu-Tang Clan would sign to one label, while its individual members would cut solo deals with other labels. RZA would be the producer for all of the releases. Using different labels, RZA correctly theorized, would mean that the several companies would deploy different marketing strategies for each of the acts and in the end supply maximum promotion for the group and its members.

The group's debut record, *Enter the Wu-Tang (36 Chambers)*, was released in November of 1993 and peaked at No. 8 on the U.S. R&B/Hip Hop chart. RZA explained the title's origins to Havelock Nelson in *Billboard*. "Young monks went to Shao Lin to study the Wu-Tang style. It was all done in secret, and students became masters only by advancing through 35 chambers in a process. One day, one of the monks decided to take the technique to the whole world. The world became the 36th chamber, which would complete a circle." Eastern philosophies were just one of the many topics addressed by the Wu-Tang Clan on the tracks, and they gained accolades for their cryptic references and poetic flourishes. The second single from the debut, "C.R.E.A.M." ("Cash Rules Everything Around Me"), hit No. 1 on the U.S. Hot Dance Music chart. Critics hailed the group's debut as the rebirth of the East Coast sound in rap, whose center had migrated to the West Coast in recent years. The album would later appear on lists of the most influential records of the decade and the most significant releases in the history of contemporary urban music. "RZA's productions created an ominous, bombed-out urban sound, with rough-cut rhythms and elegiac, hovering strings," wrote Pareles in the *New York Times*. "The music was simultaneously raw, ferocious and mournful, full of tension and bleak memories."

Expanded Wu-Tang Empire

As promised, RZA went back into the studio to produce a string of solo records for the Wu-Tang Clan artists, and nearly all of them reached the Top Ten on the U.S.

R&B/Hip Hop album charts in the mid- to late 1990s. The Wu Tang parent company also branched out into other, similarly profitable projects, with a Wu clothing line, comic-book series, and video game. RZA also teamed with three other rappers outside of the Wu-Tang Clan to form Gravediggaz, who released a widely acclaimed debut, *6 Feet Deep,* in the summer of 1994.

The Wu-Tang Clan's second release, *Wu-Tang Forever,* was a stunning double album that debuted at No. 1 in the summer of 1997 and was nominated for a Grammy award for best rap album. With that, RZA proclaimed a promise fulfilled. The combined work of the past five years had brought an unimaginable sum pouring into his bank account; he estimated that he earned $25 million in 1997 alone. At that point, he permitted himself to indulge. "That was when I started the ego thing," RZA admitted to Karen Valby in *Entertainment Weekly.* "I probably spent $100,000 a month…. I stayed in the Trump Plaza for two months once. Four rooms, my whole crew up in there. We turned the Trump Plaza into the projects."

RZA appeared on and produced another record for Gravediggaz, *The Pick, the Sickle and the Shovel,* and released his own first solo record, *Bobby Digital in Stereo,* in the fall of 1998. He made a short film starring himself as the eponymous superhero to accompany the record release and financed the $800,000 production cost himself. A play on his birth name, the alter ego Bobby Digital was imagined as "a comic hero from the early 1970's," RZA told Pareles in the *New York Times.* Through his work, RZA now hoped to provide a window for a younger generation, showing them the discipline of martial arts as an alternative to the deadly ubiquity of firearms. Nothing could ever be so "serious that you got to kill someone," he said in the same interview. "Most of the cases that you've got in these courtrooms is something that could have been handled with a smack in the face, maybe. But to actually go ahead and take this guy off the planet for something that has no value, that's not right."

Moved into Film Composing

RZA's experience in making the Bobby Digital movie whetted his appetite for more film work. Screenwriter and director Jim Jarmusch invited him to compose the score for Jarmusch's 1999 film *Ghost Dog: The Way of the Samurai.* His work with Jarmusch led RZA to a collaboration with *Pulp Fiction* director Quentin Tarantino, another martial-arts cinema buff. RZA composed the soundtrack to Tarantino's 2003 movie *Kill Bill—Vol. 1,* which was nominated in the best film music category of the British Academy of Film and Television Arts Awards, known as the BAFTAs. With that accomplishment RZA realized that he had become "a composer," he told Valby in the *Entertainment Weekly* article. "Snoop Dogg was telling me, 'You can do that … until you're 90 years old. Being a composer, trust me, there ain't a lot of black boys doing that.'"

The Wu-Tang Clan reunited in 2000 for a third record, *The W,* which failed to achieve the sales and chart marks hit by earlier releases, and followed up a year later with *Iron Flag,* which also tanked. All of the group's members, however, had gone on to extremely successful solo careers. Their accomplishments were marred by tragedy in the fall of 2004, when RZA's cousin Ol' Dirty Bastard died suddenly. ODB, as he was called, collapsed after leaving a recording studio just two days before his thirty-sixth birthday. A toxic combination of prescription painkillers and cocaine was the cause of death. RZA delivered a eulogy at his cousin's funeral in which he urged friends and family to look after one another, and in later interviews he said he felt personally responsible for the loss. "You can't neglect love," he reflected in the *Entertainment Weekly* interview. "And that's all it was. ODB's life was basically neglect. He had the wrong people hanging around. Man, I should have just pushed everybody away from him. I had a whole plan for him."

In addition to his film-composing work, RZA has also appeared before the camera. He had a cameo in *Ghost Dog* and supporting parts in the Clive Owen–Jennifer Aniston thriller *Derailed* (2005) and Denzel Washington's *American Gangster* (2007). Throughout 2009 and 2010 he appeared in several major studio releases, including Judd Apatow's *Funny People* and the Jamie Foxx comedy *Due Date.* He has studied with Sifu Shi Yan Ming, a Shaolin monk, and visited China in 1999 to scale the peaks of the actual Wu-Tang Mountains, home to numerous monasteries. He chronicled the history of the Wu-Tang Clan and then his personal philosophies in two books—*Wu-Tang Manual* (2005) and *The Tao of Wu* (2009). As a high-profile rap music star, RZA admits to being overly cautious about his personal safety and owns an armored GMC Suburban customized with the same level of protection used by U.S. presidents and other heads of state. In 2005 he was living in the Los Angeles area with four of his children. He was rumored to have several more but avoided divulging an exact number when asked by Valby in *Entertainment Weekly.* "I don't like to talk about it too much," he said. "As a musician, you can imagine how many I have. That's real. I take care of them, support 'em the best way I can. I realize now that one day off the path will change your life. A child, that's a life you got to worry about. That's 18 to 20 years you got to feed that mouth."

Selected works

LPs as Prince Rakeem

Ooh I Love You Rakeem (EP), Tommy Boy, 1991.

LPs as RZA

Birth of a Prince, Wu Records, 2003.

LPs with Wu-Tang Clan

Enter the Wu-Tang (36 Chambers), Loud/RCA, 1993.
Wu-Tang Forever, Loud/RCA, 1997.
The W, Loud/Columbia, 2000.
Iron Flag, Loud/Columbia, 2001.
8 Diagrams, SRC Records/Universal, 2007.

LPs with Gravediggaz

6 Feet Deep, Gee Street Records, 1994.
The Pick, the Sickle and the Shovel, Gee Street Records, 1997.
Nightmare in A-Minor, Empire Musicwerks, 2002.

LPs as Bobby Digital

Bobby Digital in Stereo, Gee Street Records, 1998.
Digital Bullet, Koch Records, 2001.
Digi Snacks, Koch Records, 2008.

Books

The Wu-Tang Manual, Riverhead/Berkeley Books, 2005.
The Tao of Wu, Riverhead/Berkeley Books, 2009.

Films

(Also film score composer) *Ghost Dog: The Way of the Samurai,* ARD/Channel Four Films, 1999.
Coffee and Cigarettes, Asmik/Ace Entertainment, 2003.
(Also film score composer) *Kill Bill—Vol. 1,* Miramax, 2003.
Derailed, Miramax, 2005.
Miami Vice, Universal Pictures, 2006.
American Gangster, Universal Pictures, 2007.
Funny People, Universal Pictures, 2009.
Due Date, Warner Bros., 2010.
Repo Men, Mambo Films, 2010.

Sources

Periodicals

Billboard, November 25, 1995, p. 34.
Entertainment Weekly, May 20, 2005, p. 40.
New York Times, November 5, 1998, p. E1.
Time, December 11, 2000, p. 82.
Vibe, September 1993, pp. 42–44.

—Carol Brennan

Betye Saar

1926—

Artist, educator

Betye Saar (pronounced Say-er) has been at the forefront of the art world for decades. Best known for her accomplishments in the field of mixed-media assemblage, she has been featured in solo shows at museums and galleries around the nation, including New York City's Whitney Museum of American Art (1975) and the Pennsylvania Academy of the Fine Arts (2006). "I am intrigued with combining the remnant of memories, fragments of relics and ordinary objects, with the components of technology," she noted on her Web site, BetyeSaar.net. "It's a way of delving into the past and reaching into the future simultaneously. The art itself becomes the bridge."

Saar was born Betye Irene Brown on July 30, 1926, in Los Angeles, California. When her father, Jefferson Maze Brown, died in about 1931, she moved with her mother, Beatrice Parson Brown, and siblings to the nearby city of Pasadena. She returned frequently to Los Angeles, however, to visit her grandmother in the predominately African-American neighborhood of Watts. Her experiences in that poor but vibrant community later served as an inspiration for her work. Particularly impressive to her were the Watts Towers, a series of imposing structures built by a construction worker named Simon Rodia in his spare time. Rodia's use of pottery shards, broken glass, and iron scraps were an early indication to Saar that there was beauty and utility in such items, known in the art world as "found objects."

Saar's own artistic projects began well before the age of ten. Throughout the Depression, her family's finances were fragile, and there was little money for toys. To amuse herself, Saar made dolls and other playthings out of scrap materials left over from her mother's seamstress business. Her skill in these projects was apparent, and art soon figured prominently in her career plans. At Pasadena City College and then the University of California–Los Angeles (UCLA), she studied design, earning a bachelor's degree in that subject from the latter institution in 1949.

After leaving UCLA, Saar supported herself as a social worker, pursuing art primarily as a hobby. In about 1952 she married Richard Saar, a painter, ceramist, and art conservator. The couple had three daughters—Lezley, Alison, and Tracye—before divorcing in 1968. Alison and Lezley grew up to become noted artists in their own right; Tracye became a writer.

In the late 1950s and early 1960s, Saar pursued graduate studies in art and education at the University of Southern California and California State University while raising her children. When her youngest child, born in about 1962, entered school, she was able to devote more time to the techniques she had learned in graduate school, particularly printmaking. A pivotal moment came in 1967, when she attended an exhibition of work by Joseph Cornell, a seminal figure in the history of mixed-media assemblage. Soon thereafter she began adapting Cornell's techniques to her own thematic interests, including racism, sexism, and mysticism.

Saar's breakthrough came in 1972, when she completed "The Liberation of Aunt Jemima," a work that overturned in a dramatic fashion a number of stereotypes about African-American women that were a staple of advertising until the late twentieth century. In Saar's assemblage, a toy figurine of the familiar title character is endowed with weapons and set against a backdrop of old advertisements. Amid the struggles for civil rights and women's liberation, Saar's work found a receptive audience. By the mid-1970s, major museums were competing for her assemblages. "The Liberation of Aunt Jemima" was eventually acquired by the Berkeley Art Museum at the University of California–Berkeley. Other pieces entered the collections of the Boston Museum of Fine Arts; the High Museum in Atlanta; the Smithsonian Museum of American Art in Washington, DC; and the Hirshhorn Museum and Sculpture Garden, also in Washington.

Saar's growing prominence in the art world was accompanied by a number of grants and fellowships. One of these, from the National Endowment for the Arts in 1974, enabled her to travel to Haiti and Mexico to study altars and religious ritual. Imagery drawn from those studies has had a prominent place in her work since that time. She has also shown an increasing interest in memory, both individual and collective. Old photographs, for example, are at the center of works like "Midnight Madonnas" (1996). Many of the photos have been sent to her; others she has found at flea markets and antique shops. "She'll use memories from other people," gallery director Halley K. Harrisburg remarked to Kathryn Shattuck of the *New York Times* in 2006. "She takes it in, and when it's time to create a work, she has embraced it [so that] it no longer has that specific association and now just has a deeper, richer meaning."

Widely regarded as a caring and enthusiastic mentor, Saar has had a number of teaching positions over the years, mostly at institutions near her home in Southern California. She also speaks regularly to students, gallery visitors, and art aficionados of all ages. In recognition of those efforts, and of her artistic achievements, she has received a number of awards, including honorary doctorates from the Massachusetts College of Art (1992) and other leading art schools. In 1994 she was one of two artists chosen to represent the United States at the São Paulo Biennial in Brazil. Another sign of her growing reputation abroad came eleven years later, when her work was featured at the Whitechapel Art Gallery in London and the Centre Pompidou in Paris.

Publications about Saar include a 1995 volume she co-wrote with James Christen Stewart. Donna Seaman of *Booklist* called *Betye Saar: Extending the Frozen Moment* "a richly interpretive and well-illustrated volume [that] provides an essential overview of a major artist deeply involved in conveying the texture of African American life and the nature of femininity."

As she reached her mid-eighties, Saar showed little sign of slowing down. "There are more years behind me than in front of me, but there's a sense of freedom," she told Shattuck of the *Times.* "I'm shifting into cruise control and I'm coasting along, and it's just wonderful."

Selected works

"The Liberation of Aunt Jemima," mixed-media assemblage, 1972.
"Eternity," mixed-media assemblage, 1992.
"Watching," mixed-media assemblage, 1995.
"Midnight Madonnas," mixed-media assemblage, 1996.
(With James Christen Stewart) *Betye Saar: Extending the Frozen Moment,* University of California, 2005.
"Cage (In the Beginning)," mixed-media assemblage, 2006.

Sources

Periodicals

Art in America, October 2006.
Booklist, February 1, 2006.

Essence, March 2003.
New York Times, September 12, 2006.

Online

"Betye Saar," VisionaryProject.org, http://www.vision aryproject.org/saarbetye/ (accessed November 10, 2009).

"Betye Saar (b.1926)," MichaelRosenfeldArt.com, http://www.michaelrosenfeldart.com/artists/artists _represented.php?i=56&m=history (accessed November 12, 2009).

"Statement," BetyeSaar.net, http://www.betyesaar. net/ (accessed November 10, 2009).

—R. Anthony Kugler

Marina Silva

1958—

Politician, environmental activist

Silva, Marina, photograph. AP Images.

Marina Silva has played a vital role in forcing Brazil, the world's fifth-largest nation, to adopt sound environmental policies and laws. A member of its Federal Senate since 1994, Silva spent five years as minister for the environment before stepping down in 2008 due to conflicts with the government led by President Luiz Inácio Lula da Silva. In 2009 she switched political allegiances to Brazil's Partido Verde, or Green Party, and is poised to become the country's first black presidential candidate in 2010.

Silva's trajectory of success has resonated with many Brazilians from similarly disadvantaged backgrounds. Born in 1958, she comes from a family of African descent who lived a hardscrabble existence in the remote rainforest working as rubber tappers, a backbreaking profession that involves removing the sap from the jungle's latex trees. She grew up in Seringal Baga͵o in the state of Acre in northwestern Brazil on the border of Peru and Bolivia. Much of Acre is Amazon rainforest, and until Silva reached adolescence there were no major roads nearby. The closest neighbor was an hour away by foot through the jungle, and a trip to Acre's capital might take as long as a week during the rainy season, when the muddy roads be-

came impassible. Silva was one of ten children, and because there were no schools in the area, she was illiterate until her mid-teens.

Lost Sisters to Malaria

Silva was around twelve years old when a new highway project promised a boon to the families of Seringal Bagaço. Then two of her sisters died, followed by an uncle and her cousin—all felled by malaria brought to the village by the road-building crew. "I don't know if I was conscious that the road was bringing all that," she reflected in an interview with Tom Phillips in the London *Guardian*, "but it made me write on my own flesh the consequences of what it meant to mess around with nature without giving the slightest attention to the need to look after it."

When Silva's mother died she was left to care for her siblings, then began accompanying her father and sisters into the rainforest on sap-collecting runs. They often spent twelve hours a day working, and she recalled going entire twenty-four-hour periods without food when money was scarce. "I still haven't forgotten the flavor of a good *farofa de paca*," she told *New*

At a Glance . . .

Born Maria Osmarina da Silva on February 8, 1958, in Seringal Bagaço, Acre State, Brazil; daughter of rubber tappers. *Politics:* Green Party of Brazil. *Education:* Earned degree in history from the Federal University of Acre, 1984.

Career: Worked as a domestic, after 1975, and as a teacher, after 1984; with Chico Mendes, founded the Partido dos Trabalhadores (Workers' Party of Brazil); elected to the Rio Branco municipal council and the Acre State legislature; elected to the Federal Senate of Brazil, 1994, 2002; named to the cabinet of President Luiz Inácio Lula da Silva as minister for environment, 2003 (resigned, 2008); changed political allegiance to the Partido Verde (Green Party of Brazil), 2009.

Awards: Goldman Environmental Prize (with Cristina Narbona Ruiz), 1996; Sophie Prize, Sophie Foundation, 2009.

Addresses: *Home*—Brasília and Rio Branco, Brazil. *Office*—Green Party of Brazil, SDS Edifício Miguel Badya, Bloco L, Sala 218, Brasília, Brazil.

Internationalist magazine writer Tony Samphier, who described the dish as made from "a large forest rodent, roasted with cassava."

Silva's father taught her some basic math skills, she recalled in an interview with Natalie Hoare in *Geographical* magazine, "because when we sold the latex on behalf of all of the owners, we had to discount 17 per cent of the weight to account for the moisture content. Because most people were illiterate, they used to end up taking 30 or even 40 per cent off. My father taught me how to work it out so that I could do it accurately and not be ripped off." When she was sixteen years old she contracted hepatitis and became unable to work the long hours, which involved carrying heavy buckets over several square miles every day. Her father gave her permission to move in with a cousin in Rio Branco, Acre's capital city, and she arrived in September of 1975.

Considered Becoming a Nun

Silva found a medical clinic that treated her hepatitis, and she then found a literacy program in order to begin her education. At this time in her life she was considering entering Roman Catholic religious life. She learned to read in just two weeks, then sped through the rest of her schooling in four years. For two years she lived in a convent while discerning her religious calling. Drawn to liberation theology, she left the convent and earned a degree in history from the Universidade Federal do Acre, or Federal University of Acre. Her interest in liberation theology led her into leftist politics and then into the trade union movement. With Chico Mendes, a legendary figure in Acre politics, Silva founded the first labor union in Acre.

Mendes was a compelling figure in Brazilian grassroots political organizing. He, too, came from a family of rubber tappers, and, working alongside him, Silva was drawn into the nascent environmental movement in Brazil. Activists helped raise international awareness for saving Brazil's rainforests, which were being destroyed at an alarming rate by cattle barons. Clearing the forests by fire, the cattle ranchers left rubber tappers and indigenous groups dispossessed of their land and livelihoods. Mendes was assassinated by the son of a cattle rancher in 1988.

Silva took up Mendes's mantle. She was first elected to the Rio Branco municipal council and then won a seat in the Acre state legislature. By then she was firmly established politically within Brazil's Partido dos Trabalhadores (PT), or Workers' Party, which she and Mendes had cofounded. The PT played a pivotal role in helping Brazil transition out of a military dictatorship that was in place from 1964 to 1985. In 1994 she won a seat in Brazil's eighty-one-member Federal Senate. Silva was the first legislator there to have come from a rubber tapping background, as well as the youngest woman ever to win a seat in the body.

Named Environment Minister

Another PT cofounder was Luiz Inácio Lula da Silva (no relation to Silva), who was elected president of Brazil in 2002 on a PT coalition ticket. Da Silva named Silva to serve as head of Brazil's ministry of environment. Working with a cooperative cabinet and backed by PT muscle in leadership positions within Brazil's twenty-six states and the federal district, Silva scored some major victories as environment minister. The deforestation rate plummeted, and Silva was heralded as the savior of the Amazon rainforest by scores of global watchdog groups. She also played a key role in setting up an indigenous reserve nearly equal in acreage to the American state of Texas.

Brazil's wildly popular president, known by his nickname "Lula," won a second term in 2006. With a worsening global financial recession, some of his government's policies began to shift. He sought approval for a major hydroelectric dam project that was fiercely opposed by the rural residents it would displace. Silva was head of IBAMA (Instituto Brasileiro do Meio Ambiente e dos Recursos Naturais Renováveis, or

Brazilian Institute of Environment and Renewable Natural Resources), Brazil's federal environmental protection agency, and its officials stalled on issuing the permits necessary to begin construction on the dam. This inaction provoked the president, and in 2007 he divided IBAMA into two agencies. As environment minister, Silva clashed with da Silva on two other matters: She raised alarms about the government's proposed new biofuels program and unsuccessfully fought against the introduction of genetically modified crops in Brazil.

Silva resigned her cabinet post in May of 2008. "Nongovernmental organizations were clearly alarmed over the resignation," wrote Alexei Barrionuevo in the *New York Times*. "Greenpeace Brazil called it a 'disaster' that clearly demonstrated a 'change of posture' in the government." Barrionuevo also noted that Silva's achievements had significantly raised Brazil's profile at the table when nations came together to set new climate change standards. "I was fortunate to achieve some things, but they were far short of what Brazil and the world needs us to do," Silva told the *New York Times* correspondent.

Silva returned to her seat in the federal senate as a representative of Acre. In August of 2009 she again made international headlines when she announced her decision to leave the PT in order to join the Brazilian Green Party, known as the Partido Verde, or PV. Pundits and environmental groups saw her decision as a clear sign that she would be the PV candidate in the 2010 presidential election. If that prediction proves true, Silva will be the first black Brazilian to enter the race on a major party ticket. She still recalls the lessons she learned from Mendes, her former mentor. "He knew how to listen and let everyone else speak, and only later would he make up his own mind," she said in the *New Internationalist* interview. "This is a very important lesson he left me."

Sources

Periodicals

Geographical, January 2009, p. 82.
Guardian (London), May 22, 2008.
New Internationalist, October 1995.
New York Times, May 16, 2008; August 28, 2009, p. A6.

Online

The Sophie Prize 2009, SophiePrize.org, http://www.sophieprize.org/Prize_Winners/2009/index.html (accessed January 2, 2010).

—Carol Brennan

Bruce Smith

1963—

Athlete

Bruce Smith retired from nineteen seasons in the National Football League (NFL) after setting a new league record for career sacks in 2003. A defensive end of enormous size and surprising speed, Smith played fifteen seasons with the Buffalo Bills and finished out his career on the roster of the Washington Redskins. He was inducted into the NFL's Pro Football Hall of Fame in Canton, Ohio, in 2009. Former Bills teammate Jim Kelly paid tribute to Smith on the occasion; writing in an essay that appeared on the Pro Football Hall of Fame Web site, he recalled "looking on from the sidelines, watching [Smith] terrorizing opposing offensive linemen and quarterbacks. I would sit there thinking, 'Thank God Bruce Smith is on my team,' because I would never want to see [him] rushing in on me."

Sportswriters, coaches, and fellow players have cited Smith as one of the top athletes to emerge from the Hampton Roads area of Virginia. He was born in Norfolk in 1963, one of three children in a family where both parents worked long hours but encouraged their two sons and daughter to excel in school and athletic pursuits. Smith's father worked as a shipping clerk and later drove a dirt hauling truck; he also moonlighted as a cab driver for extra income. George Washington Smith had been an amateur boxer in his younger days, while Smith's mother, Annie, played basketball in high school.

Became Hokies' "Sack Man"

Growing up, Smith loved basketball, but his increasing size was noticed by local football coaches, who encouraged him to sign up. In his 2009 induction speech at the Pro Football Hall of Fame, Smith recalled his first day of football practice for the Mighty Bookers team of Booker T. Washington High School. The coaches, he remembered, were "scouring the inner city field for broken bottles and debris that could potentially harm us. The temperature was hot. It was in the mid 90s. The humidity was high, and the training was rigorous. The first day was a nightmare, the second day I quit." More specifically, Smith failed to show up for the second day of practice, which prompted a visit to his house by the coach, who asked to speak to his father. Smith recalled in the Hall of Fame speech that afterward, George Smith asked his son if he had been sick. The teenager responded that "football is just too hard. It's too hot, and it's too painful,". Then, he remembered, "My father gave me a look that I never will forget. And in this baritone voice he said, son, whatever you do in life, don't ever quit."

Smith went on to help the Mighty Bookers win the 1980 Virginia AAA championship title as a center, and he also racked up impressive statistics in the winter season on the basketball court. At graduation he was offered several scholarships in both sports but chose to play football at Virginia Polytechnic Institute and State University in Blacksburg, more commonly known as Virginia Tech. It was there that his skills as a defensive end were honed, and he emerged as the much-feared "Sack Man" for the Hokies. In their 1983 season he tallied twenty-two quarterback sacks and was named to the All-American team by the American Football

At a Glance . . .

Born Bruce Bernard Smith on June 18, 1963, in Norfolk, VA; son of George Washington (a shipping clerk, truck driver, and taxi driver) and Annie (a bus driver) Smith; married Carmen, 1990(?); children: Alston. *Religion:* Baptist. *Education:* Studied sociology at Virginia Polytechnic Institute and State University, 1981(?)–84.

Career: Buffalo Bills, defensive end, 1985–99; Washington Redskins, defensive end, 2000–03; hotel designer in Virginia Beach, VA.

Awards: All-American, American Football Coaches Association and Newspaper Enterprise Association, 1983, 1984; Outland Trophy, Football Writers Association of America, 1984; as a National Football League player, played in eleven Pro Bowl games, was named to All-Pro teams nine times, and was named either the League's best defensive player of the year or the American Football Conference's top defensive lineman eight times; inducted into the Virginia Sports Hall of Fame, 2005, the College Football Hall of Fame, 2006, and the Pro Football Hall of Fame, 2009.

Addresses: *Home*—Virginia Beach, VA. *Office*—Armada Hoffler, 222 Central Park Ave., Ste. 2100, Virginia Beach, VA 23462.

Coaches Association and the Newspaper Enterprise Association. He won the honor again for the 1984 season and then won the Outland Trophy, the honor given to the best interior lineman in college football.

Smith ended his college career with the 1984 college bowl season; a few credits short of a sociology degree, he left Virginia Tech to make himself available for the 1985 NFL Draft. The No. 1 draft pick, he was signed by the Buffalo Bills, who chose him over Doug Flutie. In his rookie season he started in thirteen games and accumulated six and a half sacks; the Bills finished the season 2-14. By this time Smith was six feet, four inches tall and tipped the scales at nearly three hundred pounds. It took a new coaching staff, including future Pro Hall of Famer Marv Levy, to help him reach his potential. In his second season he racked up fifteen sacks and continued to hit those double-digit figures for the next twelve seasons, with the exception of 1991, when he sat out much of the season due to a knee injury. He also accumulated scores of honors, including Defensive Player of the Year from various media associations and All-Pro team votes. Over the course of his career, he played in eleven Pro Bowl games.

Maintained Fighting Weight Year-Round

As the Bills' no. 78, Smith was lauded as part of Levy's stunning lineup that won four consecutive American Football Conference (AFC) titles to make four Super Bowl appearances. In January of 1991 the Bills lost the Super Bowl to the New York Giants, 20-19. In 1992 they lost to the Washington Redskins, followed by a 1993 trouncing by the Dallas Cowboys in a 52-17 finish. The Bills secured their status as the NFL's perennial underdogs by their fourth straight loss in Super Bowl XXVIII, again to Dallas, in 1994.

Early in his pro career Smith was known as a formidable eater. Asked by Rick Telander for *Sports Illustrated* about the most food he had ever packed away, Smith replied, "In one sitting? Maybe four big plates of fried chicken, biscuits, chitlins, gravy. Then dessert. Apple pie, sweet potato pie. My mother cooked that stuff, good Southern food, and when I was 300 pounds I never missed a meal. As a kid I'd eat at my mother's house, then go down the road to my girlfriend's and eat, and then sometimes go to my friend's house and eat again. I could gain five pounds in a day." In recent years Smith had worked hard to get his weight down to about 270 and maintained a punishing workout regimen every day of the year, off-season or not. He had also given up red meat and fried foods. At Smith's home in Virginia Beach, Telander noticed a stair-climbing machine that was already beginning to rust from sweat. "In a 20-minute workout, Smith climbs the equivalent of 148 floors, running 3.5 miles, burning off 800 calories," Telander wrote.

The 1991 season was the only one of Smith's career to be hampered by injury. After undergoing knee surgery, Smith returned to the Bills' defensive lineup ready for battle once again. Five years later he was still winning Defensive Player of the Year honors and racking up impressive season statistics: In 1996 he made ninety tackles and fourteen sacks; in 1997 it was sixty-five tackles and fourteen sacks. "Every now and then there's someone for whom chronological age is not accurate," Coach Levy told Ed Miller in the *Virginian Pilot* about his thirty-three-year-old star. "He's a pretty good example of it."

Snapped Up by Redskins

Levy departed as the Bills' coach after the 1997 season. Smith departed, too, following the 1999 season, after team owner Ralph Wilson asked him to take a pay cut of more than fifty percent. Smith refused and was released from his contract along with two other Buffalo veterans, Thurman Thomas and Andre Reed.

Two days later Smith signed with the Washington Redskins, who offered him a five-year, $25 million contract.

Playing for the Redskins allowed Smith to stick closer to his hometown, and he spent the last four seasons of his pro career chasing Reggie White's career-sack record of 198, set in 2000 after White's final season with the Carolina Panthers. By the time Smith started the 2003 season, he had reached 195 sacks. He had also played in 263 NFL games and started in 259 of them. On December 7, 2003, Smith sacked Jesse Palmer of the New York Giants for his 199th career sack, surpassing White's record. He made another sack two weeks later in a game the Redskins lost to the Chicago Bears.

Smith was now forty years old and had hinted that he was considering retirement. Redskins management released him from his contract on February 24, 2004. He began a second career in Virginia Beach, where he has a wife and son, as a hotel designer in partnership with Armada Hoffler, a commercial real estate and construction company. He became eligible for the Pro Football Hall of Fame in 2009, five years after his retirement, and was voted in that same year. His induction ceremony was held at the Canton, Ohio, football shrine on August 8, 2009. In his acceptance speech he cited his late father's influence on his life and thanked other members of his family, former coaches, and fellow players for their years of support and encouragement. "If there were anything that I could share or report that I've learned over the course of my career, it would simply be one's value in life is not determined by accolades or worldly success," he said in closing. "One's worth as human beings resides in our willingness to gladly extend ourselves in service to our fellow man."

Sources

Periodicals

New York Times, February 27, 2000, p. 86.
Sports Illustrated, October 13, 2003, p. 36; September 2, 1991, p. 28.
Tampa Tribune, September 28, 2000, p. 1.
Virginian Pilot, November 3, 1996, p. C1.

Online

Brandt, Gil, "Hall Recall: Smith Was Always a Man among Boys," Pro Football Hall of Fame, http://www.nfl.com/halloffame/story?id=09000d5d811613c7&template=without-video-with-comments&confirm=true (accessed January 2, 2010).

Eisen, Rich, "Bruce Smith Enshrinement Speech Transcript," Pro Football Hall of Fame, August 9, 2009, http://www.profootballhof.com/story/2009/8/9/bruce-smith-enshrinement-speech-transcript/ (accessed January 2, 2010).

"Hall of Famers: Bruce Smith," Pro Football Hall of Fame, http://www.profootballhof.com/hof/member.aspx?PlayerId=280 (accessed January 2, 2010).

Kelly, Kim, "Jim Kelly Welcomes Former Bills Teammate Bruce Smith to Hall of Fame," Pro Football Hall of Fame, http://www.nfl.com/halloffame/story?id=09000d5d8115eacd&template=without-video&confirm=true (accessed January 2, 2010).

—Carol Brennan

Steely

1962–2009

Reggae musician

Steely Johnson is remembered as one-half of the influential production duo Steely & Clevie, who transformed reggae music in the 1980s and 1990s by introducing digital studio technology to Jamaican popular music. Together with partner Cleveland "Clevie" Browne, Steely was a pioneer of the dancehall and ragga (also known as digital dancehall) styles, which succeeded the "roots" reggae made popular by Bob Marley in the 1970s. Steely & Clevie were responsible for producing most of the memorable tracks of the dancehall genre, creating hits for artists such as Freddie McGregor, Shabba Ranks, Maxi Priest, and Gregory Isaacs, and later collaborating with international acts such as Heavy D and No Doubt.

Steely was known equally for his talents as a keyboardist. He recorded with Marley, Bunny Wailer, and the Roots Radics early in his career, and worked at all of the major recording studios in Jamaica, becoming a prolific session musician—by some accounts, he played on more tracks than anyone else in the history of reggae. Both as a musician and as a producer, Steely had a hand in thousands of reggae recordings over the course of his career, leaving an indelible mark on Jamaican music.

Born Wycliffe Johnson on August 18, 1962, in Kingston, Jamaica, and raised in the same Trench Town neighborhood where Marley had grown up. Steely had no formal training in music but instead taught himself to play the piano at age nine or ten. At age twelve, he met Cleveland Browne, a drummer, and spent countless hours at Browne's home, accompanying his drum-ming on bass and keyboards and learning from Browne's older brothers, who had formed a group called the Browne Bunch. As teenagers, the pair began hanging out at Channel One Studios in Kingston, running errands for the popular bass-and-drum duo Sly Dunbar and Robbie Shakespeare, known as Sly & Robbie.

Steely first drew notice as a keyboardist in 1978, when he appeared on Sugar Minott's album *Ghetto-ology*. At age eighteen, Steely played keyboards on Marley's recording of "Trench Town." Both Steely and Browne became key members of the Roots Radics, a studio and stage band that came to dominate Jamaican popular music in the late 1970s and early 1980s.

In the aftermath of Marley's death in 1981, a new sound began to emerge in reggae that drew on the energetic atmosphere of Kingston's live dancehalls and suddenly eclipsed the roots reggae of the previous decade. The dancehall style of reggae was less political in its subject matter and more stripped-down in its instrumentation. The Roots Radics were at the forefront of dancehall reggae, performing on seminal records such as Cocoa Tea's "I Lost My Sonia," McGregor's "Big Ship," and Yellowman's "Zungguzungguguzungguzeng." During this time, Steely worked as a session musician at most of the major recording studios in Jamaica, including Lee "Scratch" Perry's Black Ark, Minott's Youth Promotion, and Clement Coxsone Dodd's Studio One. Steely was so prolific that some music historians estimate he played on more tracks than anyone else in the history of reggae.

At a Glance . . .

Born Wycliffe Johnson on August 18, 1962, in Kingston, Jamaica; son of Alice Johnson; died on September 1, 2009, in East Patchogue, NY; children: Kerry, Shae, Shanice, Daniel, Cailon.

Career: Roots Radics, 1980s; King Jammy Studio, house band, 1980s; Steely & Clevie, producer, 1988–2009.

By the mid-1980s, the sound of reggae was changing once again, as digital studio technology made it possible to create synthesized mixes and rhythms ("riddims" in the Jamaican patois). Steely and Browne, now calling themselves Steely & Clevie, were at the vanguard of ragga, also known as digital dancehall, a style that was marked by faster rhythms and that made ample use of sampling. Working with engineer Bobby "Digital B" Dixon and songwriter-producer Mikey Bennett, Steely & Clevie became the house band at the Kingston studio run by Lloyd "King Jammy" James, with Steely on synthesizers and Browne on the drum machine. They produced a series of instrumental tracks that they called "ana-digital"—part analog, part digital—including "Punany," "Cat's Paw," and "Duck Dance," and created rhythms for most of the other producers in Kingston. Decades later, these tracks are still being sampled by younger musicians and producers.

Steely & Clevie left King Jammy's studio in 1988 to form their own record label, named for themselves. They produced such hits as "Prophecy" and "Loving Pauper" for McGregor, "It's All Over" for Buju Banton, "Love Is the Answer" for Garnett Silk, and "Pocoman Jam" for Gregory Peck, as well as tracks for reggae artists such as Beenie Man, Ranks, Johnnie P, Foxy Brown, Maxi Priest, and Bushman. By their own account, Steely & Clevie were responsible for producing roughly three-quarters of the singles on the Jamaican top 100 during the late 1980s.

After signing a publishing deal with EMI in 1990, Steely & Clevie collaborated with artists outside Jamaica, including Billy Ocean, Heavy D, Caron Wheeler, and No Doubt. In 1992 they produced the critically acclaimed album *Steely & Clevie Play Studio One Vintage,* a collection of rerecorded hits by veterans of the legendary Studio One in Kingston. The album featured a remake of the Dawn Penn classic "You Don't Love Me (No No No)," originally recorded in 1967, that made the top forty in the United States in 1994. Steely & Clevie had another international hit in 2004 with Sean Paul and Sasha's "I'm Still in Love

with You," a vintage reggae tune, which peaked in the top five.

Steely's health began to fail in December of 2008; he traveled to New York City the following summer to undergo treatment for kidney failure resulting from diabetes. Following surgery for a blood clot in the brain, he developed pneumonia and suffered a heart attack. He died on September 1, 2009, at Brookhaven Memorial Hospital in East Patchogue, New York, at the age of forty-seven.

Upon Steely's death, Jamaican culture minister Olivia Grange paid tribute to the producer; the *Jamaica Gleaner* quoted her as saying that "Jamaica has lost another brilliant musician but we must give thanks for Steely's creativity and abundance of talent which enriched our music immeasurably." Browne, according to the *Daily Telegraph,* said of his longtime partner, "He taught Jamaica, the world and me in particular a lot about music, and helped to nurture dancehall into a genre that kids still enjoy.... [He was] a great soldier of reggae music."

Selected recordings

21st Century Sound Clash, VP, 1988.
Busting Out, VP, 1988.
Can't Do the Work, VP, 1989.
Real Rock Style, VP, 1989.
Ghetto Man Skank, ROIR, 1990.
Present Wicked & Wild, Sonic Sounds, 1992.
Fast Car, VP, 1992.
Limousine, VP, 1992.
Steely & Clevie Play Studio One Vintage, Heartbeat, 1992.
Before the Time, Steely & Clevie, 1996.
High Gear, VP, 1997.
Old to the New: A Steely & Clevie Tribute to Joe Gibbs Classics, VP, 2002.
Dubbist, Prestige Elite, 2002.
Dubmissive, Rhythm Club, 2005.

Sources

Books

Chang, Kevin O'Brien, and Wayne Chen, *Reggae Routes: The Story of Jamaican Music,* Temple University Press, 1998.

Periodicals

Daily Telegraph (London), September 12, 2009.
Guardian, September 29, 2009, p. 35.
Jamaica Gleaner, September 2, 2009.
New York Times, September 6, 2009, p. A29.
Times (London), September 24, 2009, p. 52.
Washington Post, September 8, 2009.

—Deborah A. Ring

Koko Taylor

1928–2009

Blues singer, business owner

Taylor, Koko, photograph. AP Images.

Koko Taylor earned the title "Queen of Chicago Blues" from her intense live work on the South Side of the Chicago in the early 1960s. She won a record 29 W. C. Handy Awards, was nominated eight times for Grammy Awards (winning in 1984), and was inducted into the Blues Hall of Fame in 1999. In 1965 Taylor recorded "Wang Dang Doodle" for Chess Records, a million-copy seller that became her theme song. Her popularity even stretched to the white-dominated North Side of Chicago, and she proved to audiences that a woman could shout and sing the blues as well as any man. "Taylor is that rarity," noted Dave Marsh in the *New Rolling Stone Record Guide,* "a contemporary *female* Chicago blues performer."

Taylor was born Cora Walton on September 28, 1928, in Memphis, Tennessee. Her father was a sharecropper, and she grew up with her siblings working on the family farm. It was a difficult environment. The family had no electricity or running water, and Taylor's mother died in 1939. "It wasn't an easy life," she told Mark Guarino in the Arlington Heights, Illinois, *Daily Herald,* "but it was a good life." Young Cora earned the nickname "Little Koko" because of her love of chocolate. She started singing in the choir at the Baptist church her family attended, and broadened her musical education by listening to a disc jockey named B. B. King on the radio. The songs of Bessie Smith, Big Mama Thornton, and Memphis Minnie introduced her to the blues, and she mimicked their songs, while her brothers backed her up with a makeshift guitar built out of bailing wire and a harmonica fashioned from a corncob. "My father, if he catch us singing the blues," she told Marty Racine in the *Houston Chronicle,* "we'd get a good beatin'. He said that was the devil's music."

In 1953 Walton married Robert "Pops" Taylor, a truck driver. The couple boarded a Greyhound bus to Chicago, and he went to work in a slaughterhouse while she worked as a domestic servant. "I raised their children, washed their clothes, ironed, cooked, did everything," she told Paul De Barros in the *Seattle Times.* In the couple's spare time they played the blues together and attended nightclubs on Chicago's South Side. With encouragement from her husband, Taylor

At a Glance . . .

Born Cora Walton on September 28, 1928, in Memphis, TN; married Robert Taylor (deceased); married Hays Harris, 1996.

Career: Discovered by Willie Dixon, 1962; signed with Chess Records, 1964; recorded signature song, "Wang Dang Doodle," 1965; released first album on Alligator Records, *I Got What It Takes,* 1975; opened a blues club, Koko Taylor's Celebrity, 2000.

Awards: Grammy Award, 1984, for Best Traditional Blues Album; inducted into the Blues Hall of Fame, 1999; received 29 W. C. Handy Awards.

began to sit in with Muddy Waters, Buddy Guy, and Howlin' Wolf. Soon the gravelly-voiced Taylor began to achieve a reputation in the world of blues music as a woman with a powerful set of pipes.

In 1962 Taylor met songwriter and bass player Willie Dixon, who produced her first single for the U.S.A. label. He secured her a contract with Chess in 1964 and the following year wrote her most popular song for the label, "Wang Dang Doodle." At first, Taylor was reluctant to sing it: the song seemed silly to her. However, after the racier lyrics had been toned down she recorded it, and "Wang Dang Doodle," rose to number four on the R&B charts and sold more than a million copies. Jim Mcguinness noted in the Bergen County, New Jersey, *Record,* "Besides being her signature tune, the song's dance beat helped define Taylor's uplifting take on the blues that she characterizes as 'foot-stomping music.'"

Even though Taylor never had another big hit, her popular live act guaranteed that she had steady work. She also secured a job at the Wise Fools Pub, a club located on the white-dominated North Side of Chicago. Her popularity eventually allowed Taylor and her husband to quit their day jobs, and he became her manager. In 1969 she released *Koko Taylor,* an album that collected previous singles, and followed it with *Basic Soul* in 1972. Taylor also ventured outside Chicago, performing at the Ann Arbor Blues and Jazz Festival in 1972. In the early 1970s Chess Records began to experience financial difficulties, and in 1975 they went out of business. Taylor then signed with the fledgling Alligator Records, released *I Got What It Takes* in 1975, and received her first Grammy nomination. Her follow-up in 1978, *Earthshaker,* included "Hey Bartender" and "I'm a Woman," two songs that became staples of her live repertoire.

In 1980 Taylor won her first W. C. Handy Award for Best Contemporary Female Artist, and in 1984 she won her first Grammy Award, for her work on the compilation *Blues Explosion.* In 1988 tragedy struck when Taylor's touring bus missed a turn and rolled down the side of a mountain in Tennessee. Pops Taylor, injured in the accident, never regained his health and died of a heart attack a year later. "The last thing he told me," Taylor recalled to Racine, was "'I'll be dead and gone, but I want you to keep on doin' what you doin'. You love what you doin' too much. Don't give it up.'"

Taylor made her comeback in 1990, appearing at the Chicago Blues Festival. She also made a cameo appearance in David Lynch's movie *Wild at Heart.* She continued to spend a great deal of time touring, playing as many as one hundred dates a year during the 1990s. "It's not a bed of roses being out here," she told Madelyn Rosenberg in the *Roanoke Times.* "The roses come so far as I'm enjoying what I'm doing…. I look forward to performing. That's the reason I'm out here." In 1993 Taylor recorded *Force of Nature,* and she returned in 2000 with *Royal Blue,* recorded with the help of a number of young musicians like Keb' Mo' and Shemekia Copeland, who had been influenced by her career. She also opened a blues club called Koko Taylor's Celebrity, in Chicago's revitalized South Loop.

In 2002 Taylor had artery surgery after fainting during a function at her club. The following year she was presented with the Rhythym & Blues Foundation's Pioneer Award and performed "Wang Dang Doodle" at the ceremony, where she maintained, "I feel like I'm nineteen." In 2004 she was named one of Chicago's "100 Most Influential Women" by *Crain's Chicago Business* and was one of ten recipients of a National Heritage Fellowship from the National Endowment for the Arts. In 2007 she released *Old School,* which, in the words of Philip Van Vleck writing for *Billboard,* "delivers a dozen killer tunes" and "is destined to be remembered as one of the top blues albums of 2007, and, no doubt, as one of the best projects in her illustrious discography."

Despite her ongoing success, as Taylor's health continued to decline, she ran into trouble with the tax authorities, who maintained that she failed to pay her taxes in full in 1998, 2000, and 2001 and owed $400,000 in back taxes and penalties. Taylor testified in court that she had virtually no assets beyond her home and that her income had dropped significantly as failing health forced her to curtail her performance schedule. She died on June 3, 2009, as a result of complications from surgery. Nearly a thousand mourners attended her visitation and memorial service, which, appropriately, fell on the eve of the Chicago Blues Festival.

Selected discography

"Wang Dang Doodle," Chess, 1965.
Koko Taylor, Chess, 1969.
Basic Soul, Chess, 1972.
I Got What It Takes, Alligator, 1975.
Queen of the Blues, Alligator, 1975.
Earthshaker, Alligator, 1978.
(Contributor) *Blues Explosion,* Atlantic, 1984.
Force of Nature, Alligator, 1993.
Royal Blue, Alligator, 2000.
Old School, Alligator, 2007.

Sources

Books

Marsh, Dave, and John Swenson, eds., *New Rolling Stone Record Guide,* Random House, 1983, p. 505.

Periodicals

Billboard, April 14, 2007, p. 37.
Crain's Chicago Business, June 7, 2004, p. W52.
Daily Herald (Arlington Heights, IL), June 9, 2000, p. 4.
Forbes, June 2, 2008, p. 36.
Houston Chronicle, November 5, 1998, p. 8.
Jet, February 18, 2002, p. 37; June 21, 2004, p. 38; February 14, 2005, p. 58.
Los Angeles Times, June 21, 1996, p. 6.
New York Times, February 22, 2003; June 4, 2009.
Record (Bergen County, NJ), March 9, 2001, p. 14.
Roanoke Times, October 29, 1998, p. 1.
Seattle Times, November 15, 2002, p. H6.

Online

Koko Taylor, http://www.kokotaylor.com/ (accessed January 6, 2010).

—Ronnie D. Lankford Jr. and Paula Kepos

Robert Robinson Taylor

1868–1942

Architect, professor

Robert Robinson Taylor was the first African American to earn a degree in architecture in the United States. Taylor's achievement came at his 1892 graduation from the prestigious Massachusetts Institute of Technology, where he is the first black student on record at the school. He spent much of his career in Alabama at the Tuskegee Institute, whose first president, Dr. Booker T. Washington, personally recruited him to serve as the campus architect.

Taylor was born in 1868 in Wilmington, North Carolina, where his father, Henry Taylor, had a prosperous shipbuilding and general contracting business before the Civil War. Henry Taylor was apparently the son of a slave woman and a white slave owner who hired him out as a carpenter to repair ships docked at Wilmington. This experience eventually enabled Henry to found his own business as a builder of cargo ships for the Caribbean and South American trade routes. Taylor and his five sisters grew up in Wilmington, where Taylor attended the missionary schools set up in the city after the Civil War to educate African-American youth. After working with his father for a few years, he decided to pursue an architecture degree. With his father's support, he chose the Massachusetts Institute of Technology (MIT) in Cambridge, Massachusetts. It is unclear if the administration was aware that Taylor would be the school's first African-American student.

Won Scholarship

Taylor took a rigorous entrance exam to get into MIT, and he was granted conditional admittance after failing three subjects. He retook the tests in history, geometry, and the metric system during his first year, and passed all of them. During his four years at the school, he earned top grades and won two Loring scholarships to cover his tuition costs. For his graduation project he designed a soldiers' home in the French Beaux-Arts style, which was popular with institutional architects of the era.

Taylor's status as MIT's only black student and the first African American in the United States to earn a degree in architecture brought him to the attention of Booker T. Washington, who had become the first president of the Tuskegee Normal and Industrial Institute in 1881. Tuskegee was founded as a teacher training school and attracted national attention and philanthropic dollars thanks to the success of Washington's programs. Washington offered Taylor a job as the campus architect at a time when Tuskegee had launched an ambitious building program. Taylor accepted and arrived at Tuskegee in late 1892 or early 1893.

Taylor's first major building at Tuskegee was the new Science Hall (later renamed Thrasher Hall), which was finished in 1893. Following Washington's precepts that intellectual pursuits were best accompanied by manual labor, Science Hall was built by Tuskegee students from 1.2 million bricks they had made themselves. The next work to emerge from Taylor's drafting board was Butler Chapel, which was completed in 1898. "Taylor designed a complicated-to-build hammer-beam wood roof truss, which must have posed a challenge for students to erect," noted Dreck Spur-

At a Glance . . .

Born on June 8, 1868, in Wilmington, NC; died on December 13, 1942, in Tuskegee, AL; son of Henry (a boat builder and contractor) and Emily Taylor; first wife's name, Beatrice; second wife's name, Nellie (a music teacher); children: (with Beatrice) Robert Rochon, Helen, Edward, Beatrice; (with Nellie) Henry. *Religion:* Presbyterian. *Education:* Massachusetts Institute of Technology, BS, 1892.

Career: Worked as a boat builder and contractor in Wilmington, NC, before 1898; primary campus architect and instructor in architecture, Tuskegee Normal and Industrial Institute (now Tuskegee University), 1892–1900, 1902–33; architectural draftsman with the Cleveland, OH, firm of Charles W. Hopkinson, 1900(?)–02; builder in Cleveland, 1902(?)–04; Tuskegee Institute, director of mechanical industries department, 1904–21; general superintendent of industries, 1921–25; vice principal, 1925–33. American Red Cross—Tuskegee chapter, chairperson.

lock Wilson in *African-American Architects: A Biographical Dictionary, 1865–1945.* "[He] chose yellow pine for the molding, trim, chancel, pews, and gallery because it was plentiful on land owned by Tuskegee Institute and could be felled and milled by students."

Taylor left Tuskegee in 1899 after completing The Oaks, a majestic residence designated as the college president's house; it was the first new construction in Macon County, Alabama, to be wired for electricity. Dr. Washington's autocratic manner exasperated some Tuskegee staffers, and this may have been the reason for Taylor's three-year hiatus. He apparently spent the years in Cleveland, Ohio, where he worked for the architectural firm of Charles W. Hopkinson, and he was later listed as a builder in the city directory. Taylor returned to Tuskegee in 1902 to be director of mechanical industries there. Records show that Washington regularly approved salary increases to match offers Taylor received from other schools to teach architecture. He was promoted to general superintendent of industries in 1921 and to vice principal—equal to second in command after the Tuskegee president—in 1925.

Spoke at MIT Anniversary

In April of 1911 Taylor returned to MIT for the school's fiftieth anniversary celebration. He was the only African-American speaker at the "Congress of Technology" event, and he delivered a speech entitled "The Scientific Development of the Negro." In his opening remarks he noted that it had been nearly fifty years, too, since the end of slavery. "The negro was the farmer of the South," Taylor said, according to a collected volume of the congress speeches, *Technology and Industrial Efficiency.* "He raised millions of dollars' worth of cotton, the crop which has been the basis of the wealth of the South." Yet, Taylor remarked, an economic system based on bondage ultimately failed. "Executive ability or the chance to develop it by taking charge of work, of a business, laying out the plans, gathering the workmen and material, keeping everybody busy, looking ahead to avoid delays, these things which seem so natural to those with different surroundings and which are a part of their inheritance, had no part in the colored man's life," Taylor told his MIT audience. "In fact, the opposite condition seemed the perfectly natural one. Instead of keeping material on hand to avoid delays, by not having them on hand, a few idle days might result, and where bread and clothes and shelter come whether one works or not, and no more and no less whether he works or not, the chances are that with most of us under such circumstances we would welcome the idle days, especially if the weather were warm and the fishing good."

Dr. Washington died in 1915 but Taylor remained at the school for the next two decades. He continued to design significant campus landmarks as well as buildings for historically black schools in other southern states. In the late 1920s he spent time in Kakata, Liberia, overseeing the construction of the Booker T. Washington Institute. At Tuskegee he trained what scholars estimate to be half of the first generation of black architects in the United States. His students included Wallace Rayfield, who designed the historic 16th Street Baptist Church in Birmingham, Alabama, and John A. Lankford, the first practicing African-American architect in Washington, DC. In civic affairs, Taylor served as chair of the Tuskegee chapter of American Red Cross, which at the time was the only all-black chapter of the emergency relief organization. After the devastating 1927 Mississippi river floods, Taylor headed a special Red Cross "Colored Advisory Commission," which had been "organized to investigate relief efforts aimed at the more than 400,000 rural colored refugee victims of the flood," wrote Wilson in *African-American Architects.* "The commission's scathing report concluded that the efforts of the American Red Cross had largely been ineffective, minuscule, corrupt, and biased."

Taylor retired from Tuskegee in 1933 and returned to his birthplace of Wilmington, North Carolina. Seven years later he collapsed from a heart attack while attending services in the Tuskegee chapel, which he considered his best work. He died on December 13, 1942. With his first wife, Beatrice, he had four children—Robert, Helen, Edward, and Beatrice—and with his second wife, Nellie, he had a son named Henry. His first son, Robert Rochon Taylor, went on to become the first African American to head the Chicago Housing Authority; the largest public housing complex in the United States, the Robert Taylor Homes in Chicago, was named in his honor. Robert Rochon Taylor's daughter was Barbara Taylor Bowman, an expert in early childhood education. Her daughter, Valerie Bowman Jarrett, is a Chicago lawyer who became a senior advisor to President Barack Obama.

A 1957 fire destroyed Taylor's Butler Chapel; a new chapel was erected in 1969. Several of his buildings on the Tuskegee campus still stand a century after he supervised the students' efforts. These include his Administration Building from 1903; Tompkins Hall and Alexander Moss White Hall, both from 1910; the George Washington Carver Museum (originally built as the Laundry in 1915); the William G. Wilcox Trade Building from 1928; and his last project for the school, the Hollis Burke Frissell Library, completed in 1932.

Sources

Books

Technology and Industrial Efficiency: A Series of Papers Presented at the Congress of Technology, Opened in Boston, Mass., April 10, 1911, in Celebration of the Fiftieth Anniversary of the Granting of a Charter to the Massachusetts Institute of Technology, McGraw-Hill, 1911, pp. 167–68.

Wilson, Dreck Spurlock, "Robert Robinson Taylor (1868–1942)," *African-American Architects: A Biographical Dictionary, 1865–1945,* Routledge, 2004.

Online

"Robert R. Taylor," The African American Registry, http://www.aaregistry.com/detail.php?id=2660 (accessed January 2, 2009).

Williams, Clarence G., "From 'Tech' to Tuskegee: The Life of Robert Robinson Taylor, 1868–1942," Blacks at MIT History Project, Massachusetts Institute of Technology, http://libraries.mit.edu/archives/mithistory/blacks-at-mit/taylor.html (accessed January 2, 2009).

—Carol Brennan

Burl Toler

1928–2009

Educator, National Football League official

Burl Toler was the first African American to become an on-field official in the National Football League (NFL), as well as the first African American to officiate in a Super Bowl. Toler is often touted as having been the best player of the University of San Francisco's (USF) 1951 undefeated football team, the Dons, but a combination of circumstances would prevent Toler's entrance onto the professional playing field. Toler and his teammate Ollie Matson were the focus of racial discrimination when the USF Dons were snubbed by the college bowl committees after, in a show of solidarity, the team refused to leave its two black players behind to play in the Orange Bowl. Toler would become one of four members of the 1951 team to be inducted into the Bay Area Sports Hall of Fame in 2008.

Toler was drafted in the first round by the Cleveland Browns in 1952, but his dream of professional football was quashed after he sustained a serious knee injury in a College All-Star game. After returning to school, Toler turned his attention to education and taught mathematics and physical education for 17 years at the Benjamin Franklin Middle School in San Francisco, where he would eventually become the district's first African-American secondary school principal. The school closed in 2004 but was reopened in 2006 as the Burl A. Toler campus. The year 1965 marked Toler's return to professional football as an NFL linesman. Toler received numerous honors and awards, including an honorary doctorate from alma mater USF in 2006. Toler was born in Memphis, Tennessee, but San Francisco would remain his home until his death in August of 2009.

Moved from Memphis to San Francisco

Burl Abron Toler was born in Memphis on May 9, 1928, to Arnold and Annie Toler. One of four children, Toler, whose parents had a high regard for education, was encouraged to continue his education after graduating from Manassas High School. Toler had not thought about playing football until his senior year in high school, but this plan was sidelined after he severely burned his arm disposing of kitchen cooking grease. Instead, he spent his time on the playing field serving as his high school team's water boy. He briefly attended the historically black college LeMoyne-Owen, where he got his first opportunity to play organized football. In 1948 an uncle living in Oakland invited Toler to move to California, where Toler enrolled in the City College of San Francisco (CCSF). It was not long before a football coach noticed Toler in the college gym and asked him to try out for the team. It was here that Toler would become lifelong friends with the great running back Matson after tackling him on three consecutive plays. "Nobody could block Burl because he was so strong and quick," said CCSF running back Walt Jourdan to the *San Francisco Chronicle*. The team's 1948 record of 12–0 earned Toler the title of All-American Player in the Junior College Division and, along with Matson, a four-year scholarship to the University of San Francisco.

At USF Toler majored in education, but his main interest at this time was playing as a linebacker and offensive linesman with the USF Dons. In 1951 the

At a Glance . . .

Born Burl Abron Toler on May 9, 1928, in Memphis, TN; died on August 16, 2009, in Castro Valley, CA; son of Arnold (a Pullman porter) and Annie King (an educator and owner of a small store and boarding house) Toler; married Melvia Woolfolk, January 1953 (died 1991); children: Valerie D., Burl Jr., Susan A., Gregory L., Martin L., and Jennifer L. *Education:* University of San Francisco, BS, 1952, MA, 1966.

Career: San Francisco Unified School District, began as teacher and became counselor, assistant principal, and principal, 1955–74; National Football League official, 1965–90; San Francisco Community College District, director of personnel, beginning 1972 ; University of San Francisco, trustee, 1987–96, trustee emeritus, 1997–2009.

Memberships: American Federation of Teachers; Association of California Community College Administrators; National Association for the Advancement of Colored People (NAACP); African American Historical Society; Booker T. Washington Community Center, board of directors; California Teachers Association; Mount Zion Hospital, board of directors; University of San Francisco, board of governors; St. Ignatius College Preparatory School, board of regents; San Francisco Police Department, commissioner.

Awards: Isaac Hayes Achievements in Sports Award, Vanguard Club, 1972; University of San Francisco Alumnus of the Year, 1995; African American Ethnic Sports Hall of Fame, 2002; Honorary Doctorate of Humane Letters, University of San Francisco, 2006; Bay Area Sports Hall of Fame, 2008; City College of San Francisco Hall of Fame; University of San Francisco Hall of Fame.

team's head coach was Joe Kuharich, who would go on to coach Notre Dame and three professional teams, and the publicity director was Pete Rozelle, who would later become the commissioner of the NFL. The team, coined "the best team you never heard of" by *Sports Illustrated,* was undefeated, ranked in the top 20 nationally, had ten players destined for the NFL, and included three who would reach the Hall of Fame. This was during a segregated America, however, and the USF Dons were shunned by the Orange Bowl because

the team refused to leave Toler and Matson behind. The official reason cited for the snub was the team's "soft season," but according to *Sports Illustrated,* "San Francisco sportscaster Ira Blue ... was told by Gator Bowl president Sam Wolfson that the Gator, Sugar and Orange Bowl committees had all decided to avoid teams with 'Negro' players."

The loss of the $50,000 bowl bid came as a severe blow to the USF Dons, who were $70,000 in debt, and left the university with no alternative but to drop the sports program before the next season. In 2000, at the behest of California Democrat Barbara Boxer, the U.S. Senate unanimously passed a resolution acknowledging that the 1951 USF Dons were the victims of racial discrimination, and "that the treatment endured by this team was wrong and that recognition for it accomplishments is long overdue," as quoted by the *New York Times.* Years later—in 2006 at the USF commencement and in 2008 at the Fiesta Bowl—the team would be honored for taking this stand against racial injustice. "We were a family. We were all so close; there were no color barriers. There really wasn't. We lived together, played together, joked around together. When stuff happened to those two guys, we all felt it," said former teammate Bob Weibel to the *Philadelphia Daily News.* He added, "We could have sent [Toler and Matson] down to the Orange Bowl alone and they might have beat the other guys."

In 1952 Burl Toler and two of his teammates, Matson and Gino Marchetti, were invited to play in the College All-Star Game against the Los Angeles Rams at Chicago's Soldier Field. Toler was on track to being named the squad's Most Valuable Player, but his right knee was shattered in the fourth quarter, ending his dream of playing in the NFL. Toler had been drafted by the Cleveland Browns and acquired by the Cardinals in a trade, but with his knee beyond repair, he never even reported for practice.

Returned to USF

Toler decided to return to USF to complete his bachelor's degree and obtain his teaching credentials. For the next 17 years, he worked at the Benjamin Franklin Middle School, teaching math and physical education, and he eventually became the first African-American secondary school principal in the San Francisco School District. The former middle school campus would eventually become the home of two charter schools, and the campus was renamed in his honor on October 22, 2006. After completing his master's degree in educational administration in 1966, Toler became the director of personnel for the San Francisco Community College District, where he was responsible for more than 1,100 teachers and administrators.

In 1953 Toler married college sophomore Melvia Woolfolk, a social welfare major. The Toler's had six children and enjoyed a long and happy life together until Melvia's death in 1991. His grandson, Burl III, would go on to play college football with the California Golden Bears from 2001 until 2004, before going professional. "My grandfather is so modest," Burl III said to the *Washington Times* in 2007, "The lessons I've learned from him have been more life lessons than football lessons. Like always give it your all. That's where my motivation comes from—the motivation to keep going, to find a way to make this team." During the early part of his career, while he and Melvia raised their children, Toler kept his hand in football by officiating extracurricular games. In 1965 he received the call that would bring him back to the NFL.

Rozelle was now the Commissioner of the NFL, and he knew that Toler, with his thorough knowledge of the game, physical agility, and even temperament, had what it took to be an exceptional NFL official. For the next 25 years, Toler served as a field judge and head linesman of the NFL. In 1980 he became the first African American to officiate a Super Bowl. In 1982 he was the linesman at the American Football Conference championship game between the Cincinnati Bengals and the San Diego Chargers, later dubbed the "Freezer Bowl." The coldest game in history, the temperature was 59 degrees below zero with the wind chill, and Toler sustained frostbite on his fingers. For most of his career, Toler was head linesman, garnering enormous respect from coaches and players alike. "Burl Toler was a pioneer as the first African-American game official in pro sports," NFL spokesman Greg Aiello said to *USA Today*. "He was a great athlete who then became a great official. The NFL will always be proud of his contributions to football and his unique place in NFL history." After retiring in 1990, Toler remained a member of NFL's Professional Referees Association and stayed on as an observer and recruiter of NFL officials up until his death in August of 2009.

In 1972 Toler was awarded the Isaac Hayes Achievements in Sports Award by the Vanguard Club. From 1978 to 1986 Toler was also the San Francisco Police Commissioner. He served on the board of trustees of USF from 1987 to 1996 and was honored as Alumnus of Year in 1995. He was also inducted into the City College and USF Hall of Fame. In 1996 an anonymous donor established the Burl A. Toler Sr. Scholarship, an annual award to an African-American student to attend St. Ignatius College Preparatory in San Francisco. In 2008 Toler became the fourth member of the 1951 Dons to be inducted into the Bay Area Sport Hall of Fame, joining Matson, Marchetti, and Bob St. Clair. Upon Toler's passing, Marchetti said to the *San Francisco Chronicle*, "Burl Toler was the best. He had everything an athlete should have: He loved the game, he was fast and he was the best tackler I've ever seen. He would have been a hell of an NFL linebacker."

Sources

Books

Clark, Kristine Setting, *Undefeated, Untied, and Uninvited,* Griffin Publishing Group, 2002.

Periodicals

Diverse Issues in Higher Education, June 15, 2006, p. 12.
New York Times, August 21, 2009, p. A21.
Philadelphia Daily News, December 28, 2007.
San Francisco Chronicle, August 18, 2009, p. B1; August 27, 2009, p. B3.
San Jose Mercury News (San Jose, CA), May 22, 2006.
Sports Illustrated, November 12, 1990, p. 90A.
St. Petersburg Times (St. Petersburg, FL), December 28, 2006, p. 10C.
USA Today, August 17, 2009.
Washington Times, July 31, 2007, p. C01.

Online

"Remembering Burl Toler," San Francisco Photo Gallery, http://www.usfdons.com/view.gal?id=51563 (accessed December 16, 2009).

—Marie O'Sullivan

Kara Walker

1969—

Artist

Walker, Kara, photograph. AP Images.

In 1994, when she was just twenty-four, Kara Walker created a sensation in the art world when her thirteen- by fifty-foot work *Gone, An Historical Romance of a Civil War as It Occurred between the Dusky Thighs of One Young Negress and Her Heart* was included in a group exhibition at the Drawing Center in New York. Featuring nearly life-size cut-paper silhouettes, the work combined formal elegance with a bizarre tableau of characters from the antebellum South engaged in acts of sexually explicit violence and depravity. Holland Cotter, writing in the *New York Times* in 2003, characterized the work as a "picaresque blend of slave narrative, Harlequin romance, fairy-tale illustration, pornography and racial stereotyping." Since her sensational debut, Walker's work has met equally with notoriety and acclaim, as critics have called for a boycott of her art at the same time that museums and private collectors throughout the world have snapped up her works. Pieces by Walker are held in numerous public collections in the United States and abroad, including the Guggenheim Museum, the Metropolitan Museum of Art, the Museum of Modern Art, the Tate Gallery, and the Whitney Museum of American Art.

Shocked to Discover Racism

Walker was born in Stockton, California, in 1969. Her father was the chair of the art department at University of the Pacific; her mother a seamstress and amateur clothing designer. Walker was shocked to discover racism for the first time at the age of thirteen, when her father moved the family to Stone Mountain, Georgia—a historical meeting place for the Ku Klux Klan—to take a position at Georgia State University. The teenage Walker became quickly aware of the contrast between Southern gentility and the prejudice entrenched in white culture there. She began laying the groundwork for her future artworks in her daydreaming. "I started playing little games with myself, pretending what it would be like if I were a slave," she told the *New York Times Magazine..*

While attending the Atlanta College of Art, Walker began to use cut-out black silhouettes and explore graphic sexual imagery. Part of her inspiration for this artistic direction was her fascination with contemporary pulp fiction novels that took place in the antebellum

At a Glance . . .

Born Kara Elizabeth Walker in 1969, in Stockton, CA; daughter of Larry (an art professor) and Gwen Walker; married Klaus Burgel (a jewelry designer), March 1996; children: Octavia. *Education:* Atlanta College of Art, BA, 1991; Rhode Island School of Design, MFA, 1994.

Career: Artist, 1994—. Columbia University, New York, NY, faculty member in MFA program, 2002—.

Awards: Presidential Scholar, Atlanta College of Art; Ida Blank Ocko Scholarship, Atlanta College of Art; Awards of Excellence I, Rhode Island School of Design; Awards of Excellence II, Rhode Island School of Design; Individual Artist's Fellowship, Art Matters, Inc.; fellowship, John D. and Catherine T. MacArthur Foundation, 1997; Deutsche Bank Artist of the Business Year Award, 2000; U.S. representative to São Paolo Bienal, São Paulo, Brazil, 2002; Lucelia Artist Award, Smithsonian American Art Museum, 2004; Larry Aldrich Award, 2005; United States Artists Eileen Harris Norton Fellowship, 2008.

Addresses: *Home*—New York, NY. *Office*—c/o Sikkema Jenkins & Co, 530 West 22d St, New York, NY, 10011.

South, many of which featured passionate scenes of interracial love. As Walker later told *Artnews,* "My work is intended to function like Harlequin romance novels, which veil themselves in history and encourage women to participate in stories that are not in their best interests."

Made Art World Debut

In 1994 Walker earned a Master of Fine Arts degree at the Rhode Island School of Design. Intent on a career as a professor, she traveled to New York City to attend an academic conference. A friend convinced her to submit slides of her work to the Drawing Center, where the curator, Annie Philbin, found the work "astonishing" and asked her to create a wall drawing for an upcoming exhibit. *Gone, An Historical Romance of a Civil War as It Occurred between the Dusky Thighs of One Young Negress and Her Heart,* decisively changed the course of Walker's career. As Walker told Hilton Als of the *New Yorker* in 2007, "It was my proudest moment. Honestly and truly." Pursued by art

dealers eager to represent her, she chose Brent Sikkema, whose business, while small, was nevertheless known for representing women and artists of color.

Over the next three years, her works were featured in no fewer than eight solo exhibitions. The first of these was at the Brent Sikkema and Wooster Gardens galleries in New York in early 1995. Viewers were shocked by an installation drawing called "Gaining," which depicted a black girl emerging from the shadows toting what appeared to be a man's genitals. A massive exhibition at Wooster Gardens in the spring of 1996 called From the Bowels to the Bosom challenged viewers with images including a young white girl slicing off her hand, a mammy slaughtering a dog while she smoked a pipe, and black women and a baby suckling each other. The installation also included some images with moving parts, similar to old-fashioned puppets. "Like soft porn, her cutouts play coyly with concealment and disclosure," remarked Leslie Camhi in her review of the show in the *Village Voice.* "Two-dimensional with a vengeance, they draw on the tradition of racist caricature, but layer it with parody and irony, and the stories they tell are more strange than moralizing." A 1997 show at the Renaissance Society in Chicago featured startling images of a nude black woman vomiting human body parts and another black woman having intercourse with a white master while smiling and picking cotton, among others.

Became Focus of Controversy

That same year Walker became one of the youngest recipients of a fellowship by the MacArthur Foundation—commonly known as a "genius grant"—which provided her with a $500,000 stipend over five years. Her rising profile provoked a backlash among black artists and critics who objected to the debasement of blacks portrayed in her works. African-American artist Betye Saar undertook a letter-writing campaign to publicize what she saw as the damage being done by Walker's work, imploring others in the art world to boycott her art. As she told Juliette Harris, the editor of the *International Review of African American Art,* "The trend today is to be as nasty as you want to be…. The goal is to be rich and famous. There is no personal integrity…. Kara is selling us down the river."

Walker also had prominent defenders, including Henry Louis Gates Jr., who stated, "No one could mistake the images of Kara Walker . . . as realistic images! Only the visually illiterate could mistake their post-modern critiques for realistic portrayals, and that is the difference between the racist original and the post-modern, signifying, anti-racist parody that characterizes this genre of artistic expression." The controversy generated a 1998 symposium at Harvard entitled *Change the Joke and Slip the Yoke: A Harvard University Conference on Racist Imagery.* According to Eleanor Heartney, writing in *Art in America* in 2007, the symposium "exposed an intergenerational divide within the black art community.... Walker's critics, many of them African-Americans who had been involved in the civil rights struggles of the '50s and '60s, saw her work as a refutation of their own efforts to bury the degrading and racist cliches that made slavery and, later, segregation possible." Walker is not surprised by people taking offense at her art. "I can understand it, and I can't even really talk my way out of it," she remarked to Julia Szabo in the *New York Times Magazine.* "I can't say, 'well, you shouldn't be offended.'"

The controversy did not slow the rise of Walker's fortunes. In 2002 she became a faculty member in the MFA program at Columbia University and was chosen to represent the United States at the São Paulo Bienal. She was awarded a $25,000 Lucelia Artist Award from the Smithsonian American Art Museum in 2004 and a $25,000 Larry Aldrich Award in 2005. She moved into multimedia and adapted her silhouettes into shadow puppets to create short films, including *Eight Possible Beginnings Or: The Creation of African-America, Parts 1-8, A Moving Picture By: Kara E. Walker, 2005,* which was first screened at the Sikkema Jenkins gallery.

Curated Show at Metropolitan Museum of Art

In 2005 the Metropolitan Museum of Art offered Walker the opportunity to curate an exhibition using her works alongside works from its collection. Inspired in large part by the racial inequalities exposed by Hurricane Katrina, the exhibition, which opened in 2006, was called After the Deluge. Walker interspersed works of African, European, and American art from the Met's collection with her own pieces, focusing on themes of water and race throughout history. Critically well received, the show was characterized by the *New York Times* as "a small tour de force of curatorial creativity."

In 2007 Walker had a mid-career retrospective which opened at the Walker Art Center in Minneapolis, Minnesota, before moving on to the ARC/Musée d'Art Moderne de la Ville de Paris and the Whitney Museum of American Art in New York. Entitled My Complement, My Enemy, My Oppressor, My Love, the exhibition included Walker's signature cut-paper tableaux as well as drawings, collages, texts, wall projections, and short films. Holland Cotter of the *New York Times* evaluated the survey of Walker's work as follows: "if Ms. Walker retired today she would leave behind one of the most trenchant and historically erudite bodies of art produced by any American in the last 15 years.... So fiercely imagined and resolved is her work that one tends to forget she was only in her 20s when she first startled us with its newness. Now she is two years shy of 40, and she is certain to do so again."

Selected works

Solo exhibitions

The High and Soft Laughter of the Nigger Wenches at Night, Wooster Gardens/Brent Sikkema, New York, 1995.

From the Bowels to the Bosom, Wooster Gardens/ Brent Sikkema, New York, 1996.

Upon My Many Masters—An Outline, San Francisco Museum of Modern Art, 1997.

Benefit of Enlightened Audiences Wherever Such May Be Found, By Myself, Missus K.E.B. Walker, Colored; The Renaissance Society, The University of Chicago; 1997.

American Primitive, Brent Sikkema, New York, 2001.

The Emancipation Approximation, The Tel Aviv Museum of Art, Tel Aviv, Israel, 2001.

Kara Walker, Slavery!, Slavery!; 25th International Bienal of São Paulo, Brazil; 2002.

Kara Walker at the Met: After the Deluge, The Metropolitan Museum of Art, New York, 2006.

Kara Walker: My Complement, My Enemy, My Oppressor, My Love; The Walker Art Center, Minneapolis, MN; ARC/ Musée d'Art Moderne de la Ville de Paris, France; Whitney Museum of American Art, New York, 2007–08.

The Black Road, CAC Málaga, Centro de Arte Contemporáneo de Málaga, Spain, 2008.

Books

Kara Walker: After the Deluge, Rizzoli, 2007.

Kara Walker: Bureau of Refugees, Charta/Sikkema Jenkins & Co., 2008.

Sources

Books

Berry, Ian, *Kara Walker: Narratives of a Negress,* Rizzoli, 2007.

Jenkins, Sidney, *Slice of Hand: The Silhouette Art of Kara Walker,* Center for Curatorial Studies, Bard College, 1995.

Reid-Pharr, Robert, et al., *Kara Walker: Pictures from Another Time,* D.A.P./Distributed Art Publishers/ University of Michigan Museum of Art, 2002.

Shaw, Gwendolyn DuBois, *Seeing the Unspeakable: The Art of Kara Walker,* Duke University Press, 2004.

Vergne, Philippe, et al., *Kara Walker: My Complement, My Enemy, My Oppressor, My Love,* Walker Art Center, 2007.

Walker, Kara, *Kara Walker: After the Deluge,* Rizzoli, 2007.

———, *Kara Walker: Bureau of Refugees,* Charta/ Sikkema Jenkins & Co., 2008.

Periodicals

Art Bulletin, December 2008.

Art Forum, September 1996, pp. 92–93.

Art in America, September 1996, pp. 106–107; November 2006; October 2007.

Art in New England, December 1995/January 1996, pp. 26–27.

Artnews, January 1997, p. 136.

Commonweal, January 18, 2008.

Ebony, June 2007.

Grand Street, Fall 1996, p. 34.

International Review of African American Art, 1997.

New Art Examiner, May 1996, pp. 49–50; April 1997, pp. 41–42.

New York Times, May 5, 1995, p. C30; April 5, 1996, p. C2; May 9, 2003; March 24, 2006; October 12, 2007; March 30, 2008.

New York Times Magazine, March 23, 1997, pp. 48–50.

New Yorker, Oct 8, 2007.

Village Voice, April 9, 1996, p. 81.

Online

"Kara Walker," Art 21, http://www.pbs.org/art21/art ists/walker/index.html (accessed January 6, 2010).

"Kara Walker," Sikkema Jenkins & Co., http://sikke majenkinsco.com/karawalker.html (accessed January 6, 2010).

"Kara Walker at the Met: After the Deluge," Metropolitan Museum of Art, http://www.metmuseum.org/special/se_event.asp?OccurrenceId= (accessed January 6, 2010).

—Ed Decker and Paula Kepos

Wyatt Tee Walker

1929—

Minister, civil rights activist, writer

Walker, Wyatt Tee, photograph. AP Images.

Civil rights leader, minister, and writer Wyatt Tee Walker is internationally recognized for his contributions to human rights issues. Appointed by Dr. Martin Luther King Jr., Walker was the executive director from 1960 to 1964 of the Southern Christian Leadership Conference (SCLC), where he helped raise more than one million dollars for the organization and served as King's key strategist. He is credited with organizing the major civil rights campaigns during this period and was often at the forefront of marches and sit-ins. His most notable success was "Project C," a strategic plan for the mass marches on Birmingham in April 1963.

After resigning from the SCLC in 1964, Walker returned to the ministry, which led to his position in 1967 as senior pastor of Harlem's Canaan Baptist Church of Christ. In this capacity he continued to champion the causes of African Americans for the next 37 years and assumed leading positions in a number of organizations, such as president and publisher at the Negro Heritage Library. As special assistant for urban affairs under Governor Nelson Rockefeller, Walker planned the construction of the Adam Clayton Powell State Office Building Plaza in Harlem. In 1975 Walker earned his doctor of ministry (DMin) degree, and subsequently published numerous books dealing with human rights, religion, and African-American music. By the 1980s Walker was involved in the antiapartheid movement and helped to bring about free elections in South Africa. Serving on the National Committee of the American Committee on Africa (ACOA), Walker hosted several African leaders, including Nelson Mandela, at Canaan Baptist Church. Walker has visited more than 90 countries and has preached on every continent, with the exception of Australia. After suffering a series of strokes in 2002 and 2003, Walker regretfully resigned his position as senior pastor and retired to Chester, Virginia, just outside Richmond.

Entered the Ministry

The tenth of eleven children, Wyatt Tee Walker was born on August 16, 1929, in Brockton, Massachusetts, to John Wise and Maude Pinn Walker. Walker's father had moved from the South to escape the Jim Crow segregation laws but found little change in the North. While still an infant, Walker's parents moved the family from Massachusetts to New Jersey, and it was here that Walker would stage his first protest. At nine years of age, he and his siblings challenged the establishment when they entered a "white only" movie theater and took their rightful seats among the audience. Walker returned to the South in 1946 to study at Virginia Union University (VUU), where he often refused to ride in the back of public transport, resulting in Walker's unceremonious removal on several occasions. In 1950, after graduating magna cum laude with a BS in chemistry and physics, Walker entered VUU's graduate school of religion. That same year, he married his lifelong partner, Theresa Edwards, on December 24. It was at an Inter-Seminary Movement meeting that he met and became fast friends with the president of the student body, Martin Luther King Jr.

Walker earned his master of divinity degree in 1953 (summa cum laude) and became the pastor of Gillfield Baptist Church in Petersburg, Virginia, shortly thereafter, where he served for the next eight years. It was during this period that Walker became heavily involved in civil rights issues. With his stirring sermons from the pulpit, he urged his congregation to contribute to the cause. In 1957 Walker was one of a group of black men who established the Southern Christian Leadership Conference (SCLC) to promote integration and civil rights for African Americans through nonviolent means. The following year, he cofounded and served as state director of the Congress for Racial Equality (CORE), and he also served for five years as branch president of the National Association for the Advancement of Colored People (NAACP).

Walker founded the protest organization, Petersburg Improvement Association (PIA), and experienced the first of his numerous arrests when he led a group of blacks, which included his wife and two of their children, through the doors of the "whites only" Petersburg Public Library. Walker is often referred to as "the architect of the civil rights movement," and his successful march on Richmond to protest the closing of public schools to avoid segregation attracted the attention of Martin Luther King Jr., with the PIA becoming the model for SCLC movement centers throughout the state.

Worked for King Jr.

In 1960 Walker left Gillfield Baptist Church for Atlanta, Georgia, when King appointed him as the first full-time executive director of the SCLC, a position he would hold for the next four years. Walker was given complete administrative authority, and his first objective was to bring order to the chaotic organization. During his tenure he developed fundraising activities that helped to raise more than 1 million dollars for the organization, increased the staff from 5 to 100 employees, introduced personnel policies and procedures, and implemented sound financial reporting practices. As chief strategist, Walker was at the forefront of the civil rights movement, and he controlled sit-ins, marches, protests, and freedom rides via a network of walkie-talkies. Often in the front lines of civil rights events, Walker endured police beatings and was arrested 17 times. His most notable campaign was "Project C," a detailed three-phase plan designed to expose Birmingham's federally supported segregation practices and disrupt its economy during the Easter season of 1963.

According to the Wyatt Tee Walker Web site (www.wyattteewalker.com), some SCLC staff found his style "aggressive, arrogant and heavy-handed," and Walker left the organization in 1964 to become the marketing specialist for the Negro Heritage Library, where he was promoted to president two years later. He was also the vice president of an African-American studies publisher, Educational Heritage Inc. For a brief period he served as minister of Adam Clayton Powell's Abyssinian Baptist Church in New York City. In 1965 Walker was appointed Governor Nelson Rockefeller's special assistant for urban affairs, a position he would hold for 10 years. In this capacity, he assisted with the peaceful desegregation of schools, helped ease racial tensions surrounding labor disputes, and oversaw Harlem's new state office building project. Walker found his home when, in December of 1966, he became the interim minister of the Canaan Baptist Church in Harlem. As CEO of the Church Housing Development Fund, Walker launched construction projects to provide housing to senior citizens and low-income families. On September 1, 1967, Walker was appointed senior pastor, a position he would hold for the next 37 years.

Moved to Canaan Baptist Church

On August 29, 1972, Walker signed an agreement with Clinton Utterbach and Eugene Cooper, new musicians for his Canaan church. This venture added a dimension to the music department, which would lead to the church's first choral albums. It was during this time that Walker was also pursuing his PhD at Colgate-Rochester Divinity School, with a specialization in African-American musical traditions. After earning his DMin in 1975, Walker went on to write numerous books about African-American music and its relation to social change and black spirituality. From 1977 to 1987 he also served as chairman of the board of the Freedom National Bank. Now defunct, it was once the largest and most profitable minority-owned bank in America.

In 1978 Walker turned his attention to international humanitarian issues as an antiapartheid activist and advocate for the Palestinians. In addition to organizing International Freedom Mobilization to publicize the plight of apartheid victims in South Africa, Walker also was the first African American to meet with Yassar Arafat after the demilitarization of the Gaza Strip. Walker served as chairman of the board of ACOA, renamed Africa Action, and raised funds for Mandela and the African National Conference (ANC). Upon his first visit to the United States as South Africa's presi-

dent, Mandela made Walker's church his first port of call. In 2001 Walker became president of the Religious Action Network (RAN), a consortium of congregations dedicated to achieving freedom and peace in Africa. On the home front, Walker continued his tireless efforts to improve conditions for the underprivileged and was active in the Consortium for Central Harlem Development.

Over the course of his distinguished career, Walker was honored many times. In 1993 an *Ebony* magazine poll listed Reverend Walker as one of "The 15 Greatest Black Preachers" in the United States. He has received honorary doctorates from Princeton University and Virginia Union University. In March of 2005 the Sisulu Children's Academy was renamed the "Sisulu-Walker Charter School of Harlem." On October 2, 2006, Harlem's St. Nicholas Avenue, located between 115th and 116th Streets, was renamed in his honor. Walker was inducted into the International Civil Rights Walk of Fame in 2008 and the International Gospel Music Hall of Fame and Museum in 2009. On January 18, 2009, Walker was the recipient of the "Keepers of the Flame" Award at the African-American Church inaugural ball in Washington, DC.

Walker has also enjoyed a rich and rewarding personal life with his wife of 58 years, Theresa, and their four children. In the latter part of his career, Walker suffered some ill health, and a series of cerebral strokes in 2002 and 2003 left him partially paralyzed on his left side. In 2004 he made the difficult decision to step down as senior pastor of the Canaan Baptist Church. As pastor emeritus, Walker and his wife decided to retire to Chester, Virginia. Between 2006 and 2008 Walker continued to make occasional appearances at speaking engagements.

Selected writings

(With Harold A. Carter and William A. Jones Jr.) *The Black Church Looks at the Bicentennial,* Progressive National Baptist Publishing House, 1976.

Somebody's Calling My Name: Black Sacred Music and Social Change, Judson Press, 1979.

The Soul of Black Worship: A Trilogy—Preaching, Praying, Singing, Martin Luther King Fellows Press, 1984.

The Road to Damascus: A Journey of Faith, Martin Luther King Fellows Press, 1985.

Common Thieves: A Tithing Manual for Black Christians and Others, Martin Luther King Fellows Press, 1986.

Gospel in the Land of the Rising Sun, foreword by Hishashi Kajiwara, Aaron Press, 1991.

Occasional Papers of a Revolutionary, Martin Luther King Fellows Press, 1992.

The Harvard Paper: The African-American Church & Economic Development, Martin Luther King Fellows Press, 1994.

Soweto Diary: The Free Elections in South Africa: Featuring the Original Poetry of Nathan Wright, Jr., foreword by Michael Battle, Martin Luther King Fellows Press, 1994.

A Prophet from Harlem Speaks: Sermons & Essays, foreword by W. Franklyn Richardson and introduction by Al Sharpton, Martin Luther King Fellows Press, 1997.

Race, Justice & Culture: Pre-Millennium Essays, Martin Luther King Fellows Press, 1998.

Millennium End Papers: The Walker File '98–'99, foreword by Andrew Billingsley and introduction by Floyd H. Flake, Martin Luther King Fellows Press, 2000.

Spirits That Dwell in Deep Woods: The Prayer and Praise Hymns of the Black Religious Experience, Gia Publications, 2004.

Sources

Books

Branham, Charles R., *Profiles of Great African Americans,* Publications International Ltd., 1998.

Franklin, John Hope, and Alfred A. Moss Jr., *From Slavery to Freedom: A History of African Americans,* 7th ed., McGraw-Hill, 1994.

Hampton, Henry, and Steve Fayer, *Voices of Freedom: An Oral History of the Civil Rights Movement from the 1960s to the 1980s,* Bantam Books, 1991.

Houck, Davis W., and David E. Dixon, *Rhetoric, Religion and the Civil Rights Movement, 1954–1965,* Baylor University Press, 2006, pp. 533-542.

Morris, Aldon D., *The Origins of the Civil Rights Movement: Black Communities Organizing for Change,* Free Press, 1984.

Patterson, Lillie, *Martin Luther King Jr. and the Freedom Movement,* Facts on File, 1993.

Powledge, Fred, *Free at Last: The Civil Rights Movement and the People Who Made It,* Harper Perennial, 1992.

Weisbrot, Robert, *Freedom Bound: A History of America's Civil Rights Movement,* Norton, 1990.

Woodward, C. Vann, *Strange Career of Jim Crow,* Oxford Press, 1974.

Periodicals

Black Music Research Journal, Spring–Fall 2005, pp. 43–72.

Jet, April 3, 2006, p. 30; June 5, 2006, p. 38; October 2, 2006, p. 15; September 8, 2008, p. 13.

Online

"Africa Action Is Born," University of Pennsylvania African Studies Center, http://www.africa.upenn.edu/Urgent_Action/apic-032101.html (accessed December 19, 2009).

"International Civil Rights Walk of Fame Announces 2008 Inductees," Georgia Informer Inc., http://www.gainformer.com/Files/International%20Civil%20Rights%20Walk%20of%20Fame%20Inductees.htm (accessed December 19, 2009).

"The 13th Annual Induction Celebration and Fundraiser: 2009 Honored Inductees," International Gospel Music Hall of Fame and Museum, http://www.igmhf.org/website/html_pages/home_page.html (accessed December 19, 2009).

—Marie O'Sullivan

Kim Wayans

1961—

Comedian, actress, writer, producer, director

Wayans, Kim, photograph. AP Images.

Kim Wayans, the multitalented sister of the famous Wayans brothers, first grabbed attention in 1990 on the ensemble comedy sketch show *In Living Color.* With perfect timing and sharp wit, Wayans brought an array of characters to life, such as Bonita Buttrell, the gossipy neighbor, and Li'l Magic, the namesake of Wayans's production company. Wayans started out doing stand-up on the comedy club circuit before landing a small role in *Robert Townsend's Hollywood Shuffle* (1987). The following year Wayans showed off her voice when she played the part of a nightclub singer in *I'm Gonna Git You, Sucka,* where she also served as production assistant to the director, her brother Keenen Ivory. An accomplished comedian, actor, director, and producer, with numerous film and television credits both behind and in front of the camera, Wayans professes her first love was writing. Wayans returned to this passion on *In Living Color* and *My Wife and Kids,* and it was on the latter that she met her future husband and writing partner, Kevin Knotts. Wayans and Knotts went on to create the successful children's book series *Amy Hodgepodge,* about the trials and tribulations of a multiracial fourth grader. Wayans's tour de force is her autobiographical play, *A Handsome Woman Retreats,* which she not only wrote but has produced and performed in cities throughout the nation since its 2007 premier.

Kim Wayans, the fourth of ten children, was born on October 8, 1961, in the Chelsea section of New York City to Howell and Elvira Wayans. In her autobiographical, one-woman play *A Handsome Woman Retreats,* Wayans reveals that her father was a strict Jehovah's Witness who instilled in his children the fear of a vengeful Lord. Wayans attributes her and her siblings' sense of humor and flair for comedy to Elvira, whose warmth and sensibilities brought balance to the household. "She is really funny, especially when she is not trying to be funny. I think there is a lot of comedy in lack…. Things were always tight financially, and I think we found a lot to laugh at in that. You either laugh or cry, and we chose to laugh," said Wayans in a 2009 *News & Record* interview. The Wayans children also inherited a strong work ethic and a respect for family from their parents; the siblings would emerge as one of the most powerful families in Hollywood with estimated combined domestic box office takings of over 1 billion dollars.

Kim Wayans' writing abilities were first noticed when she was a fifth grade student, and her teacher asked her to read her collection of short stories to the first and second grade students. Wayans also possessed a natural talent for acting and performed in community plays from a very young age. By Wayans' own admission, she thought she was the only one in the family who was interested in the entertainment business and was surprised when her brothers took the same route, with Keenen and Damon heading out West before her. After graduating from high school, Wayans won a scholarship to study at Wesleyan University in Middletown, Connecticut, where she wrote a book of short stories as her senior thesis and graduated with honors. After a few stints of office temping, Wayans decided to follow her brothers to California and try her hand at stand-up comedy.

Comedy gigs at the Laugh Factory and the Improv caught the attention of an agent, and in 1987 Wayans landed her first bit part in *Robert Townsend's Hollywood Shuffle*. In that same year, she broke into television with a recurring role on the sitcom *A Different World*. In 1988 she appeared alongside her brothers, Damon and Marlon, in *I'm Gonna Git You, Sucka*, a film directed by her brother Keenen, where she also served as his production assistant. Wayans's big break came in 1990 when she joined her brothers on the groundbreaking comedy sketch show *In Living Color*. For the next three years she captivated audiences with her uproarious parodies of high profile celebrities, such as Oprah Winfrey and Whitney Hous-

ton, and her array of hilarious original characters. Wayans had hit the big time as was evidenced in 1992 when she was featured in the humorous documentary *Wise Cracks*, alongside such luminaries as Ellen DeGeneres and Whoopi Goldberg.

By 1993 Keenen and Damon had already left the show when Kim was suspended for refusing to perform a skit that she deemed offensive. Wayans held her ground and quit, with the show closing shortly thereafter, in 1994. Over the next few years, Wayans appeared in a number of films, including: the independent film *Talking about Sex; A Low Down Dirty Shame*, which was written and directed by Keenen; and *Don't Be a Menace to South Central While Drinking Your Juice in the Hood*, written by and starring brothers Marlon and Shawn. From 1995 to 1998 Wayans appeared opposite LL Cool J in the television sitcom *In the House*. During this time, she also lent her voice to the animated cartoon series *Waynehead*, produced by her brother Damon. Other television shows followed before Wayans returned to film in 2002 in the basketball comedy *Juwanna Mann*.

Also in 2002, Wayans joined her brother, Damon, on the hit sitcom *My Wife and Kids* as story editor. During her tenure here, Wayans had the opportunity to write, direct, and produce, earning her BET Comedy nominations for both writing and directing in 2005. It was on this show that Wayans met her future husband and writing partner, Kevin Knotts. After working on the Wayans family's children's animation series *Thugaboo*, Wayans and Knotts were inspired to write their own series of children's books. Drawing on the experiences of their large and culturally diverse family of 38 nieces and nephews, they collaborated on the *Amy Hodgepodge* series, a hugely successful series about multiracial children and their daily challenges.

Wayans returned to film in 2009 in another Wayans family production, *Dance Flick*, an irreverent parody of the musical genre. In 2007 Wayans gave a voice to her own personal journey when she penned, produced, and acted in the autobiographical play *A Handsome Woman Retreats*. Inspired by a 10-day meditation retreat that Wayans took in order to overcome frequent panic attacks, this revealing play is in memory of her grandmother who told her as a young girl "that I would grow up to be a handsome woman," Wayans told the *News & Record*. Wayans grew up to be much more than that and would appear to have a lot more in store. As she said in the 2009 *News & Record* interview, "Who is to say what is in the future, on the horizon? I stay open and creative and see which way the wind blows me."

Selected works

Book author

(With Kevin Knotts) *All Mixed Up: Amy Hodgpodge Series #1*, Grosset & Dunlap, 2008.

(With Kevin Knotts) *Happy Birthday to Me: Amy Hodgpodge Series #2,* Grosset & Dunlap, 2008.

(With Kevin Knotts) *Lost and Found: Amy Hodgpodge Series #3,* Grosset & Dunlap, 2008.

(With Kevin Knotts) *Playing Games: Amy Hodgpodge Series #4,* Grosset & Dunlap, 2008.

(With Kevin Knotts) *The Secret's Out: Amy Hodgpodge Series #5,* Grosset & Dunlap, 2009.

(With Kevin Knotts) *Digging Up Trouble: Amy Hodgpodge Series #6,* Grosset & Dunlap, 2010.

Television writing

(With others) *In Living Color,* Fox, 1991–92.

(With others) *My Wife and Kids* (also known as *Wife and Kids*), ABC, 2002–05.

Stage writing

(And producer and actor) *A Handsome Woman Retreats* (one-woman show), Lil' Magic Productions and Bee-Be Smith Johnson (premier), 2007.

Television Work

My Wife and Kids (also known as *Wife and Kids*), ABC, story editor, 2001–02, executive story editor, 2002–03, supervising producer, 2003–05, director of episodes between 2004 and 2005.

Television appearances

A Different World, NBC, 1987–88.

In Living Color, Fox, 1990–93.

In the House, NBC, 1995–96, UPN, 1996–98.

Waynehead (animated), The WB, 1996–97.

Specials appearances

The Best of Robert Townsend & His Partners in Crime, HBO, 1991.

It's Hot in Here: UPN Fall Preview, UPN, 1996.

The Steadfast Tin Soldier: An Animated Special from the "Happily Ever After: Fairy Tales for Every Child" Series (animated), HBO, 2000.

Awards presentation appearances

Soul Train Comedy Awards, 1993.

American Comedy Honors, Fox, 1997.

BET Comedy Awards, Black Entertainment Television, 2004.

The Second Annual BET Comedy Awards (also known as *BET Comedy Awards*), Black Entertainment Television, 2005.

Episodic television appearances

"Lost and Found: Parts 1 & 2," *China Beach,* ABC, 1988.

"Over Your Dead Body," *Dream On,* HBO, 1990.

Soul Train (host), syndicated, 1993.

"Farmer's Daughter," *The Wayans Bros.,* The WB, 1995.

"A Country Christmas," *The Wayans Bros.,* The WB, 1998.

"There's Something about Rhonda," *Getting Personal,* Fox, 1998.

Random Acts of Comedy, Fox Family Channel, 1999.

"New Kids on the Planet," *Cousin Skeeter,* Nickelodeon, 2000.

The Oprah Winfrey Show (also known as *Oprah;* guest), syndicated, 2004.

The Wayans Family Presents: Thugaboo (animated movie series), 2006.

What News? 2007.

Pilot appearances

In Living Color, Fox, 1990.

Not the Bradys, NBC, 2003.

Film appearances

Robert Townsend's Hollywood Shuffle, Samuel Goldwyn, 1987.

(Uncredited) *Eddie Murphy Raw* (also known as *Raw*), Paramount, 1987.

(And production assistant) *I'm Gonna Git You, Sucka,* Metro-Goldwyn-Mayer, 1988.

Wisecracks, Alliance International Pictures, 1992.

Talking about Sex, 1994.

A Low Down Dirty Shame (also known as *Mister Cool*), Buena Vista, 1994.

"Unemployment," *Floundering,* A-pix Entertainment/Strand Releasing, 1994.

Don't Be a Menace to South Central While Drinking Your Juice in the Hood (also known as *Don't Be a Menace*), Miramax, 1996.

Critics and Other Freaks (also known as *Critics Choice*), Niuwirth Pictures, 1997.

Juwanna Mann, Warner Bros., 2002.

Dance Flick, Paramount, 2009.

Sources

Periodicals

Back Stage West, February 7, 2008, p. 23.

Entertainment Weekly, October 8, 1993, p. 61; June 30, 2006, p. 27.

Film Journal International, August 2002, p. 46; July 2009, p. 43.

Jet, March 1, 1993, p. 60.

News & Record (Greensboro, NC), July 31, 2009.

People, May 7, 1990, p. 11.

Online

Black Film, http://www.blackfilm.com (accessed December 21, 2009).

Dungan, Isabelle, "The Wayans Brothers' Sister Stands Alone in Her One-Woman Show," instantCast, http://www.instantcast.com/LearnAbout/Articles/

InstantCast_Journeys_with_Kim_Wayans.asp (accessed December 21, 2009).

"Interview with Kim Wayans," Teen Project RACE, http://www.projectrace.com/teenprojectrace/kim-wayans-interview.php (accessed December 21, 2009).

Kim Wayans, http://www.kimwayans.com (accessed December 21, 2009).

"Kim Wayans," Yahoo Movies, http://movies.yahoo.com/movie/contributor/1800214619/bio (accessed December 21, 2009).

Scott, Lucile, "A Handsome Woman Retreats," nythea tre.com, June 18, 2008, http://nytheatre.com/nytheatre/solo_rev2008.php?0=S&1=297 (accessed December 21, 2009).

Tarie, "Author Interview: Kim Wayans and Kevin Knotts," July 16, 2009, http://peteredmundlucy7.blogspot.com/2009/07/author-interview-kim-wayans-and-kevin.html (accessed December 21, 2009).

Wayans Family Presents Amy Hodgepodge, http://www.amyhodgepodge.com (accessed December 21, 2009).

—Marie O'Sullivan

Cornel West

1953—

Educator, social critic, writer

West, Cornel, photograph. AP Images.

Cornel West has impressed audiences from scholars and activists to students and churchgoers with his analytical speeches and writings on issues of morality, race relations, cultural diversity, and progressive politics. A scholar, activist, and teacher of religion, West combines his theological concerns with his Marxist political convictions in an attempt to "uphold the moral character of the black freedom struggle in America," he said in *Emerge*. His writings, which reflect the theories of historian Sacvan Bercovitch, combine a dual castigation for moral failure with an optimism that insists on the possibility—through struggle—of making real a world of higher morality.

Influenced by Christian and Marxist Ideals

West was born on June 2, 1953, in Tulsa, Oklahoma, the grandson of the Reverend Clifton L. West Sr., pastor of the Tulsa Metropolitan Baptist Church. West's mother, Irene Bias West, was an elementary school teacher (and later principal), and his father, Clifton L. West Jr., was a civilian Air Force administra-

tor. From his parents, siblings, and community, young West derived "ideals and images of dignity, integrity, majesty, and humility," he wrote in the introduction to *The Ethical Dimensions of Marxist Thought*. West wrote that the basis for his "life vocation" lies in three essential components of the Christian outlook with which he was raised: "a Christian ethic of love-informed service to others, ego-deflating humility about oneself owing to the precious yet fallible humanity of others, and politically engaged struggle for social betterment."

In *Ethical Dimensions,* West examined his own experiences and those of his ancestors against a broad historical backdrop. His views on what he calls the "Age of Europe" are informed by his descent from seven generations of Africans who were "enslaved and exploited, devalued and despised" by Euro-Americans, and three more generations who were "subordinated and terrorized" by the legal racist practices of Jim Crow laws in the South. He recounted that both of his parents were born into a place and time—Louisiana during the Great Depression—when Jim Crow laws of segregation were thriving.

At a Glance . . .

Born Cornel Ronald West on June 2, 1953, in Tulsa, OK; son of Clifton L. Jr. (a civilian Air Force administrator) and Irene (a school teacher; maiden name, Bias) West; divorced twice; married Elleni (a social worker); children: Clifton Louis, Dilan Zeytun. *Politics:* Democratic Socialists of America. *Religion:* Baptist. *Education:* Harvard College, AB (magna cum laude), 1973; Princeton University, MA, 1975, PhD, 1980.

Career: Assistant professor of philosophy of religion at Union Theological Seminary, 1977–83 and 1988, Yale Divinity School, 1984–87, and University of Paris VIII, spring 1987; director of Afro-American studies and professor of religion at Princeton University, 1989–94; Professor of religion and African-American studies, Harvard University, 1994–2002; Class of 1943 University Professor in the Center for African American Studies, Princeton University, 2002—.

Awards: Four Freedoms Medal, Franklin and Eleanor Roosevelt Institute, 2005; named among the 100 Most Influential Black Americans, *Ebony,* 2005. .

Addresses: *Office*—Center for African American Studies, Princeton, NJ 08544.

West was raised in Sacramento, California, where his community of friends and family participated actively in the struggle to overturn racist laws. His earliest political actions included marching with his family in a civil rights demonstration and coordinating with three other Sacramento high school students a strike to demand courses in black studies. In his youth, West admired "the sincere black militancy of Malcolm X, the defiant rage of the Black Panther Party, and the livid black theology of James Cone [a noted writer and professor of religion at Union Theological Seminary]."

Robert S. Boynton highlighted in the *New York Times Magazine* the role the Panthers played in refining West's progressive international perspective: they taught him the importance of community-based struggle; introduced him to the writings of Ghanaian anticolonial philosopher Kwame Nkrumah; and acquainted him with the principles of critical Marxist thought, which called for the achievement of a classless society. Still, West recalled in his introduction to *Ethical Dimensions* that he never fully agreed with these groups and thinkers, since he longed for more of the self-critical humility found in the life and work of Martin Luther King Jr.

Developed Critical Thinking and Political Action

At age seventeen West enrolled in Harvard as an undergraduate. By taking eight courses per term as a junior, he was able to graduate one year early, achieving magna cum laude in Near Eastern languages and literature. While there, he once wrote a spontaneous fifty-page essay to work through the differences between Immanuel Kant and George Wilhelm Friedrich Hegel's conceptions of God. He even dreamed of philosophical concepts taking form and battling one another.

West credited his time at Harvard with fueling a reexamination of his world views. Over those three years, he surveyed his own thoughts and actions and pursued a rigorous study of new ideas. In class he developed a passionate interest in the effects of time and culture on philosophical thought and historical actions. Outside of class, he participated in discussion groups, took weekly trips to Norfolk State Prison, and worked with the Black Student Organization, which was responsible for the 1972 takeover of Massachusetts Hall to both protest Harvard's investments in Gulf Oil and show support for liberation forces operating in the southwest African country of Angola. However, West attributed his greatest intellectual influences on political matters to a variety of philosophers such as nineteenth-century Serbian political writer Svetozar Marković. He continued, however, to recognize the limits of "book knowledge" and to value dedication in action.

After Harvard, West began pursuing a doctorate in philosophy at Princeton University. There, he discovered that the values most precious to him were those of individuality and democracy. In the introduction to *Ethical Dimensions,* he defined individuality as "the sanctity and dignity of all individuals shaped in and by communities," and explained democracy as a way of living as well as a way of governing. The work of Richard Rorty, a philosopher at Princeton, also impressed West. West called Rorty's attention to history "music to my ears" and subsequently developed his own vision of Rorty's favorite philosophical tradition— American pragmatism—in his 1989 book *The American Evasion of Philosophy: A Genealogy of Pragmatism.* In this book, West defined his own version of pragmatism, called "prophetic pragmatism," which he considered vital in promoting the formation of a democracy that both recognizes and extols the virtues of individual morality, autonomy, and creativity. Philosopher K. Anthony Appiah, writing in the *Nation,* considered the book "a powerful call for philosophy to play its role in building a radical democracy in alliance with the wretched of the earth" and deemed West possibly "the pre-eminent African-American intellectual of our generation."

Gained Renown as Teacher and Writer

West began writing during the late 1970s, and his works began to be published in the early 1980s. During his mid-twenties, he left Princeton, returned to Harvard to finish his dissertation, and then began his first tenure-track teaching job as an assistant professor of philosophy of religion at Union Theological Seminary in New York City. While at Harvard, West married and had a son, Clifton. Both this marriage and a later one ended in divorce.

While teaching at Union, West remained active in racial and progressive causes and traveled to Brazil, Costa Rica, Jamaica, Mexico, Europe, and South Africa. In the early 1980s West encountered Michael Harrington's Democratic Socialists of America (DSA), an organization that shaped the version of democratic socialism he would subsequently promote. West described the DSA in *Ethical Dimensions* as "the first multiracial, socialist organization close enough to my politics that I could join."

West wrote *The Ethical Dimensions of Marxist Thought* during his time at Union, but it was not published until 1991. In the book, he traced Karl Marx's intellectual development to reveal how Marx incorporated the growing consciousness of history in modern thought with values of individuality and democracy. West combined his interests in Marxism and religion in his 1982 book *Prophesy Deliverance! An Afro-American Revolutionary Christianity*, in which he outlined the potential in prophetic Christianity for meaningful opposition to racism and oppression.

In 1984 West assumed a post at the Yale Divinity School that eventually became a joint appointment with the institution's American Studies Department. He participated in a campus drive for clerical unionism and against Yale's investments in South African companies and was arrested and jailed during one campus protest. West viewed his political actions at Yale as "a fine example for my wonderful son, Clifton," whereas the Yale administration punished West by canceling his leave and requiring him to teach a full load of two courses in the spring of 1987.

Before his leave was canceled, West had already arranged to teach African-American thought and American pragmatism at the University of Paris, so in order to fulfill his responsibilities to both schools, he commuted to Paris for his three courses there while teaching his two courses at Yale. He also served as the American correspondent for *Le Monde diplomatique* at Yale. In 1988 West returned to Union. One year after that move, he accepted a position at Princeton University as professor of religion and director of the Afro-American studies program. West continued to write and edit books on philosophy throughout the 1980s and early 1990s. In his 1985 publication *Post-*

Analytic Philosophy, which he edited with John Rajchman, West reflected on the crisis in American philosophy. *Prophetic Fragments,* addresses such subjects as theology, sex, suicide, and violence in contemporary U.S. culture. In 1991's *Breaking Bread: Insurgent Black Intellectual Life,* coauthors West and bell hooks focused on the problems of creating black male-female dialogue and an effective black intellectual community while suggesting practical solutions to communication problems.

Promoted the "Power of Diversity"

West's impassioned and insightful writings make a resounding appeal for cross-cultural tolerance and unity, urging individuals to recognize the power of diversity within society. As a member of the editorial collective for *Boundary 2: An International Journal of Literature and Culture,* West related Marxist thought to cultural politics of difference, including differences in race, gender, sexual orientation, and age. In addition, he wrote a column for the progressive Jewish journal *Tikkun.* West also wrote commentary on contemporary subjects for popular journals, such as his essay on the 1992 Los Angeles riots for the *New York Times Magazine.*

West continued his exploration of race relations and cultural diversity in *Race Matters* (1993), which his publisher, Beacon Press, promoted as a "healing vision for the crisis of racial politics today." Resolute in his belief that people of color must struggle for a better future, he persisted in his quest to create an effective, black, progressive leadership. After his return to Harvard, West produced *The Future of the Race* and *The African American Century: How Black Americans Have Shaped Our Country,* both coauthored with his colleague Henry Louis Gates Jr. The latter comprises approximately 100 biographies of prominent African Americans, including some obscure notables such as the first black woman aviator, Bessie Coleman. For the book, the authors wrote, "At the dawn of the twenty-first century ... we cannot imagine a truly American culture that has not, in profound ways, been shaped by the contributions of African Americans."

In 1996 West, along with feminist and economist, Sylvia Ann Hewlett, created the Task Force of Parent Empowerment, and later, West and Hewlett coauthored *The War against Parents: What We Can Do for America's Beleaguered Moms and Dads* and *Taking Parenting Public: The Case for a New Social Movement,* which was edited by Hewlett. Both books address how American government policies and the American media work against families. West and Hewlett have called for a Parent Bill of Rights, which includes paid parenting leave, help with housing, and tax relief for families.

West also recorded a CD that included rap and spoken word, *Sketches of My Culture.* In 2004 he followed with *Street Knowledge,* saying at the time in *Jet,* "I am a teacher, so I use different avenues to express my passion to communicate." In 2007 he issued another rap CD, *Never Forget: A Journey of Revelations,* which featured guest performances by such artists as Prince, KRS-One, and Gerald Levert and included tracks on the war in Iraq, homophobia, and the presidency of George W. Bush.

Maintained High-Paced Career after Cancer

In 2003, at the special request of film directors Andy and Larry Wachowski, West created the role of Councillor West in *the Matrix Reloaded* and *The Matrix Revolutions.* That same year West successfully battled prostrate cancer, and he later told Patrik Henry Bass in *Essence* that beating this medical diagnosis was his greatest challenge. In an interview with Terrence McNally on AlterNet.com, West described the impact of the disease on his thinking. "I think that in some way my struggling with cancer was an intensifying of my dance with mortality. And death has a way of arresting the mind, as Samuel Johnson put it. So there's no doubt ... the near death experience of cancer made me think about the life that I had lived."

In 2005 West received the Franklin and Eleanor Roosevelt Institute Four Freedoms Medal for freedom of worship at the Franklin D. Roosevelt Presidential Library and Museum in Hyde Park, New York. He was also named among the 100 most influential black Americans by *Ebony* magazine that year. He wrote *Democracy Matters: Winning the Fight against Imperialism,* a work of philosophy and social criticism that blamed three characteristics in U.S. society for impeding progress toward the ideals of freedom and democracy outlined in the Constitution. The three impediments, according to West, are an increasingly greedy free-market capitalism, militarism, and authoritarianism. He maintains that the key to combating these trends lies in engaging in genuine debate of social issues based on the Socratic method of philosophical inquiry, the Judeo-Christian concept of justice, and lessons learned through the epic struggle for African-American equality.

On the eve of the election of Barack Obama to the presidency in November 2008, West's *Hope on a Tightrope: Words and Wisdom* was published. It compiles excerpts from West's speeches, letters, and essays, along with photographs and an audio CD, on such topics as courage, faith, family, freedom, music, and philosophy. While a supporter of Obama's candidacy, West was a cautious ally who in *Hope on a Tightrope* renewed his challenge to Americans to do more than talk about social change, but to engage in the daily work of making it happen. He followed in 2009 with the autobiography *Brother West: Living and Loving Out Loud, A Memoir.* The book traces his life beginning with his birth into a tight-knit religious family to his early activism, Ivy League education, influential career, and battle with cancer. West told McNally, "I am a person with my own individuality, and I try to forge my own voice and style, but I'm very much a part of a tradition. I'm not a self-made man, that American myth that goes back to Ben Franklin. There are even elements of it in Frederick Douglass. I am the opposite of that, I am in no way self-made, I come out of a tradition, a community of struggle, a heritage that exemplifies struggle for justice and freedom. I'm very blessed to be a part of that family and that traditional community."

A prolific writer, provocative speaker, and outspoken activist, West is among the most influential representatives of progressive thinking in the United States and a relentless advocate for social justice and racial equality. In addition to his many speaking engagements and television appearances, since 2002 he has served as the Class of 1943 University Professor in the Center for African American Studies at Princeton University. Reflecting on his friend's intellectual strengths, Gates noted, "One of Professor West's great gifts is that he can engage in conversation with almost anyone, whatever their ideology. His keen-edged analysis forces us to remember what he has to say. There's no one from whom I've learned more than Cornel West. One of the most important things that he has to teach, I think, is that being a Black intellectual doesn't have to mean mindless, pompous cheerleading."

Selected works

Albums

Sketches of My Culture, 2001.
Street Knowledge, Roc Diamond Records, 2004.
(With BMWMB) *Never Forget: A Journey of Revelations,* Hidden Beach, 2007.

Books

Black Theology and Marxist Thought, Theology in the Americas, 1979.
Prophesy Deliverance! An Afro-American Revolutionary Christianity, Westminster Press, 1982.
(Coeditor) *Theology in the Americas,* Orbis Books, 1982.
(Coeditor with John Rajchman) *Post-Analytic Philosophy,* Columbia University Press, 1985.
Prophetic Fragments, Eerdmans, 1988.
The American Evasion of Philosophy: A Genealogy of Pragmatism, University of Wisconsin Press, 1989.
(Coeditor) *Out There: Marginalization and Contemporary Cultures,* New Museum of Contemporary Art/Massachusetts Institute of Technology, 1990.
(With bell hooks) *Breaking Bread: Insurgent Black Intellectual Life,* South End Press, 1991.

The Ethical Dimensions of Marxist Thought, Monthly Review Press, 1991.

Beyond Eurocentrism and Multiculturalism, Common Courage Press, 1993.

Keeping Faith: Philosophy and Race in America, Routledge, 1993.

Race Matters, Beacon Press, 1993.

(With Henry Louis Gates Jr.) *Future of the Race,* Vintage, 1997.

(With Kevin Shawn Sealey) *Restoring Hope: Conversations on the Future of Black America,* Beacon Press, 1997.

(With Sylvia Ann Hewlett) *The War against Parents: What We Can Do for America's Beleaguered Moms and Dads,* Houghton Mifflin, 1998.

The Cornel West Reader, Basic Civitas Books, 1999.

(With Henry Louis Gates Jr.) *The African-American Century: How Black Americans Have Shaped Our Country,* Free Press, 2000.

Cornel West: A Critical Reader, edited by George Yancy, Blackwell, 2001.

Democracy Matters: Winning the Fight against Imperialism, Penguin Press, 2004.

Hope on a Tightrope: Words and Wisdom, SmileyBooks, 2008.

Brother West: Living and Loving Out Loud, A Memoir, SmileyBooks, 2009.

Films

The Matrix Reloaded, Warner Brothers, 2003.
The Matrix Revolutions, Warner Brothers, 2003.

Sources

Books

West, Cornel, *The Ethical Dimensions of Marxist Thought,* Monthly Review Press, 1991.

Periodicals

America, November 8, 2004, p. 26.
Black Enterprise, February 2005, p. 176.
Christian Century, July 12, 2005, p. 35.
Commonweal, December 20, 1985, p. 708.
Ebony, June 2004, p. 44; May 2005, p. 52.
The Economist, January 5, 2002.
Emerge, March 1993.
Essence, June 1996, p. 42; February 2005, p. 210.
Jet, December 13, 2004, p. 26.
Nation, April 9, 1990, pp. 496–08.
National Review, January 28, 2002.
Newsweek, June 7, 1993, p. 71.
New York Times Magazine, September 15, 1991.
Poughkeepsie Journal, October 23, 2005.
The Progressive, January 1997, p. 26.
Publishers Weekly, March 30, 1998, p. 60; October 16, 2000, p. 57.
Religious Studies Review, April 1992, p. 103.
Time, January 14, 2002, p. 14.
USA Today, August 28, 2007, p. D3.
Voice Literary Supplement, December 1988, pp. 3–4.

Online

Cornel West Official Web Site, 2009, http://www.cornelwest.com/ (accessed December 28, 2009).

McNally, Terrence, "Always Controversial Cornel West Disses Obama, Survives Cancer and Almost Spent His Life in Prison," AlterNet.com, December 18, 2009, http://www.alternet.org/rights/144569/always_controversial_cornel_west_disses_obama,_survives_cancer_and_almost_spent_his_life_in_prison/?page=1 (accessed December 28, 2009).

—Nicholas S. Patti, Christine Miner Minderovic, and Laurie DiMauro

Armond White

1954(?)—

Film, music critic

Armond White is a leading film critic whose conservative, and often contrary, views have raised the hackles of many cineasts over the years. His criticisms of popular films, such as *The Dark Knight, Slumdog Millionaire,* and *Iron Man,* have caused storms of controversy on movie review Web sites. Love him or loathe him, White gets people arguing about films and talking about Armond White, to which he confidently replies, "Shows I'm doing my job," as quoted by Marc Jacobson in *New York Magazine.* A writer for the *New York Press* since 1997, White is also a university lecturer of cinema studies and a curator of the Film Society at Lincoln Center. He has served on the juries of various film festivals, and in 2009 White was re-elected chairman of the New York Film Critics Circle, a position he held 15 years earlier. White has contributed to a variety of publications and monographs and has published three books of his own. His first book, *The Resistance: Ten Years of Pop Culture that Shook the World,* is a thought-provoking collection of essays that traces the developments in film, hip-hop, and theater from 1984 to 1994. In *Rebel for the Hell of It: The Life of Tupac Shakur,* published in 2002, White takes an in-depth look at rap and the ghetto culture. *Keep Moving: The Michael Jackson Chronicles* is a collection of essays compiled over 25 years that not only examines the meaning behind the artist's music but successfully captures White's development as a critic through the evolution of his own analyses of Jackson's work.

Grew Up in Detroit

Armond White was the youngest of seven children raised in Detroit, Michigan, during the civil rights movement and the Motown era. White and his family were the first African Americans to move into their northwest Detroit neighborhood, which was once predominantly Jewish. White's father, a piano player, owned a gas station and a pool hall before deciding to take a more secure day job at the Ford Motor Factory. Both of his parents were devout Baptists before converting to Pentecostal, and religion played a very large part in the children's upbringing. The family members were avid moviegoers, and classics, such as *The Long Hot Summer* and *Cat on a Hot Tin Roof,* made lasting impressions on the young White. From the family home, White was able to receive Canadian television, and he enjoyed watching international films from Federico Fellini, Vittorio De Sica, Luchino Visconti, and other artistic geniuses. "If you cut me open, that's what you'd find: the movies, Bible verses, and Motown lyrics," White said to Jacobson.

Before White had ever heard of film criticism, he was putting down his interpretations of films using an old manual typewriter. White would draw cartoon panels to map out a movie without knowing about storyboards. In his senior year of high school, White found his muse when he was assigned to write a report on any book of his choice. He found a copy of Pauline Kael's *Kiss Kiss Bang Bang* in a local drugstore, a collection of the

At a Glance . . .

Born in 1954(?) in Detroit, MI. *Religion:* Baptist. *Education:* Wayne State University, BA; Columbia University, MFA.

Career: *City Sun* (now defunct), arts editor, 1984–96; *New York Press,* film critic and writer, 1997—; teacher of cinema studies at Columbia University, Fordham University, and Long Island University; curator and lecturer for Film Society of Lincoln Center; writer for numerous publications, including *Essence, Film Comment, Nation, New York Times, Rolling Stone,* and *Vibe.*

Memberships: National Society of Film Critics; New York Film Critics Circle, chairman, 1994, 2009; member of juries at the Sundance Film Festival, Tribeca Film Festival, and the National Endowment for the Arts.

Awards: ASCAP-Deems Taylor Award, 1996, for music criticism.

Addresses: *Web*—http://www.nypress.com.

acerbic film critic's reviews, and he was hooked. Kael, who became one of White's greatest inspirations as well as a personal friend in the years to come, would be responsible for his nomination for membership in the Film Critics Circle in 1986.

While an undergraduate at Wayne State University, White reviewed films for the school newspaper. It was during this time that he covered Steven Spielberg's *Close Encounters of the Third Kind,* and his lifelong fascination with the director's work was established. In the Jacobson interview, White considers Spielberg to be "the greatest of all American humanist directors, every bit the equal of John Ford ... the measure by which all films and filmmakers must be judged." In 1980 White went to Columbia University to study for a masters degree in film history, theory, and criticism. It was here that Stefan Sharff completely changed the way White looked at film. Using a stop-projection projector, Sharff analyzed films frame-by-frame, stressing that film was a visual medium, and a good director could tell a story without any sound. Andew Sarris, one of Kael's greatest rivals, was another of White's mentors at Columbia University and would become his second great inspiration after Kael. In a *Senses of Cinema* interview, White enthused about Kael and Sarris, remarking that there was nothing more exciting to him as a young student then discovering one of their

obscure recommendations, such as the 1916 film *Intolerance* by D. W. Griffith.

Joined Staff of Radical Newspaper

After graduating from Columbia, White joined the staff of the now-defunct *City Sun,* a weekly radical black newspaper based in Brooklyn, New York. As arts editor from 1984 to 1996, White wrote elaborate prose, at times lamenting mainstream filmmakers as banal, and praising the work that he deemed artistically worthy. With Kael and Sarris as his mentors, White went where few black critics of his generation dared to go, which was essentially to critique art for arts sake and not give in to the Hollywood hype. One example is his scathing review of Spike Lee's *Malcolm X,* which appears in *The Resistance: Ten Years of Pop Culture that Shook the World*: "Because Spike Lee has white people on the brain, his new film is about the shock wave Malcolm X created in American society, not a biography of the martyred Black Muslim spokesman. At three hours plus, it's a movie with a theme but not a subject." This is in contrast to his review of Lee's *Do the Right Thing,* which, according to an interview with Steven Boone on the *Big Media Vandalism* blog spot, White considered to be "the film [Lee] was put on the planet to do." Although White's detractors have said that he is "contrarian for the sake of being contrary," as noted by Boone, White has dismissed these comments by drawing a distinction between the reviewer and the critic. "A reviewer is someone who decides whether it's enjoyable, whereas a critic is one who concerns him or herself with the ideas and aesthetics ... and the way it affects society," White said to *Senses of Cinema's* Jeremiah Kipp.

During the 1990s White wrote film and music reviews for several publications, including the *New York Times, Film Comment, Essence, Rolling Stone, Vibe,* and the *Nation.* Since 1993 White has also produced and presented a music video program for the Film Society of Lincoln Center's annual video festival. White's series, which examines the music video as a postmodern art form, has been the center's most popular program and has attracted international attention. Although most of his presentations have been compilations of the works of acclaimed filmmakers, musicians, and singers, he has dedicated two presentations to a singular artist, Michael Jackson. The latest was in 2009, titled *Keep Moving: Michael Jackson's Video Art,* and coincided with the publication of his collection of Michael Jackson essays, *Keep Moving: The Michael Jackson Chronicles.* In 1996 White won the ASCAP-Deems Taylor Award for music criticism.

Generated Controversy

White's negative reviews of films, such as *District 9* and *Precious: Based on the Novel "Push" by Sap-*

phire, have generated a barrage of hate mails to Internet movie Web sites, such as Rotten Tomatoes. *The Reader, American Gangster, In Bruges,* and *Milk* are other notable films that have made it on to White's "bad" list, while films such as *Norbit, What Happens in Vegas, Transformers 2,* and *I Now Pronounce You Chuck and Larry* have been featured on White's list of "likes." Reviews such as these prompted Roger Ebert to write in his *Chicago Sun-Times* article, "I am forced to conclude that White is, as charged, a troll. A smart and knowing one, but a troll." However, White's contention has been that reviewers, such as Ebert, "promote a film culture of consumption rather than inquiry and sensitivity," as he was quoted in *Cineaste.*

White's work has been included in a number of National Society of Film Critics anthologies, including *The A List, The X List, They Went Thataway, Foreign Affairs,* and *Love and Hisses.* White's writings can also be found on DVD liners of a broad range of films, such as Ernst Lubitsch's *Trouble in Paradise* (1932) and Samuel Fuller's controversial *White Dog* (1982). Since 1997 White has been the film critic for the *New York Press* and has been a cinema studies lecturer at the universities of Columbia, Fordham, and Long Island.

Selected works

Books

The Resistance: Ten Years of Pop Culture That Shook the World, Overlook Press, 1995.
(Contributor) *Birth of a Nation'hood: Gaze, Script, and Spectacle in the O. J. Simpson Case,* Pantheon, 1997.
(Contributor) *Alfred Hitchcock's Rear Window,* Cambridge University Press, 2000.
(Contributor) *Doomed Bourgeois in Love: Essays on the Films of Whit Stillman,* Intercollegiate Studies Institute, 2001.
Rebel for the Hell of It: The Life of Tupac Shakur, Da Capo Press, 2002.
(Contributor) *New York Calling: From Blackout to Bloomberg,* Reaktion Books, 2007.
Keep Moving: The Michael Jackson Chronicles, Resistance Works, WDC, 2009.

Periodicals

(Writer and editor with Stanley Aronowitz, Benj DeMott, and Charles O'Brien) *First of the Month,* http://www.firstofthemonth.org.

Television documentaries appearances

Baadassss Cinema, Film One Productions, 2002.
Headliners & Legends: Denzel Washington, MSNBC, 2002.

Urban Soul: The Making of Modern R&B, 2004.
50 Films to See Before You Die (also), known as *Film4's 50 Films to See Before You Die* Film4 (U.K.), 2006.

Sources

Books

Lopate, Philip, *American Movie Critics: From the Silents until Now,* Library of America, 2006.
White, Armond, *The Resistance: Ten Years of Pop Culture that Shook the World,* Overlook Press, 1995.

Periodicals

Chicago Sun-Times, August 14, 2009.
Cineaste, Winter 2000, p. 27.
Filmmaker Magazine, Winter 2004.
Los Angeles Times, November 5, 2009.
New York Entertainment, August 14, 2009.
New York Magazine, February 15, 2009.

Online

Boone, Steven, "'In a World That Has *The Darjeeling Limited,* Sidney Lumet Should Be Imprisoned!': Armond White Conversation, Part I," December 10, 2007, "Phonies, Cronies, American Ironies, American Gangsters: Armond White Conversation, Part II," December 14, 2007, "Sweet Lime and 'Sour Grapes': Armond White Conversation, Part III," December 18, 2007, Big Media Vandalism, http://bigmediavandal.blogspot.com/search?q=armond (accessed December 22, 2009).
Boone, Steven, "White Power: Ten Armond White Quotes That Shook My World," The House Next Door, December 10, 2007, http://www.thehousenextdooronline.com/2007/12/white-power-ten-armond-white-quotes.html (accessed December 22, 2009).
Kessler, Ben, "Critic Armond White's New Book *Keep Moving* Chronicles MJ's Career," Graphic Design Forum, August 25, 2009, http://blogs.graphicpdesignforum.com/bkessler/2009/08/critic-armond-w.html (accessed December 22, 2009).
Kipp, Jeremiah, "Beyond Entertainment: An Interview with Film Critic Armond White," Senses of Cinema, April 2002, http://archive.sensesofcinema.com/contents/02/20/armond.html (accessed December 22, 2009).
White, Armond, "Things Done Changed," First of the Month Quarterly, July 2008, http://www.firstofthemonth.org/archives/2008/07/things_done_cha_2.html (accessed December 22, 2009).

—Marie O'Sullivan

Claude Williams

1908–2004

Jazz musician

Claude "Fiddler" Williams was one of the greatest jazz violinists to grace the world stage. His illustrious career spanned eight decades, but it was in his later years that his star reached its zenith. By the age of ten, Williams was playing the guitar, banjo, mandolin, and cello. The violin became Williams's instrument of choice after listening to the jazz violinist Joe Venuti. Williams developed a distinctive bluesy, hard-swinging style, and by the 1930s he was playing with Nat King Cole, Count Basie, and other greats from that era. Refusing to conform to the styles of his contemporaries, such as the classically polished tones of Stéphane Grappelli or the melodic improvisations of Stuff Smith, Williams produced a vigorous, no-frills sound that earned him plaudits throughout the jazz age and critical acclaim in the latter part of his career. At 85 years of age, Williams was asked by Mark O'Connor to teach at his annual fiddle camp. "He's a legend and he should be there," O'Connor said to *JazzTimes*. "And it was a great call. So many kids were able to be around him. Whenever he'd pick up his violin, it was like a history lesson." Williams continued to tour internationally, teach, record, and play the jazz festival circuit well into his nineties.

Started Early

Claude Gabriel Williams was the youngest of six children, born in Muskogee, Oklahoma, to Lee and Laura Williams on February 22, 1908. Williams had a natural talent, and at a very early age he was taught by his brother-in-law Ben Johnson to play stringed instru-

ments. By about eight years of age, Williams, who was already playing the guitar, mandolin, cello, and banjo, joined his brother-in-law's string band. When the jazz violinist Joe Venuti visited Williams's hometown to play a concert in the segregated city park, Williams watched and listened with fascination through a hole in the fence. Williams was in no doubt that this was the instrument for him, and he exchanged his cello for a violin the following day. He practiced tirelessly and studied other artists, such as the harmonic improvisations of Louis Armstrong, to develop his own style.

Williams played in local hotels with various bands, including Oscar Pettiford's, before heading to Oklahoma City in 1927 to join trumpeter Terence Holder and his Clouds of Joy. Due to bad money management, Holder was soon replaced by tuba player Andy Kirk as the band's leader. Within two years the band was a major player on the Kansas City jazz scene, and Williams, now the top violinist in Kansas City, would regularly play alongside Charlie Parker and enter into jam sessions with visiting musicians, such as Stuff Smith.

When the Clouds of Joy went on to tour the East Coast, Williams was mainly playing the banjo and violin, although Kirk was pushing him toward the guitar. When Williams injured his leg on the road, Kirk abruptly replaced him with a rhythm guitarist, and Williams returned to Kansas City. After gigging there for a short time, he moved to Chicago, where he joined the Cole brother trio, with Nat King Cole on piano. In 1936 Count Basie asked him to join his band as their

At a Glance . . .

Born Claude Gabriel Williams on February 22, 1908, in Muskogee, OK; died on April 25, 2004, in Kansas City, MO; son of Lee J. (a blacksmith) and Laura (a homemaker) Williams; married Blanche Y. Fouse (second wife); children: Michael. *Military service:* Inducted into service, 1944; discharged after nine months.

Career: Played with several bands, including Clouds of Joy (also known as 11 Clouds of Joy, 12 Clouds of Joy, and Dark Clouds of Joy), 1927–30, Alphonse Trent band, 1932, George E. Lee band, 1933, Chick Stevens band, 1934–35, Eddie and Nat King Cole's Combo, and Count Basie's bands, 1936–37; formed a swing trio, the Three Swing Men of Swing, 1938; played with jazz groups with the Works Progress Administration (WPA), beginning 1938; played with Four Shades of Rhythm, beginning 1944; played electric guitar with Roy Milton's Solid Senders, early 1950s; played with several musicians, including Jay McShann (pianist), Eddie "Cleanhead" Vinson (saxophonist), and Hank Jones (pianist), 1950s–60s; toured and recorded with McShann, 1970–79; cast of stage production *Black & Blue,* Paris, 1989; appeared with his own band at numerous jazz festivals, including the Monterey Jazz Festival, the Nice Jazz Festival, and the Smithsonian Institution's Festival of American Folk Life; instructor at the Mark O'Connor Annual Fiddle Camp, 1993–2004; appeared in hundreds of personal performances at venues throughout the United States and Europe; recorded numerous albums and is featured on many other recordings.

Awards: Oklahoma Jazz Hall of Fame, 1989; Oklahoma Music Hall of Fame, 1997; National Heritage Fellowship Award, 1998.

guitar player, and he was soon recognized as "Guitarist of the Year" in a *Downbeat* magazine poll. "Claude was there at the most important moments in American music. Every note he played was the real thing. I never heard him play one false or unswinging note. He's the guy we all aspired to be like," Matt Glaser, jazz violinist and chair of the string department at Boston's Berklee College of Music, was quoted as saying in an All about Jazz piece after Williams's passing.

When Basie's band, which now had 14 musicians, made its New York debut, reviews were lukewarm, with the exception of Williams's guitar solos. John Hammond, the band's talent scout, felt that Williams was taking attention away from Basie, and he was replaced by Freddie Green, a rhythm guitarist. Williams returned to Kansas City, where he focused on violin and formed the Three Swing Men of Swing. In 1938 Williams moved to Flint, Michigan, where he took a day job welding tanks, and played with the Works Progress Administration (WPA) at night. In 1944 Williams was inducted into the service, only to be discharged nine months later.

Williams returned to Chicago, where his career continued in relative obscurity for nearly three decades. He joined up with the Four Shades of Rhythm for a short time, playing in Chicago, Cleveland, and Flint. In 1951 Williams headed out to Los Angeles, touring the West Coast, as well as the Midwest, playing electric guitar in a rhythm and blues band, Roy Milton's Solid Senders. When the work dried up, Williams returned to Kansas City, where he took another day job and played the Blue Room, the Orchid Room, Fandango, and other small venues at night. Some of the musicians he played with during this period included saxophonist Eddie "Cleanhead" Vinson and pianists Hank Jones and Jay McShann.

Recorded with McShann

Williams's second career was launched when he played a gig with McShann in the early 1970s. This was also the first time in nearly 30 years that he had the opportunity to make a record, *The Man from Muskogee.* Throughout the 1970s Williams toured the United States and Europe with McShann's band, and in the 1980s he embarked on a very successful solo career. In 1985 a short documentary was made about him called *Fiddler's Dream.* When Broadway beckoned in 1989, Williams joined the Paris production of *Black and Blue,* a musical about the famous Cotton Club in Harlem, New York. Williams never made it to Broadway, however, returning instead to Kansas City to care for his sick wife. In this same year, he performed in a tour called "Masters of the Folk Violin" and was inducted into the Oklahoma Jazz Hall of Fame.

In 1990 he and Dr. Billy Taylor, a jazz educator and performer, were featured on the *CBS News Sunday Morning* television show. Gone were the days of the small, smoke-filled nightclubs, as Williams was now playing to packed audiences at such prominent venues as New York City's Carnegie Hall and Lincoln Center. He was invited to play for President Bill Clinton on two occasions—his first inauguration, in 1993, and five years later in the East Room of the White House. Between 1992 and 1996 Williams was also touring schools and colleges with The Statesmen of Jazz, a vibrant and energetic all-star group of elderly musicians.

Throughout the 1990s, Williams was a regular on the international jazz festival circuit and made numerous recordings. His band appeared in the Smithsonian Institution's Festival of American Folk Life, and in 1994 Mark O'Connor invited him to teach at his fiddle camp in Nashville, Tennessee. About Williams's contributions to the camp, O'Connor once said, as quoted by All about Jazz, "He fit about ninety years of music and stories in at the camp for us younger folks, especially the kids. We all learned from a music legend who gave us example after example of what the dawn of great American music sounded like up close."

Williams received several honors, including induction into the Oklahoma Music Hall of Fame in 1997 and a National Heritage Fellowship from the National Endowment for Arts in 1998. His energy knew no bounds and, at 89 years of age, Williams said, as quoted on the Oklahoma Music Hall of Fame Web site, "I don't see any reason to quit playing. I'll be doing this at least till I get to a hundred and something." Unfortunately, Williams never achieved this dream; he passed away on April 25, 2004, after contracting pneumonia at the age of 96. Williams, as quoted on the Arhoolie Web site, once said, "When I started playing, they weren't even calling it jazz!" "What they were calling 'it,'" the site quoted jazz critic Chuck Berg, "was swinging and bluesy and when all other linguistic tropes failed great and just plain terrific!"

Selected works

Albums

(With Jay McShann, Paul Gunther, and Don Thompson) *The Man from Muskogee,* Sackville, 1972.
Live at J's, Part 1, Arhoolie Records, 1989.
Live at J's, Part 2, Arhoolie Records, 1989.
The Fiddler, Steeplechase, 1994.
Swingtime in New York, Progressive Records, 1994.
(With others) *Masters of the Folk Violin,* Arhoolie Records, 1995.
(With Joe Ascione, Dave Green, and Norris Turney) *Echoes of Spring,* Sackville, 1998.
Swingin' the Blues, Bullseye Blues, 2000.
My Silent Love, Disques Black & Blue, 2002.

Singles

"Smooth Sailing," 1993.
"These Foolish Things Remind Me of You," 1995.
"That Certain Someone," 1999.
(With Eric Reed, Herlin Riley, and Reginald Veal) "Gossipin' Hens," 1999.

Sources

Books

Mel Bay Fiddler Magazine's Favorites: Tunes from

and Interviews with 36 of the World's Greatest Fiddlers, Mel Bay Publications, 1999.

Periodicals

Guardian (London), April 30, 2004.
Independent (London), July 19, 2004.
Jet, July 27, 1998, p. 32.

Online

Albin, Scott, "Claude Williams: Cherokee," Jazz.com, http://www.jazz.com/music/2009/8/3/claude-williams-cherokee (accessed December 15, 2009).
"Claude 'Fiddler' Williams Collection," LaBudde Special Collections Dept., University of Missouri–Kansas City, http://library.umkc.edu/spec-col-collections/williams-claude (accessed December 15, 2009).
"Claude 'Fiddler' Williams," Hot Jazz Management & Production, http://hotjazznyc.com/williams.html (accessed December 15, 2009).
"Claude 'Fiddler' Williams," 1998 NEA National Heritage Fellowships, National Endowment for the Arts, http://arts.endow.gov/honors/heritage/fellows/fellow.php?id=1998_10 (accessed December 15, 2009).
"Claude Williams," Arhoolie, http://www.arhoolie.com/titles/406.shtml (accessed December 15, 2009.)
"Claude Williams News," NME Artists, NME.com, http://www.nme.com/artists/claude-williams (accessed December 15, 2009).
"Claude Williams—1997 Inductee," Oklahoma Music Hall of Fame and Museum, http://www.oklahomamusichalloffame.com/Inductees/BYYEAR/tabid/86/ItemID/3/Default.aspx (accessed December 15, 2009).
"Claude Williams Papers," Smithsonian Institute Archives Center, http://americanhistory.si.edu/archives/AC0909.htm (accessed December 15, 2009).
"Jazz Legend Claude 'Fiddler' Williams Dies," All about Jazz Publicity, http://www.allaboutjazz.com/php/news.php?id=3605 (accessed December 15, 2009).
"Jazz Profiles from NPR: Claude 'Fiddler' Williams (1908–2004)," NPR, http://www.npr.org/programs/jazzprofiles/archive/williams_c.html (accessed December 15, 2009).
Joyce, Mike, "Online Exclusive: Mark O'Connor," JazzTimes, http://jazztimes.com/articles/25137-online-exclusive-mark-o-connor (accessed December 15, 2009).
"1989 Inductees," Oklahoma Jazz Hall of Fame, http://www.okjazz.org/index.cfm?id=20 (accessed December 15, 2009).

Other

Fiddler's Dream (documentary film), MT Productions, 1985.

—Marie O'Sullivan

Juan Williams

1954—

Journalist, writer

Juan Williams is a political journalist who is best known as the author of *Eyes on the Prize: America's Civil Rights Years, 1954–1965* and other nonfiction works chronicling the civil rights movement and African-American institutions. An award-winning journalist who straddles partisan lines, he contributes to both liberal and conservative news organizations and was a national and White House correspondent for the *Washington Post* for twenty-three years. In addition to *Eyes on the Prize,* his best-selling books include *My Soul Looks Back in Wonder: Voices of the Civil Rights Experience* and the controversial *Enough: The Phony Leaders, Dead-end Movements, and Culture of Failure That Are Undermining Black America—and What We Can Do about It.* A news analyst on National Public Radio (NPR) and a contributor to numerous political opinion shows, Williams is a weekend news anchor on the Fox News Channel.

Juan Williams was born to Rogelio L. and Alma Geraldine Williams on April 10, 1954 in Colon, Panama. His father was an accountant, and his mother worked as a secretary. Williams moved with his family to Brooklyn, New York, in 1958. He won a scholarship

Williams, Juan, photograph. Brendan Hoffman/Getty Images.

to Oakwood Friends School, a Quaker boarding school in Poughkeepsie, New York. One of the few black students at the school during the early 1970s, Williams credited his experiences at Oakwood with allowing him to exceed the vision he had held for himself. He told an audience there in 2006 that "Oakwood is where I got a sense of life's potential and where I learned the Quaker spirit of caring." He went on to Haverford College in Philadelphia after graduating from Oakwood in 1972. Williams majored in philosophy at Haverford and graduated in 1976 with a bachelor's degree.

Began Career as a Political Journalist

Williams began his career in journalism by interning at the *Washington Post* in 1976. He was then hired full-time by the newspaper and worked as an editorial writer, national correspondent, columnist, and White House reporter during his twenty-three years there. It was while covering White House affairs during the Ronald Reagan administration that Williams became interested in civil rights. Among other issues, President Reagan, who originally opposed the idea, presided

At a Glance . . .

Born Juan Williams on April 10, 1954, in Colon, Panama; son of Rogelio L., an accountant, and Alma Geraldine (Elias), a secretary; married Susan Delise, July 1, 1978; children: Antonio Mason, Regan Almina. *Religion:* Episcopal. *Education:* Haverford College, BA, philosophy, 1976.

Career: *Washington Post,* columnist and reporter, 1976–99: Fox News, contributor and anchor, 1997—; National Public Radio, host and contributor, 2000—. Contributor to radio and television news and political programs, including *NewsHour with Jim Lehrer* (PBS), *Nightline* (ABC), *Capital Gang* (CNN), and *Crossfire* (CNN).

Memberships: Aspen Institute of Communications and Society; Haverford College Board of Trustees; New York Civil Rights Coalition; Washington Journalism Center.

Awards: Front Page Award, Washington-Baltimore Newspaper Guild, 1979; Education Writers of America, 1979; Columnist of the Year, *Washingtonian,* 1982; Emmy Award, 1989; Outstanding Memorial Book, Myers Center for the Study of Human Rights in the United States; Best National Book, *Time*; political commentary award, American Association of University Women; honorary doctorates, Haverford College and State University of New York.

Addresses: *Home*—Washington, DC. *Office*—National Public Radio, 635 Massachusetts Ave. NW, Washington, DC 20001. *E-mail*—yourcomments@foxnews.com.

over the declaration of Martin Luther King Jr. Day in 1983. When Williams spoke to students at the University of Nevada–Reno in 2001 he recalled, "There was a lot of tension between black and white reporters. There was a lot of the tension in society in the newsroom." He said that journalism had allowed him to move into white-dominated areas and that when he served as a White House reporter earlier in his career he was "a novelty" at the time: "Here was a black man talking about events at the White House."

In 1987 Williams's book, *Eyes on the Prize: America's Civil Rights Years, 1954–1965* was published by

Viking. Each chapter was devoted to specific civil rights events during those years, such as the *Brown v. Board of Education* school desegregation case in Topeka, Kansas. This was the case that brought fame to Thurgood Marshall, the NAACP lawyer who became the first black Supreme Court justice. Other events covered in the best-selling book include the march on Washington in 1963, the desegregation of Little Rock, Arkansas, schools in 1957, and the 1955 bus boycott in Montgomery, Alabama. The book was a companion volume to the six-part public television series of the same name and traced events of the civil rights movement from its start, including various facets of the movement, many of the people involved, as well as the changes that resulted. Williams also incorporated numerous interviews he had conducted with people who had been involved in the movement, including little-known but important people who had struggled for equal rights.

Williams hosted *Talk of the Nation,* an NPR call-in radio program, for eighteen months in 2000–01. As part of the program, he traveled throughout the United States and held town hall meetings to discuss current events and issues. These discussions became part of the NPR series *The Changing Face of America,* which focused on cultural, economic, and political trends in the United States at the turn of the millennium.

When Supreme Court nominee Clarence Thomas was defending himself sexual against harassment charges in 1995, Williams supported him in his writings and on television as a co-host on the CNN panel show *Crossfire.* However, Williams soon found himself the subject of unflattering news stories, accused of verbally harassing female coworkers at the *Washington Post.* The allegations resulted in disciplinary actions and an apology from Williams.

Wrote Biography of Thurgood Marshall

Williams took time off from the *Post* to write *Thurgood Marshall: American Revolutionary.* Published by Times Books in 1998, the work was based on a series of interviews Williams conducted in 1989 with Marshall, who served as a Supreme Court Justice from 1967 to 1991. Marshall died two years after stepping down from the Court and had led a life at the forefront of the civil rights movement: he fought racial discrimination many times as lead attorney for the National Association for the Advancement of Colored People (NAACP) between 1938 and 1961. His best-known case was the *Brown v. Board of Education of Topeka, Kansas,* in which he was victorious in helping desegregate schools. He went on to serve as federal appeals court judge and solicitor general before being appointed to the Supreme Court by President Lyndon Johnson.

Reviewers of the work praised the personal aspects of *Thurgood Marshall,* but found weakness in its discussion of cases that came before Marshall during his Supreme Court years. In the *National Review,* John O. McGinnis wrote, "Williams's book is most successful in re-creating the vanished world of Marshall's upbringing. Williams draws a picture of a community that maintained the quiet dignity of self-reliance even in the face of economic hardship and social prejudice." Williams, according to Brian Lamb in the Duquesne University *Times,* noted that his interviews with Marshall had taken place "at the end of his career, the end of his life, and it was a rich time and one in which he was willing to talk. It has been a great gift to me."

In *This Far by Faith: Stories from the African-American Religious Experience* (2003), Williams and coauthor Quinton Dixie profile notable African-American religious leaders of various faith traditions, including Sojourner Truth, the former slave who became a preacher, Denmark Vesey, a church leader who was executed in South Carolina in the 1800s for inciting a slave revolt, Noble Drew Ali, who encouraged African Americans to reject the religion of their former masters and reassert of their historical African identity, and Albert Cleage, a preacher from Detroit who combined Christianity with black nationalism and advocated the idea of a black Jesus. In *The Christian Century* Williams explained, "African-American religious experience offers us a strong unifying vision that has been the basis for the freedom struggle, for political organizing, for resilient personal identity and for education. It has given our lives meaning and helped create an American community of greater equality, purpose and opportunity. I hope the book, in a small way, helps the black church claim its proud heritage and put that wealth of experience to good purpose within the black community and the broader society."

Wrote about Civil Rights, Black Leadership

Williams's next book, *My Soul Looks Back in Wonder: Voices of the Civil Rights Experience,* was published in 2004 and comprises eyewitness accounts of significant events in the civil rights movement. The book features the stories of everyday people, including a teenager who was attending services at the Sixteenth Street Baptist Church in Birmingham, Alabama, on the morning in September of 1963 when four of her friends were killed in a bombing. Events include the key moments in school desegregation cases, the Memphis sanitation workers' strike, and the Chicago riot of 1946. These events are connected with the broader struggle for rights by including similar stories from other minority populations, including Asians and Hispanics.

Williams followed with a work that celebrated an institution central to African-American political and social life: historically black colleges and universities. In *I'll Find a Way or Make One: A Tribute to Histori-cally Black Colleges and Universities,* Williams and his coauthor, Dwayne Ashley, offer a history of black higher education in the United States. Included are profiles of more than 100 institutions of higher learning and discussion of some of the schools' most prominent graduates, including Martin Luther King Jr. and Spike Lee (Morehouse College), Oprah Winfrey (Tennessee State University), Langston Hughes (Lincoln University).

In 2006 Williams produced perhaps his most controversial work to date. In *Enough: The Phony Leaders, Dead-end Movements, and Culture of Failure That Are Undermining Black America—and What We Can Do about It,* Williams argued that African-American political and cultural leaders have largely failed to reap meaningful results from the achievements of the civil rights movement. Williams wrote the book in part to support Bill Cosby, whose criticisms of black society drew harsh criticism from many African-American organizations and leaders. For his part, Williams criticizes urban schools, rap music stars, black elected officials and the notion that African Americans cannot achieve success in the United States because they are victims of racism. Williams, like Cosby, believes that education, employment, and postponing children until marriage are all keys to realizing the dreams of the civil rights generation.

Abigail Thernstrom in the *National Review,* called *Enough* "a brave and wonderful book," but others, like Eugene Kane in the *Milwaukee Journal Sentinel* thought the book offered "little new material for the debate about the state of black America, other than Williams' assertion that phony black leaders should be held more accountable." Discussing the book with Eric Deggans in the *St. Petersburg Times,* Williams noted, "The mainstream message, the one that comes from the established national civil rights leadership, says, 'Black people are victims, there's nothing we can do about it. Wait for the next Dr. King, wait for the next government program.' I think there's a lot of lives being lost. I think it's time to try something new."

Selected works

Eyes on the Prize: America's Civil Rights Years, 1954–1965, Viking, 1987.
Thurgood Marshall: American Revolutionary, Times Books, 1998.
(With Quinton Dixie) *This Far by Faith: Stories from the African-American Religious Experience,* William Morrow, 2003.
My Soul Looks Back in Wonder: Voices of the Civil Rights Experience, AARP/Sterling, 2004.
(With Dwayne Ashley) *I'll Find a Way or Make One: A Tribute to Historically Black Colleges,* Amistad/HarperCollins, 2004.
(With John Francis Ficara) *Black Farmers in America,* University Press of Kentucky, 2006.

Enough: The Phony Leaders, Dead-end Movements, and Culture of Failure That Are Undermining Black America—and What We Can Do about It, Crown , 2006.

Sources

Periodicals

America, April 10, 1999, p. 32.
Black Issues in Higher Education, October 21, 2004, p. 40.
Booklist, May 15, 2004, p. 1584; March 15, 2006, p. 14.
Christian Century, May 31, 2003, p. 45.
Christianity Today, June 2003, p. 55.
Duquesne University Times, March 20, 2000.
Library Journal, August 1, 2006, p. 110.
Milwaukee Journal Sentinel, September 3, 2006, p. A2.
National Review, December 7, 1998, p. 62; November 6, 2006, p. 50.
Newsweek, October 28, 1991, p. 33.
New York Amsterdam News, August 30, 2001, p. 35.

Oak Leaves (Poughkeepsie, NY), summer 2006, p. 1.
Publishers Weekly, May 10, 2004, p. 50; October 11, 2004, p. 66; June 19, 2006, p. 56.
St. Petersburg Times (St. Petersburg, FL), February 7, 2007, p. B2.
Time, October 28, 1991, p. 30.
USA Today, May 2007, p. 81.
Zephyr (University of Nevada–Reno), 2001.

Online

Cohen, Jeff, and Norman Solomon, "TV Reality," Tucson Weekly, December 7, 1995, http://www.tucsonweekly.com/tw/12-07-95/curr3.htm (accessed December 31, 2009).
"Juan Williams," NPR, 2007, http://www.npr.org/templates/story/story.php?storyId=1930705 (accessed December 31, 2009).
"*Washington Post* Writer Juan Williams to Discuss Latest Book, *Thurgood Marshall: American Revolutionary,*" Library of Congress, December 10, 1999, http://www.loc.gov/today/pr/1999/99-184.html (accessed December 31, 2009).

—Sandy J. Stiefer and Laurie DiMauro

Harry Wills

1889(?)–1958

Boxer

Wills, Harry, photograph. Topical Press Agency/Getty Images.

Known as the "Black Panther" or "Brown Panther," Harry Wills was considered one of the greatest heavyweight contenders between the years of 1915 and 1927, a period in which he lost only one fight in more than 50 bouts. Standing at six feet, three inches tall, and weighing 215 pounds, Wills was a formidable, intimidating, and powerful opponent who possessed great skill, speed, and cunning. Wills fought many great fights but is best known for the one that eluded him because of his race: For six years he and his manager, Paddy Mullins, tried to get a fight with the reigning heavyweight champion, Jack Dempsey. Wills was also an articulate and dignified man who "reinforced that image by downplaying the significance of race in his quest for the title," wrote Jeffrey T. Sammons in *Beyond the Ring: The Role of Boxing in American Society.* Dempsey was very willing to fight Wills, but because of racial barriers, the event never took place. Dempsey would later write in his autobiography that he thought Wills was unjustly denied a chance at winning the title because of his race.

Harrison Coleman Wills, born the son of Strother G. Wills and Georgie B. Kenner in New Orleans, Louisi-

ana, is generally believed to have been born on May 15, 1889, although some sources cite his birth date as January 20, and the birth year as 1892. The confusion over the birth year came in 1922 when Wills was the leading contender for the heavyweight championship, and, as his manager, Mullins shaved a few years off his age in order to quell any concerns that he was past his prime. Wills grew up near the New Orleans docks where he worked as a stevedore as a teenager. He also spent a lot of time around the New Orleans horseracing tracks and had ambitions of becoming a jockey. These dreams were quashed when he soon grew too tall and developed a powerful physique through his labor.

After his time as a dock hand, Wills went to work on freighters, and it was during these voyages that he was introduced to boxing. At 16 years of age, he began boxing in rundown gymnasiums in the impoverished neighborhoods of New Orleans. His first recorded fight was in 1910, when he knocked out Kid Rayarro in the first round. Wills eventually headed north, where he worked as a stevedore on the Brooklyn and Hoboken docks in between fights. In 1913 and 1914 Wills began to garner attention as he either won or drew matches with some of the better-known fighters of the day, such as Joe Jeannette, Jeff Clark, Sam McVea, and the legendary Sam Langford. In 1916 Wills married Sarah, a model and schoolteacher, whom he met on a church outing his first weekend in New York. Sarah took control of handling the family finances and, after Wills's retirement from boxing in 1932, the couple had enough money to invest in real estate, eventually buying six apartment houses in New York City.

Defeated White Opponents

Wills's fights took him to Cuba, Mexico, Panama, South America, and throughout the United States, where he made sure to barely win against white opponents so as not to enrage the predominantly white spectators. African-American fighter Jack Johnson was the reigning heavyweight champion, and his victory against Jim Jeffries in 1910 had sparked race riots. Between 1911 and 1921, out of 87 recorded fights, Wills won 56 bouts, and 32 of these were knockouts. With only four recorded losses, the remaining fights were either undecided or uncontested. During this period he fought Sam Langford 16 times, with a record of five wins and two losses. Once Johnson was dethroned in 1915 by Jess Willard, a white fighter, the racial lines in boxing were clearly drawn. As a result, all of Wills's fights between 1915 and 1918 were with black opponents, as were the majority of his fights throughout his career.

Wills suffered a temporary setback when he broke his arm in a fight with "Battling" Jim Johnson in 1917, and the match was called after two rounds. He went on to win a rematch and proceeded to win most of his bouts up until 1926. By 1920 Wills was dubbed the "Brown Panther" and was considered to be the unofficial black heavyweight champion. Between 1922 and 1927 Wills was at his peak and was the obvious choice to contest the heavyweight championship against Jack

Dempsey. On July 11, 1922, Wills's and Dempsey's managers signed an agreement, but by October 1, 1923, the fight still had not taken place and Wills was growing despondent.

The previous February, the New York State Boxing Commission signed a declaration preventing Dempsey from fighting Wills in New York. This suited Jack Kearns, Dempsey's manager, and Tex Rickard, the leading boxing promoter, neither of whom were in favor of the match. Particularly satisfied was Rickard, who was responsible for the 1910 Johnson-Jeffries fight and who did not wish to see a repetition of the riots, or the blame that was leveled at him for humiliating the white race. Meanwhile, Dempsey's reputation was taking a bashing, as rumors were circulating that he was afraid to fight Wills. "All this talk around New York that I am afraid to fight Harry Wills is beginning to get on my nerves.... Just let me get in the ring with Harry Wills and I'll win in a round or two," Dempsey is quoted as saying in the January 7, 1924, issue of *Time.*

Failed to Fight Dempsey for Championship

Wills continued to fight other major contenders and, in February of 1924, signed an agreement with Luis Angel Firpo, "the Pampas Bull of the Argentine," to fight for an estimated purse of $250,000. The bout took place on September 11, 1924, in Jersey City before 80,000 fans and was deemed a draw after twelve rounds, but a newspaper decision called it a Wills win. Wills's strong showing against Firpo earned him $150,000 and bolstered the argument that Wills was the one to fight Dempsey. Then, in 1925 Wills knocked out two white contenders, Charley Weinert and Floyd Johnson, prompting the New York State Boxing Commission to do an about face, ordering Dempsey to fight Wills or face being barred from fighting in the state. Kearns would have none of it, and instead he arranged a fight between Dempsey and Gene Tunney.

This prompted Wills to publicly accuse Dempsey of being a coward, not something that would bode well with the heavyweight champion of the world. Finally, in October of 1925, history was made when the promoter, Floyd Fitzsimmons, got Wills and Dempsey to sign a contract in Niles, Michigan, outside of New York and away from Rickard's and Kearn's control. The ten-round, no-decision contest was to take place in September of 1926 and had a forfeit clause providing for $100,000 to Dempsey, and $50,000 to Wills. The match was never fought, and Wills reluctantly took the $50,000. After Tunney defeated Dempsey in a later match-up, Wills's dream of being a contender for the heavyweight championship of the world disintegrated.

These events took their toll on Wills, and he never fought to his same high standard again. On October

12, 1926, he suffered a brutal beating at the hands of the younger, faster Jack Sharkey, and after losing every round, Wills was finally disqualified in the thirteenth round. On July 13, 1927, Wills fought the little known Spanish fighter Paulino Uzcudun but was knocked out in the fourth round. Wills only fought three minor fights after that, with his last on August 4, 1932, when he knocked out the virtually unknown Vinko Jankassa in the first round.

Wills retired from boxing and made his home in one of the apartment houses that he and his wife had purchased. They lived a quiet, unassuming life, although Wills still attracted attention with his annual one-month fasts, in which he drank only water to lose approximately 30 pounds and drain the "impurities" from his body. Wills was elected to the Boxing Hall of Fame in 1970 and the International Boxing Hall of Fame in 1992. The general consensus is that, had the Dempsey-Wills bout taken place, Dempsey would have won, but there is no doubt that Wills was robbed of his opportunity due to racial tensions. Wills was admitted to the hospital on December 8, 1958, suffering from acute appendicitis. He died on December 21, 1958, at the age of 68, from diabetes with his daughter, Gladys, and her husband at his bedside.

Sources

Books

Dempsey, Jack, and Barbara Piattelli, *Dempsey,* Harper & Row, 1977.
Donelson, Thomas, *Boxing in the Shadows,* iUniverse, 2007.
Fleischer, Nat, *Jack Dempsey, The Idol of Fistiana: An Intimate Narrative,* Kessinger Publishing, 2008.
Fleischer, Nat, *Sockers in Sepia: A Continuation of the Drama of the Negro in Pugilistic Competition,* Ring Athletic Library, 1947.
Roberts, James, and Alexander Scott, *The Boxing Register: International Boxing Hall of Fame Official Record Book,* McBooks Press, 2006.
Sammons, Jeffrey T., *Beyond the Ring: The Role of Boxing in American Society,* University of Illinois Press, 1990.

Periodicals

American Heritage, April 1994, p. 132.
Jet, January 27, 1992, p. 48.
New York Daily News, September 12, 2003.
New York Times, July 22, 1922, p. 15.
Time, April 28, 1923, p. 26; September 17, 1923, p. 22; October 1, 1923, p. 23; January 7, 1924, p. 30; February 25, 1924, p. 27; April 7, 1924, p. 26; June 16, 1924, p. 29; October 12, 1925, p. 34; July 25. 1927, p. 35.

Online

Davis, Luckett V., "Harry Wills," African American National Biography, January 1, 2008, http://www.mywire.com/a/African-American-National-Biography/Wills-Harry/9465258/ (accessed December 22, 2009).
"Harry Wills," International Boxing Hall of Fame, http://www.ibhof.com/pages/about/inductees/oldtimer/wills.html (accessed December 22, 2009).
Matsune, Jon, "Boxing Great Harry Wills," Suite101.com, September 9, 2009, http://boxing.suite101.com/article.cfm/boxing_great_harry_wills#ixzz0YMn2eHLi (accessed December 22, 2009).

—Marie O'Sullivan

Cumulative Nationality Index

Volume numbers appear in **bold**

American

Aaliyah **30**
Aaron, Hank **5**
Abbott, Robert Sengstacke **27**
Abdul-Jabbar, Kareem **8**
Abdur-Rahim, Shareef **28**
Abele, Julian **55**
Abernathy, Ralph David **1**
Aberra, Amsale **67**
Abu-Jamal, Mumia **15**
Ace, Johnny **36**
Adams, Eula L. **39**
Adams, Floyd, Jr. **12**
Adams, Jenoyne **60**
Adams, Johnny **39**
Adams, Leslie **39**
Adams, Oleta **18**
Adams, Osceola Macarthy **31**
Adams, Sheila J. **25**
Adams, Yolanda **17, 67**
Adams-Campbell, Lucille L. **60**
Adams Earley, Charity **13, 34**
Adams-Ender, Clara **40**
Adderley, Julian "Cannonball" **30**
Adderley, Nat **29**
Adebimpe, Tunde **75**
Adkins, Rod **41**
Adkins, Rutherford H. **21**
Adu, Freddy **67**
Agyeman, Jaramogi Abebe **10, 63**
Ailey, Alvin **8**
Akil, Mara Brock **60**
Akon **68**
Al-Amin, Jamil Abdullah **6**
Albright, Gerald **23**
Alcorn, George Edward, Jr. **59**
Alert, Kool DJ Red **33**
Alexander, Archie Alphonso **14**
Alexander, Clifford **26**
Alexander, Elizabeth **75**
Alexander, Joyce London **18**
Alexander, Khandi **43**
Alexander, Margaret Walker **22**
Alexander, Sadie Tanner Mossell **22**
Alexander, Shaun **58**
Ali, Hana Yasmeen **52**
Ali, Laila **27, 63**
Ali, Muhammad **2, 16, 52**
Ali, Rashied **79**
Ali, Tatyana **73**
Allain, Stephanie **49**
Allen, Byron **3, 24**
Allen, Claude **68**

Allen, Debbie **13, 42**
Allen, Ethel D. **13**
Allen, Eugene **79**
Allen, Marcus **20**
Allen, Robert L. **38**
Allen, Samuel W. **38**
Allen, Tina **22, 75**
Allen, Will **74**
Allen-Buillard, Melba **55**
Alston, Charles **33**
Amaker, Norman **63**
Amaker, Tommy **62**
Amaki, Amalia **76**
Amerie **52**
Ames, Wilmer **27**
Amos, Emma **63**
Amos, John **8, 62**
Amos, Wally **9**
Anderson, Anthony **51, 77**
Anderson, Carl **48**
Anderson, Charles Edward **37**
Anderson, Eddie "Rochester" **30**
Anderson, Elmer **25**
Anderson, Jamal **22**
Anderson, Lauren **72**
Anderson, Marian **2, 33**
Anderson, Michael P. **40**
Anderson, Mike **63**
Anderson, Norman B. **45**
Anderson, William G(ilchrist), D.O. **57**
Andrews, Benny **22, 59**
Andrews, Bert **13**
Andrews, Raymond **4**
Andrews, Tina **74**
Angelou, Maya **1, 15**
Ansa, Tina McElroy **14**
Anthony, Carmelo **46**
Anthony, Wendell **25**
Appiah, Kwame Anthony **67**
Archer, Dennis **7, 36**
Archer, Lee, Jr. **79**
Archie-Hudson, Marguerite **44**
Ardoin, Alphonse **65**
Arkadie, Kevin **17**
Armstrong, Louis **2**
Armstrong, Robb **15**
Armstrong, Vanessa Bell **24**
Arnez J **53**
Arnold, Tichina **63**
Arnwine, Barbara **28**
Arrington, Richard **24**
Arroyo, Martina **30**
Artest, Ron **52**

Asante, Molefi Kete **3**
Ashanti **37**
Ashe, Arthur **1, 18**
Ashford, Calvin, Jr. **74**
Ashford, Emmett **22**
Ashford, Evelyn **63**
Ashford, Nickolas **21**
Ashley-Ward, Amelia **23**
Asim, Jabari **71**
Atkins, Cholly **40**
Atkins, Erica **34**
Atkins, Juan **50**
Atkins, Russell **45**
Atkins, Tina **34**
Aubert, Alvin **41**
Auguste, Donna **29**
Austin, Gloria **63**
Austin, Jim **63**
Austin, Junius C. **44**
Austin, Lovie **40**
Austin, Patti **24**
Autrey, Wesley **68**
Avant, Clarence **19**
Avery, Byllye Y. **66**
Ayers, Roy **16**
Babatunde, Obba **35**
Bacon-Bercey, June **38**
Badu, Erykah **22**
Bahati, Wambui **60**
Bailey, Buster **38**
Bailey, Chauncey **68**
Bailey, Clyde **45**
Bailey, DeFord **33**
Bailey, Philip **63**
Bailey, Radcliffe **19**
Bailey, Xenobia **11**
Baines, Harold **32**
Baiocchi, Regina Harris **41**
Baisden, Michael **25, 66**
Baker, Anita **21, 48**
Baker, Augusta **38**
Baker, Dusty **8, 43, 72**
Baker, Ella **5**
Baker, Gwendolyn Calvert **9**
Baker, Houston A., Jr. **6**
Baker, Josephine **3**
Baker, LaVern **26**
Baker, Matt **76**
Baker, Maxine B. **28**
Baker, Thurbert **22**
Baker, Vernon Joseph **65**
Baldwin, Cynthia A. **74**
Baldwin, James **1**
Ballance, Frank W. **41**

Ballard, Allen Butler, Jr. **40**
Ballard, Hank **41**
Baltimore, Richard Lewis, III **71**
Bambaataa, Afrika **34**
Bambara, Toni Cade **10**
Bandele, Asha **36**
Banks, Ernie **33**
Banks, Jeffrey **17**
Banks, Michelle **59**
Banks, Paula A. **68**
Banks, Tyra **11, 50**
Banks, William **11**
Banner, David **55**
Baquet, Dean **63**
Baraka, Amiri **1, 38**
Barbee, Lloyd Augustus **71**
Barber, Ronde **41**
Barber, Tiki **57**
Barboza, Anthony **10**
Barclay, Paris **37**
Barden, Don H. **9, 20**
Barker, Danny **32**
Barkley, Charles **5, 66**
Barlow, Roosevelt **49**
Barnes, Ernie **16, 78**
Barnes, Melody **75**
Barnes, Roosevelt "Booba" **33**
Barnes, Steven **54**
Barnett, Amy Du Bois **46**
Barnett, Etta Moten **56**
Barnett, Marguerite **46**
Barney, Lem **26**
Barnhill, David **30**
Barrax, Gerald William **45**
Barrett, Andrew C. **12**
Barrett, Jacquelyn **28**
Barrino, Fantasia **53**
Barry, Marion S(hepilov, Jr.) **7, 44**
Barthé, Earl **78**
Barthe, Richmond **15**
Basie, Count **23**
Basquiat, Jean-Michel **5**
Bass, Charlotta Spears **40**
Bass, Karen **70**
Bassett, Angela **6, 23, 62**
Baszile, Jennifer **79**
Bates, Daisy **13**
Bates, Karen Grigsby **40**
Bates, Peg Leg **14**
Bath, Patricia E. **37**
Batiste, Alvin **66**
Battle, Kathleen **70**
Baugh, David **23**
Baylor, Don **6**

Cumulative Occupation Index

Volume numbers appear in **bold**

Art and design

Abele, Julian **55**
Aberra, Amsale **67**
Adjaye, David **38, 78**
Allen, Tina **22, 75**
Alston, Charles **33**
Amaki, Amalia **76**
Amos, Emma **63**
Anderson, Ho Che **54**
Andrews, Benny **22, 59**
Andrews, Bert **13**
Armstrong, Robb **15**
Ashford, Calvin, Jr. **74**
Bailey, Preston **64**
Bailey, Radcliffe **19**
Bailey, Xenobia **11**
Baker, Matt **76**
Barboza, Anthony **10**
Barnes, Ernie **16, 78**
Barthé, Earl **78**
Barthe, Richmond **15**
Basquiat, Jean-Michel **5**
Bearden, Romare **2, 50**
Beasley, Phoebe **34**
Bell, Darrin **77**
Benberry, Cuesta **65**
Benjamin, Tritobia Hayes **53**
Biggers, John **20, 33**
Biggers, Sanford **62**
Blackburn, Robert **28**
Bond, J. Max, Jr. **76**
Brandon, Barbara **3**
Brown, Donald **19**
Brown, Robert **65**
Burke, Selma **16**
Burroughs, Margaret Taylor **9**
Camp, Kimberly **19**
Campbell, E. Simms **13**
Campbell, Mary Schmidt **43**
Catlett, Elizabeth **2**
Chase-Riboud, Barbara **20, 46**
Colescott, Robert **69**
Collins, Paul **61**
Cortor, Eldzier **42**
Cowans, Adger W. **20**
Cox, Renée **67**
Crichlow, Ernest **75**
Crite, Alan Rohan **29**
De Veaux, Alexis **44**
DeCarava, Roy **42**
Delaney, Beauford **19**
Delaney, Joseph **30**
Delsarte, Louis **34**

Donaldson, Jeff **46**
Douglas, Aaron **7**
Driskell, David C. **7**
du Cille, Michel **74**
Dwight, Edward **65**
Edwards, Melvin **22**
El Wilson, Barbara **35**
Ewing, Patrick **17, 73**
Fax, Elton **48**
Feelings, Tom **11, 47**
Fine, Sam **60**
Freeman, Leonard **27**
Fuller, Meta Vaux Warrick **27**
Gantt, Harvey **1**
Garvin, Gerry **78**
Gilles, Ralph **61**
Gilliam, Sam **16**
Golden, Thelma **10, 55**
Goodnight, Paul **32**
Green, Jonathan **54**
Guyton, Tyree **9**
Hammons, David **69**
Harkless, Necia Desiree **19**
Harrington, Oliver W. **9**
Harrison, Charles **72**
Hathaway, Isaac Scott **33**
Hayden, Palmer **13**
Hayes, Cecil N. **46**
Holder, Geoffrey **78**
Honeywood, Varnette P. **54**
Hope, John **8**
Hudson, Cheryl **15**
Hudson, Wade **15**
Hunt, Richard **6**
Hunter, Clementine **45**
Hutson, Jean Blackwell **16**
Jackson, Earl **31**
Jackson, Mary **73**
Jackson, Vera **40**
John, Daymond **23**
Johnson, Jeh Vincent **44**
Johnson, William Henry **3**
Jones, Lois Mailou **13**
Jones, Paul R. **76**
King, Robert Arthur **58**
Kitt, Sandra **23**
Knight, Gwendolyn **63**
Knox, Simmie **49**
Lawrence, Jacob **4, 28**
Lee, Annie Frances **22**
Lee-Smith, Hughie **5, 22**
Lewis, Edmonia **10**
Lewis, Norman **39**
Lewis, Samella **25**

Lovell, Whitfield **74**
Loving, Alvin, Jr., **35, 53**
Manley, Edna **26**
Marshall, Kerry James **59**
Mayhew, Richard **39**
McCullough, Geraldine **58, 79**
McDuffie, Dwayne **62**
McGee, Charles **10**
McGruder, Aaron **28, 56**
Mitchell, Corinne **8**
Moody, Ronald **30**
Morrison, Keith **13**
Motley, Archibald, Jr. **30**
Moutoussamy-Ashe, Jeanne **7**
Mutu, Wangechi **44**
Myles, Kim **69**
Ndiaye, Iba **74**
Neals, Otto **73**
N'Namdi, George R. **17**
Nugent, Richard Bruce **39**
O'Grady, Lorraine **73**
Olden, Georg(e) **44**
Ormes, Jackie **73**
Ouattara **43**
Perkins, Marion **38**
Pierre, Andre **17**
Pindell, Howardena **55**
Pinder, Jefferson **77**
Pinderhughes, John **47**
Pinkney, Jerry **15**
Piper, Adrian **71**
Pippin, Horace **9**
Pope.L, William **72**
Porter, James A. **11**
Prophet, Nancy Elizabeth **42**
Puryear, Martin **42**
Reid, Senghor **55**
Ringgold, Faith **4**
Roble, Abdi **71**
Ruley, Ellis **38**
Saar, Alison **16**
Saar, Betye **80**
Saint James, Synthia **12**
Sallee, Charles **38**
Sanders, Joseph R., Jr. **11**
Savage, Augusta **12**
Scott, John T. **65**
Sebree, Charles **40**
Serrano, Andres **3**
Shabazz, Attallah **6**
Shonibare, Yinka **58**
Simmons, Gary **58**
Simpson, Lorna **4, 36**
Sims, Lowery Stokes **27**

Sklarek, Norma Merrick **25**
Sleet, Moneta, Jr. **5**
Smith, Bruce W. **53**
Smith, Marvin **46**
Smith, Morgan **46**
Smith, Vincent D. **48**
Steave-Dickerson, Kia **57**
Stout, Renee **63**
Sudduth, Jimmy Lee **65**
Tanksley, Ann **37**
Tanner, Henry Ossawa **1**
Taylor, Robert Robinson **80**
Thomas, Alma **14**
Thrash, Dox **35**
Tolliver, Mose **60**
Tolliver, William **9**
Tooks, Lance **62**
VanDerZee, James **6**
Verna, Gelsy **70**
Wagner, Albert **78**
Wainwright, Joscelyn **46**
Walker, A'lelia **14**
Walker, Kara **16, 80**
Washington, Alonzo **29**
Washington, James, Jr. **38**
Weems, Carrie Mae **63**
Wells, James Lesesne **10**
White, Charles **39**
White, Dondi **34**
White, John H. **27**
Wiley, Kehinde **62**
Williams, Billy Dee **8**
Williams, Clarence **70**
Williams, O. S. **13**
Williams, Paul R. **9**
Williams, William T. **11**
Wilson, Ellis **39**
Withers, Ernest C. **68**
Woodruff, Hale **9**

Business

Abbott, Robert Sengstacke **27**
Abdul-Jabbar, Kareem **8**
Abiola, Moshood **70**
Adams, Eula L. **39**
Adams, Jenoyne **60**
Adkins, Rod **41**
Ailey, Alvin **8**
Akil, Mara Brock **60**
Al-Amin, Jamil Abdullah **6**
Alexander, Archie Alphonso **14**
Allen, Byron **24**
Allen-Buillard, Melba **55**
Ames, Wilmer **27**

Touré, Faya Ora Rose **56**
Tribble, Israel, Jr. **8**
Trotter, Donne E. **28**
Trotter, Monroe **9**
Tsvangirai, Morgan **26, 72**
Tubman, Harriet **9**
Tucker, C. Delores **12, 56**
Tucker, Cynthia **15, 61**
Tucker, Rosina **14**
Tutu, Desmond **6**
Tyree, Omar Rashad **21**
Van Peebles, Melvin **7**
Vanzant, Iyanla **17, 47**
Vaughn, Viola **70**
Vega, Marta Moreno **61**
Velez-Rodriguez, Argelia **56**
Vincent, Marjorie Judith **2**
Waddles, Charleszetta "Mother" **10, 49**
Walcott, Derek **5**
Walker, A'lelia **14**
Walker, Alice **1, 43**
Walker, Bernita Ruth **53**
Wallace, Joaquin **49**
Wallace, Michele Faith **13**
Wallace, Phyllis A. **9**
Wallace, William **75**
Washington, Booker T. **4**
Washington, Ebonya **79**
Washington, Fredi **10**
Washington, Harold **6**
Waters, Maxine **3, 67**
Wattleton, Faye **9**
Wells, Henrietta Bell **69**
Wells, James Lesesne **10**
Wells-Barnett, Ida B. **8**
Welsing, Frances Cress **5**
West, Cornel **5, 33, 80**
White, Michael R. **5**
White, Reggie **6, 50**
White, Walter F. **4**
White, Willye **67**
White-Hammond, Gloria **61**
Wideman, John Edgar **5**
Wilkins, Roger **2**
Wilkins, Roy **4**
Williams, Armstrong **29**
Williams, Evelyn **10**
Williams, Fannie Barrier **27**
Williams, George Washington **18**
Williams, Hosea Lorenzo **15, 31**
Williams, Maggie **7, 71**
Williams, Montel **4, 57**
Williams, Patricia **11, 54**
Williams, Robert F. **11**
Williams, Stanley "Tookie" **29, 57**
Williams, Walter E. **4**
Williams, Willie L. **4**
Wilson, August **7, 33, 55**
Wilson, Margaret Bush **79**
Wilson, Phill **9**
Wilson, Sunnie **7, 55**
Wilson, William Julius **22**
Withers, Ernest C. **68**
Wiwa, Ken **67**
Wolfe, George C. **6, 43**
Woodson, Robert L. **10**
Worrill, Conrad **12**
Wright, Charles H. **35**
Wright, Louis Tompkins **4**
Wright, Nathan, Jr. **56**
Wright, Richard **5**
Wyatt, Addie L. **56**

X, Malcolm **1**
Xuma, Madie Hall **59**
Yancy, Dorothy Cowser **42**
Yarbrough, Camille **40**
Yeboah, Emmanuel Ofosu **53**
Yoba, Malik **11**
Young, Andrew **3, 48**
Young, Jean Childs **14**
Young, Whitney M., Jr. **4**
Youngblood, Johnny Ray **8**
Zulu, Princess Kasune **54**

Sports
Aaron, Hank **5**
Abdul-Jabbar, Kareem **8**
Abdur-Rahim, Shareef **28**
Adams, Paul **50**
Adu, Freddy **67**
Alexander, Shaun **58**
Ali, Laila **27, 63**
Ali, Muhammad **2, 16, 52**
Allen, Marcus **20**
Amaker, Tommy **62**
Amos, John **8, 62**
Anderson, Elmer **25**
Anderson, Jamal **22**
Anderson, Mike **63**
Anderson, Viv **58**
Anthony, Carmelo **46**
Artest, Ron **52**
Ashe, Arthur **1, 18**
Ashford, Emmett **22**
Ashford, Evelyn **63**
Ashley, Maurice **15, 47**
Baines, Harold **32**
Baker, Dusty **8, 43, 72**
Banks, Ernie **33**
Barber, Ronde **41**
Barber, Tiki **57**
Barkley, Charles **5, 66**
Barnes, Ernie **16, 78**
Barnes, John **53**
Barnes, Steven **54**
Barney, Lem **26**
Barnhill, David **30**
Baylor, Don **6**
Beamon, Bob **30**
Beasley, Jamar **29**
Bekele, Kenenisa **75**
Bell, James "Cool Papa" **36**
Belle, Albert **10**
Bettis, Jerome **64**
Bickerstaff, Bernie **21**
Bing, Dave **3, 59, 78**
Bivins, Michael **72**
Black, Joe **75**
Blair, Paul **36**
Blake, James **43**
Blanks, Billy **22**
Blanton, Dain **29**
Bogues, Tyrone "Muggsy" **56**
Bol, Manute **1**
Bolt, Usain **73**
Bolton-Holifield, Ruthie **28**
Bonaly, Surya **7**
Bonds, Barry **6, 34, 63**
Bonds, Bobby **43**
Bowe, Riddick **6**
Brand, Elton **31**
Brandon, Terrell **16**
Branham, George, III **50**
Brashear, Donald **39**
Brathwaite, Fred **35**

Briscoe, Marlin **37**
Brock, Lou **18**
Brooks, Aaron **33**
Brooks, Derrick **43**
Brown, James **22**
Brown, Jim **11**
Brown, Mike **77**
Brown, Sean **52**
Brown, Willard **36**
Bruce, Isaac **26**
Bryant, Kobe **15, 31, 71**
Buchanan, Ray **32**
Bush, Reggie **59**
Butler, Leroy, III **17**
Bynoe, Peter C.B. **40**
Campanella, Roy **25**
Carew, Rod **20**
Carnegie, Herbert **25**
Carter, Anson **24**
Carter, Butch **27**
Carter, Cris **21**
Carter, Joe **30**
Carter, Kenneth **53**
Carter, Rubin **26**
Carter, Vince **26**
Cash, Swin **59**
Catchings, Tamika **43**
Chamberlain, Wilt **18, 47**
Chaney, John **67**
Charleston, Oscar **39**
Cheeks, Maurice **47**
Cherry, Deron **40**
Cheruiyot, Robert **69**
Christie, Linford **8**
Claiborne, Loretta **34**
Clay, Bryan **57, 74**
Clemons, Michael "Pinball" **64**
Clendenon, Donn **26, 56**
Clifton, Nathaniel "Sweetwater" **47**
Coachman, Alice **18**
Coleman, Leonard S., Jr. **12**
Cooper, Andy "Lefty" **63**
Cooper, Charles "Chuck" **47**
Cooper, Cynthia **17**
Cooper, Michael **31**
Copeland, Michael **47**
Corley, Tony **62**
Cottrell, Comer **11**
Crennel, Romeo **54**
Crooks, Garth **53**
Croom, Sylvester **50**
Culpepper, Daunte **32**
Cunningham, Randall **23**
Dandridge, Ray **36**
Dantley, Adrian **72**
Davis, Ernie **48**
Davis, Mike **41**
Davis, Milt **74**
Davis, Piper **19**
Davis, Shani **58**
Davis, Terrell **20**
Dawes, Dominique **11**
Day, Leon **39**
DeFrantz, Anita **37**
DeGale, James **74**
Delaney, Joe **76**
Devers, Gail **7**
Dibaba, Tirunesh **73**
Dickerson, Eric **27**
Dixon, George **52**
Doby, Lawrence Eugene, Sr. **16, 41**
Doig, Jason **45**
Dorrell, Karl **52**

dos Santos, Manuel Francisco **65**
Drew, Charles Richard **7**
Drexler, Clyde **4, 61**
Drogba, Didier **78**
Dumars, Joe **16, 65**
Duncan, Tim **20**
Dungy, Tony **17, 42, 59**
Dunn, Jerry **27**
Durant, Kevin **76**
Dye, Jermaine **58**
Edwards, Harry **2**
Edwards, Herman **51**
Edwards, Teresa **14**
Elder, Lee **6**
Ellerbe, Brian **22**
Elliott, Sean **26**
Ellis, Dock **78**
Ellis, Jimmy **44**
Ervin, Anthony **66**
Erving, Julius **18, 47**
Eto'o, Samuel **73**
Ewing, Patrick **17, 73**
Farr, Mel **24**
Faulk, Marshall **35**
Felix, Allyson **48**
Fielder, Cecil **2**
Fielder, Prince Semien **68**
Flood, Curt **10**
Flowers, Vonetta **35**
Ford, Cheryl **45**
Foreman, George **1, 15**
Forrest, Vernon **40, 79**
Foster, Andrew **79**
Fowler, Reggie **51**
Fox, Rick **27**
Frazier, Joe **19**
Frazier-Lyde, Jacqui **31**
Freeman, Cathy **29**
Freeman, Marianna **23**
Fuhr, Grant **1, 49**
Fuller, Vivian **33**
Futch, Eddie **33**
Gaines, Clarence E., Sr. **55**
Gaither, Alonzo Smith (Jake) **14**
Garnett, Kevin **14, 70**
Garrison, Zina **2**
Gaston, Cito **71**
Gebrselassie, Haile **70**
Gentry, Alvin **23**
George, Eddie **80**
Gervin, George **80**
Gibson, Althea **8, 43**
Gibson, Bob **33**
Gibson, Josh **22**
Gibson, Truman K., Jr. **60**
Gilliam, Frank **23**
Gilliam, Joe **31**
Gooden, Dwight **20**
Gorden, W. C. **71**
Goss, Tom **23**
Gourdine, Meredith **33**
Gourdine, Simon **11**
Granderson, Curtis **66**
Grand-Pierre, Jean-Luc **46**
Gray, Yeshimbra "Shimmy" **55**
Green, A. C. **32**
Green, Darrell **39, 74**
Green, Dennis **5, 45**
Greene, Joe **10**
Greene, Maurice **27, 77**
Gregg, Eric **16**
Gregory, Ann **63**
Grier, Mike **43**

Cumulative Subject Index

Volume numbers appear in **bold**

Actuarial science

Hill, Jesse, Jr. 13

ACT UP

See AIDS Coalition to Unleash Power

ADC

See Agricultural Development Council

Addiction Research and Treatment Corporation

Cooper, Andrew W. 36

Thomas, Arthur Ray 52

American Choral Directors Association
Adams, Leslie 39

American Civil Liberties Union (ACLU)
Baugh, David 23
Murphy, Laura M. 43
Murray, Pauli 38
Norton, Eleanor Holmes 7
Pincham, R. Eugene, Sr. 69

American Communist Party
Patterson, Louise 25

American Community Housing Associates, Inc.
Lane, Vincent 5

American Composers Alliance
Tillis, Frederick 40

American Counseling Association
Mitchell, Sharon 36

American Economic Association
Loury Glenn 36

American Enterprise Institute
Woodson, Robert L. 10

American Express Company
Adams, Eula L. 39
Chenault, Kenneth I. 4, 36

American Federation of Labor and Congress of Industrial Organizations (AFL-CIO)
Fletcher, Bill, Jr. 41
Holt Baker, Arlene 73
Randolph, A. Philip 3

American Guild of Organists
Adams, Leslie 39

American Heart Association (AHA)
Cooper, Edward S. 6
Grant, Augustus O. 71
Richardson, Donna 39

American Idol
Hudson, Jennifer 63
Jackson, Randy 40

American Institute for the Prevention of Blindness
Bath, Patricia E. 37

American Library Association (ALA)
Franklin, Hardy R. 9
Hayden, Carla D. 47
Jones, Clara Stanton 51
Josey, E. J. 10
McFadden, Bernice L. 39
Rollins, Charlamae Hill 27
Wedgeworth, Robert W. 42

American Management Association
Cooper, Andrew W. 36

American Negro Academy
Grimké, Archibald H. 9
Schomburg, Arthur Alfonso 9

American Negro Theater
Martin, Helen 31

American Nuclear Society
Wilkens, J. Ernest, Jr. 43

American Nurses Association (ANA)
Kennedy, Adrienne 11
Staupers, Mabel K. 7

American Postal Workers Union
Burrus, William Henry "Bill" 45

American Psychological Association
Anderson, Norman B. 45
Mitchell, Sharon 36

American Red Cross
Bullock, Steve 22
Drew, Charles Richard 7

American Society of Magazine Editors
Curry, George E. 23

American Tennis Association
Gibson, Althea 8, 43
Peters, Margaret and Matilda 43

American Writers Association
Schuyler, George Samuel 40

America's Promise Alliance
Powell, Colin 1, 28, 75

Amistad Freedom Schooner
Pinckney, Bill 42

Amos Fraser Bernard Consultants
Amos, Valerie 41

Amsterdam News
Cooper, Andrew W. 36
Holt, Nora 38
Tatum, Elinor R. 78
Tatum, Wilbert 76

ANA
See American Nurses Association

ANC
See African National Congress

Anglican church hierarchy
Akinola, Peter Jasper 65
Tutu, Desmond Mpilo 6, 44

Angolan government
dos Santos, José Eduardo 43
Neto, António Agostinho 43

Anheuser-Busch distribution
Cherry, Deron 40

Anthropology
Asante, Molefi Kete 3
Bunche, Ralph J. 5
Cole, Johnnetta B. 5, 43
Davis, Allison 12
Diop, Cheikh Anta 4
Dunham, Katherine 4, 59

Hansberry, William Leo 11
Morrison, Toni 2, 15
Primus, Pearl 6
Robeson, Eslanda Goode 13
Rodriguez, Cheryl 64

Antoinette Perry awards
See Tony awards

APA
See American Psychological Association

Apartheid
Abrahams, Peter 39
Ashe, Arthur 18
Berry, Mary Frances 7
Biko, Steven 4
Brutus, Dennis 38
Butler, Jonathan 28
Howard, M. William, Jr. 26
Ka Dinizulu, Mcwayizeni 29
Kuzwayo, Ellen 68
LaGuma, Alex 30
Luthuli, Albert 13
Mahlasela, Vusi 65
Makeba, Miriam 2, 50, 74
Mandela, Nelson 1, 14, 77
Mandela, Winnie 2, 35
Masekela, Hugh 1
Mathabane, Mark 5
Mbeki, Thabo 14, 73
Mbuende, Kaire 12
McDougall, Gay J. 11, 43
Mhlaba, Raymond 55
Mphalele, Es'kia 40
Nkoli, Simon 60
Ntshona, Winston 52
Nyanda, Siphiwe 21
Nzo, Alfred 15
Plaatje, Sol. T. 80
Ramaphosa, Cyril 3
Ramphele, Maphela 29
Robinson, Randall 7, 46
Sisulu, Albertina 57
Sisulu, Walter 47
Sullivan, Leon H. 13, 30
Tutu, Desmond Mpilo 6, 44

Apollo Theater
Sims, Howard 48
Sutton, Percy E. 42

Apollo
Williams, O. S. 13

APWU
See American Postal Workers Union

Arab-Israeli conflict
Bunche, Ralph J. 5

Architecture
Abele, Julian 55
Adjaye, David 38, 78
Bond, J. Max, Jr. 76
Gantt, Harvey 1
Johnson, Jeh Vincent 44
King, Robert Arthur 58
McKissack, Leatrice 80
Sklarek, Norma Merrick 25
Taylor, Robert Robinson 80

Williams, Paul R. 9

Argonne National Laboratory
Massey, Walter E. 5, 45
Quarterman, Lloyd Albert 4

Ariel Capital Management
Hobson, Mellody 40
Rogers, John W., Jr. 5, 52

Arista Records
Lattimore, Kenny 35
Reid, Antonio "L.A." 28

Arkansas government
Elders, Joycelyn 6

Armed Forces Communications and Electronics Associations (AFCEA)
Gravely, Samuel L., Jr. 5, 49

Art history
Amaki, Amalia 76
Benjamin, Tritobia Hayes 53
Campbell, Mary Schmidt 43

Arthur Andersen
Scott, Milton 51

Asheville (NC) city government
Bellamy, Terry 58

Association for Constitutional Democracy in Liberia (ACDL)
Sawyer, Amos 2

Association of Tennis Professionals (ATP)
Blake, James 43

Astronauts
Anderson, Michael P. 40
Bluford, Guy 2, 35
Bolden, Charles Frank, Jr. 7, 78
Gregory, Frederick 8, 51
Jemison, Mae C. 1, 35
Lawrence, Robert H., Jr. 16
McNair, Ronald 3, 58
Wilson, Stephanie 72

Astronomy
Pitts, Derrick 77

Astrophysics
Alcorn, George Edward, Jr. 59
Carruthers, George R. 40

Atco-EastWest
Rhone, Sylvia 2

ATD Publishing
Tyson, Asha 39

Athletic administration
Goss, Tom 23
Littlepage, Craig 35

Atlanta Association of Black Journalists
Pressley, Condace L. 41

Atlanta Baptist College
See Morehouse College

Atlanta Board of Education
Mays, Benjamin E. 7

Atlanta Braves baseball team
Aaron, Hank 5
Baker, Dusty 8, 43, 72

Payne, Ethel L. 28

Chicago Defender Charities
Joyner, Marjorie Stewart 26

Chicago Eight
Seale, Bobby 3

Chicago Housing Authority (CHA)
Lane, Vincent 5

Chicago Library Board
Williams, Fannie Barrier 27

Chicago Negro Chamber of Commerce
Fuller, S. B. 13

Chicago Police Department
Hillard, Terry 25
Holton, Hugh, Jr. 39

Chicago Reporter
Washington, Laura S. 18

Chicago Tribune
Page, Clarence 4

Chicago White Sox baseball team
Baines, Harold 32
Bonds, Bobby 43
Doby, Lawrence Eugene, Sr. 16, 41
Johnson, Clifford "Connie" 52
Thomas, Frank 12, 51
Williams, Ken 68

Chicago Women's Club
Williams, Fannie Barrier 27

Child Care Trust
Obasanjo, Stella 32, 56

Child Welfare Administration
Little, Robert L. 2

Children's Defense Fund (CDF)
Edelman, Marian Wright 5, 42
Williams, Maggie 7, 71

Children's literature
Asim, Jabari 71
Berry, James 41
Bryan, Ashley F. 41
Common 31, 63
De Veaux, Alexis 44
Feelings, Muriel 44
Graham, Lorenz 48
Greenfield, Eloise 9
Johnson, Angela 52
Mollel, Tololwa 38
Myers, Walter Dean 8, 20
Okara, Gabriel 37
Palmer, Everard 37
Yarbrough, Camille 40

Chi-Lites
Record, Eugene 60

Chiropractics
Ford, Clyde W. 40
Reese, Milous J., Jr. 51
Westbrooks, Bobby 51

Chisholm-Mingo Group, Inc.
Chisholm, Samuel J. 32
Mingo, Frank 32

Choreography
Acogny, Germaine 55
Ailey, Alvin 8
Alexander, Khandi 43
Allen, Debbie 13, 42
Atkins, Cholly 40
Babatunde, Obba 35
Beatty, Talley 35
Brooks, Avery 9
Byrd, Donald 10
Campbell-Martin, Tisha 8, 42
Collins, Janet 33, 64
Davis, Chuck 33
de Lavallade, Carmen 78
de Passe, Suzanne 25
De Shields, André 72
Dove, Ulysses 5
Dunham, Katherine 4, 59
Ellington, Mercedes 34
Fagan, Garth 18
Faison, George 16
Glover, Savion 14
Hall, Arthur 39
Henson, Darrin 33
Jamison, Judith 7, 67
Johnson, Virginia 9
Jones, Bill T. 1, 46, 80
King, Alonzo 38
LeTang, Henry 66
Manning, Frankie 78
Miller, Bebe 3
Mitchell, Arthur 2, 47
Nicholas, Fayard 20, 57
Nicholas, Harold 20
Pomare, Eleo 72
Primus, Pearl 6
Rhoden, Dwight 40
Richardson, Desmond 39
Robinson, Cleo Parker 38
Robinson, Fatima 34
Rodgers, Rod 36
Spears, Warren 52
Tyson, Andre 40
Zollar, Jawole 28

Christian Financial Ministries, Inc.
Ross, Charles 27

Christian Science Monitor
Khanga, Yelena 6

Chrysler Corporation
Colbert, Virgis William 17
Farmer, Forest 1
Gilles, Ralph 61
Richie, Leroy C. 18

Church of God in Christ
Franklin, Robert M. 13
Hayes, James C. 10
Patterson, Gilbert Earl 41

CIAA
See Central Intercollegiate Athletic Association

Cincinnati city government
Berry, Theodore M. 31
Mallory, Mark 62

Cincinnati Reds baseball team
Baker, Dusty 8, 43, 72
Blair, Paul 36
Larkin, Barry 24
Morgan, Joe Leonard 9
Reese, Pokey 28
Robinson, Frank 9
Sanders, Deion 4, 31

Cinematography
Dickerson, Ernest 6, 17

Citadel Press
Achebe, Chinua 6

Citigroup
Gaines, Brenda 41
Jones, Thomas W. 41
McGuire, Raymond J. 57

Citizens Federal Savings and Loan Association
Gaston, Arthur George 3, 38, 59
Willie, Louis, Jr. 68

Citizens for Affirmative Action's Preservation
Dillard, Godfrey J. 45

City Capital Corporation
Taylor, Ephren W., II 61

City government--U.S.
Archer, Dennis 7, 36
Barden, Don H. 9, 20
Barry, Marion S. 7, 44
Berry, Theodore M. 31
Bosley, Freeman, Jr. 7
Bradley, Jennette B. 40
Bradley, Thomas 2, 20
Brown, Lee P. 1, 24
Burris, Chuck 21
Caesar, Shirley 19
Clayton, Constance 1
Cleaver, Emanuel 4, 45, 68
Coleman, Michael 28, 79
Craig-Jones, Ellen Walker 44
Evers, Myrlie 8
Fauntroy, Walter E. 11
Fields, C. Virginia 25
Ford, Jack 39
Ford, Johnny 70
Gibson, Kenneth Allen 6
Goode, W. Wilson 4
Harmon, Clarence 26
Hayes, James C. 10
Jackson, Maynard 2, 41
James, Sharpe 23, 69
Jarvis, Charlene Drew 21
Johnson, Eddie Bernice 8
Johnson, Harvey, Jr. 24
Kirk, Ron 11, 75
Lowery, Myron 80
Mallett, Conrad, Jr. 16
McPhail, Sharon 2
Metcalfe, Ralph 26
Millender-McDonald, Juanita 21, 61
Morial, Ernest "Dutch" 26
Morial, Marc H. 20, 51
Murrell, Sylvia Marilyn 49
Patterson, J. O., Jr. 80
Powell, Adam Clayton, Jr. 3
Powell, Debra A. 23
Rice, Norm 8
Sayles Belton, Sharon 9, 16

Schmoke, Kurt 1, 48
Stokes, Carl 10, 73
Street, John F. 24
Usry, James L. 23
Washington, Harold 6
Webb, Wellington 3
White, Michael R. 5
Williams, Anthony 21
Young, Andrew 3, 48

City Sun newspaper
Cooper, Andrew W. 36

City University of New York
Ballard, Allen Butler, Jr. 40
Davis, George 36
Gayle, Addison, Jr. 41
Shabazz, Ilyasah 36

Civil rights
Abbott, Diane 9
Abernathy, Ralph 1
Agyeman, Jaramogi Abebe 10, 63
Al-Amin, Jamil Abdullah 6
Alexander, Clifford 26
Ali, Ayaan Hirsi 58
Ali, Muhammad 2, 16, 52
Amaker, Norman 63
Angelou, Maya 1, 15
Anthony, Wendell 25
Aristide, Jean-Bertrand 6, 45
Arnwine, Barbara 28
Baker, Ella 5
Baker, Houston A., Jr. 6
Baker, Josephine 3
Ballance, Frank W. 41
Barbee, Lloyd Augustus 71
Bashir, Halima 73
Bass, Charlotta Spears 40
Bates, Daisy 13
Baugh, David 23
Beals, Melba Patillo 15
Belafonte, Harry 4, 65
Bell, Derrick 6
Bell, James Madison 40
Bennett, Lerone, Jr. 5
Berry, Mary Frances 7
Berry, Theodore M. 31
Bevel, James L. 75
Biko, Steven 4
Bishop, Sanford D., Jr. 24
Bond, Julian 2, 35
Booker, Simeon 23
Boyd, John W., Jr. 20, 72
Bradle, David Henry, Jr. 39
Bridges, Ruby 77
Brooks, Tyrone 59
Brown, Byrd 49
Brown, Elaine 8
Brown, Homer S. 47
Brown, Tony 3
Brown, Wesley 23
Brown, Willa 40
Burks, Mary Fair 40
Caldwell, Earl 60
Cameron, James 80
Campbell, Bebe Moore 6, 24, 59
Carmichael, Stokely 5, 26
Carr, Johnnie 69
Carter, Mandy 11
Carter, Rubin 26
Carter, Stephen L. 4
Cary, Mary Ann Shadd 30
Cayton, Horace 26

Shipp, E. R. **15**
Sleet, Moneta, Jr. **5**
Walker, Alice **1, 43**
Walker, George **37**
White, John H. **27**
Wilkins, Roger **2**
Wilson, August **7, 33, 55**

PUP
See Party for Unity and Progress (Guinea)

Puppeteer
Clash, Kevin **14**

PUSH
See People United to Serve Humanity

Quiltmaking
Benberry, Cuesta **65**
Ringgold, Faith **4**

Qwest Records
Jones, Quincy **8, 30**

Race car driving
Hamilton, Lewis **66**
Lester, Bill **42**
Ribbs, Willy T. **2**
Scott, Wendell Oliver, Sr. **19**

Race relations
Abbott, Diane **9**
Achebe, Chinua **6**
Alexander, Clifford **26**
Anthony, Wendell **25**
Asante, Molefi Kete **3**
Baker, Ella **5**
Baker, Houston A., Jr. **6**
Baldwin, James **1**
Beals, Melba Patillo **15**
Bell, Derrick **6**
Bennett, Lerone, Jr. **5**
Bethune, Mary McLeod **4**
Bobo, Lawrence **60**
Booker, Simeon **23**
Bosley, Freeman, Jr. **7**
Boyd, T. B., III **6**
Bradley, David Henry, Jr. **39**
Branch, William Blackwell **39**
Brown, Elaine **8**
Bunche, Ralph J. **5**
Butler, Paul D. **17**
Butts, Calvin O., III **9**
Carter, Stephen L. **4**
Cary, Lorene **3**
Cashin, Sheryll **63**
Cayton, Horace **26**
Chavis, Benjamin **6**
Clark, Kenneth B. **5, 52**
Clark, Septima **7**
Cobbs, Price M. **9**
Cochran, Johnnie **11, 39, 52**
Cole, Johnnetta B. **5, 43**
Comer, James P. **6**
Cone, James H. **3**
Conyers, John, Jr. **4, 45**
Cook, Suzan D. Johnson **22**
Cook, Toni **23**
Cosby, Bill **7, 26, 59**
Cunningham, Evelyn **23**
Darden, Christopher **13**
Davis, Angela **5**
Davis, Benjamin O., Jr. **2, 43**

Davis, Benjamin O., Sr. **4**
Dee, Ruby **8, 50, 68**
Delany, Martin R. **27**
Dellums, Ronald **2**
Diallo, Amadou **27**
Dickerson, Debra J. **60**
Divine, Father **7**
DuBois, Shirley Graham **21**
Dunbar, Paul Laurence **8**
Dunbar-Nelson, Alice Ruth Moore **44**
Dyson, Michael Eric **11, 40**
Edelman, Marian Wright **5, 42**
Elder, Lee **6**
Ellison, Ralph **7**
Esposito, Giancarlo **9**
Farmer, James **2, 64**
Farmer-Paellmann, Deadria **43**
Farrakhan, Louis **2**
Fauset, Jessie **7**
Franklin, John Hope **5, 77**
Fuller, Charles **8**
Gaines, Ernest J. **7**
Gibson, William F. **6**
Goode, W. Wilson **4**
Graham, Lawrence Otis **12**
Gregory, Dick **1, 54**
Grimké, Archibald H. **9**
Guinier, Lani **7, 30**
Guy, Rosa **5**
Haley, Alex **4**
Hall, Elliott S. **24**
Hampton, Henry **6**
Hansberry, Lorraine **6**
Harris, Alice **7**
Hastie, William H. **8**
Haynes, George Edmund **8**
Hedgeman, Anna Arnold **22**
Henry, Aaron **19**
Henry, Lenny **9, 52**
Hill, Oliver W. **24, 63**
hooks, bell **5**
Hooks, Benjamin L. **2**
Hope, John **8**
Howard, M. William, Jr. **26**
Ingram, Rex **5**
Innis, Roy **5**
Jeffries, Leonard **8**
Johnson, James Weldon **5**
Jones, Elaine R. **7, 45**
Jordan, Vernon E. **3, 35**
Khanga, Yelena **6**
King, Bernice **4**
King, Coretta Scott **3, 57**
King, Martin Luther, Jr. **1**
King, Yolanda **6**
Lane, Charles **3**
Lee, Spike **5, 19**
Lee-Smith, Hughie **5, 22**
Lorde, Audre **6**
Mabuza-Suttle, Felicia **43**
Mandela, Nelson **1, 14, 77**
Martin, Louis E. **16**
Mathabane, Mark **5**
Maynard, Robert C. **7**
Mays, Benjamin E. **7**
McDougall, Gay J. **11, 43**
McKay, Claude **6**
Meredith, James H. **11**
Micheaux, Oscar **7**
Moore, Harry T. **29**
Mosley, Walter **5, 25, 68**
Muhammad, Khallid Abdul **10, 31**

Norton, Eleanor Holmes **7**
Page, Clarence **4**
Perkins, Edward **5**
Pitt, David Thomas **10**
Poussaint, Alvin F. **5, 67**
Price, Frederick K.C. **21**
Price, Hugh B. **9, 54**
Robeson, Paul **2**
Robinson, Spottswood W., III **22**
Sampson, Edith S. **4**
Shabazz, Attallah **6**
Sifford, Charlie **4, 49**
Simpson, Carole **6, 30**
Sister Souljah **11**
Sisulu, Sheila Violet Makate **24**
Smith, Anna Deavere **6, 44**
Sowell, Thomas **2**
Spaulding, Charles Clinton **9**
Staples, Brent **8**
Steele, Claude Mason **13**
Taulbert, Clifton Lemoure **19**
Till, Emmett **7**
Tutu, Desmond Mpilo **6, 44**
Tutu, Nontombi Naomi **57**
Tyree, Omar Rashad **21**
Walcott, Derek **5**
Walker, Maggie **17**
Washington, Booker T. **4**
Washington, Harold **6**
Wells-Barnett, Ida B. **8**
Welsing, Frances Cress **5**
Wideman, John Edgar **5**
Wiley, Ralph **8, 78**
Wilkins, Roger **2**
Wilkins, Roy **4**
Williams, Fannie Barrier **27**
Williams, Gregory **11**
Williams, Hosea Lorenzo **15, 31**
Williams, Patricia **11, 54**
Williams, Walter E. **4**
Wilson, Sunnie **7, 55**
Wright, Richard **5**
Young, Whitney M., Jr. **4**

Radio
Abrahams, Peter **39**
Abu-Jamal, Mumia **15**
Alert, Kool DJ Red **33**
Anderson, Eddie "Rochester" **30**
Banks, William **11**
Bates, Karen Grigsby **40**
Beasley, Phoebe **34**
Blayton, Jesse B., Sr. **55**
Booker, Simeon **23**
Branch, William Blackwell **39**
Crocker, Frankie **29**
Dee, Ruby **8, 50, 68**
Dre, Dr. **10, 14, 30**
Elder, Larry **25**
Fuller, Charles **8**
Gibson, Truman K., Jr. **60**
Goode, Mal **13**
Greene, Petey **65**
Gumbel, Greg **8**
Hamblin, Ken **10**
Haynes, Trudy **44**
Holt, Nora **38**
Hughes, Cathy **27**
Jackson, Hal **41**
Jarrett, Vernon D. **42**
Joe, Yolanda **21**
Joyner, Tom **19**
Kelley, Cliff **75**

Keyes, Alan L. **11**
Lewis, Delano **7**
Lewis, Ramsey **35, 70**
Ligging, Alfred, III **43**
Love, Ed **58**
Lover, Ed **10**
Ludacris **37, 60**
Madison, Joseph E. **17**
Majors, Jeff **41**
Mickelbury, Penny **28**
Moss, Carlton **17**
Parr, Russ **51**
Pressley, Condace L. **41**
Quivers, Robin **61**
Samara, Noah **15**
Smiley, Rickey **59**
Smiley, Tavis **20, 68**
Smith, Greg **28**
Steinberg, Martha Jean "The Queen" **28**
Taylor, Billy **23**
Tirico, Mike **68**
Whack, Rita Coburn **36**
Williams, Armstrong **29**
Williams, Wendy **62**
Woods, Georgie **57**
Yarbrough, Camille **40**

Radio Jamaica
Abrahams, Peter **39**

Radio One Inc.
Hughes, Cathy **27**
Ligging, Alfred, III **43**
Majors, Jeff **41**

Radio-Television News Directors Association
Pressley, Condace L. **41**

Ragtime
Blake, Eubie **29**
Europe, James Reese **10**
Joplin, Scott **6**
Robinson, Reginald R. **53**
Sissle, Noble **29**

Rainbow Coalition
Chappell, Emma **18**
Jackson, Jesse **1, 27, 72**
Jackson, Jesse, Jr. **14, 45**
Moore, Minyon **45**

Rap music
Alert, Kool DJ Red **33**
Baker, Houston A., Jr. **6**
Bambaataa, Afrika **34**
Banner, David **55**
Benjamin, Andre **45**
Big Daddy Kane **79**
Black Thought **63**
Blow, Kurtis **31**
Bow Wow **35**
Brown, Foxy **25**
Butts, Calvin O., III **9**
Cee-Lo **70**
Chuck D. **9**
Combs, Sean "Puffy" **17, 43**
Common **31, 63**
Deezer D **53**
DJ Jazzy Jeff **32**
DMX **28, 64**
Dre, Dr. **10, 14, 30**
Dupri, Jermaine **13, 46**
Dyson, Michael Eric **11, 40**

Cumulative Name Index

Volume numbers appear in **bold**